A GENERATION
LOST

A GENERATION LOST

CHINA UNDER THE CULTURAL REVOLUTION

ZI-PING LUO

AVON BOOKS ◢ NEW YORK

AVON BOOKS
A division of
The Hearst Corporation
105 Madison Avenue
New York, New York 10016

Copyright © 1990 by Zi-ping Luo
Cover photographs courtesy of AP/Wide World Photos
Published by arrangement with Henry Holt and Company, Inc.
Library of Congress Catalog Card Number: 89-36056
ISBN: 0-380-71377-2

The Henry Holt and Company edition contains the following Library of Congress
Cataloging in Publication Data:

Luo, Zi-ping.
  A generation lost: China under the Cultural Revolution / Zi-ping Luo.—1st ed.
  p.   cm.
1. China—History—Cultural Revolution, 1966–1969—Personal narratives.
2. Luo, Zi-ping.   I. Title.
DS778.7.L86   1990
951.05′6—dc20   89-36056
                                                                                    CIP

First Avon Books Trade Printing: June 1991

AVON TRADEMARK REG. U.S. PAT. OFF. AND IN OTHER COUNTRIES, MARCA REGISTRADA,
HECHO EN U.S.A.

Printed in the U.S.A.

OPM   10   9   8   7   6   5   4   3   2   1

In memory of my parents
and for the others who were persecuted
during the Grand Cultural Revolution as well.

Acknowledgments

I would like to express my gratitude to all those who made this book possible:

Miss Susan E. Mustonen, a fellow chemist who helped rewrite the final English version with great accuracy and who made the process both enjoyable and educational; Dr. Brian G. R. T. Treco and Dr. Kimberly A. Schugart, who worked with me on the original English version although their specialty is also chemistry; Mr. D. E. Steward, author, for his assistance and good advice; Mr. Jack Macrae and Ms. Amy Hertz at Henry Holt and Co., for their professional efforts and personal encouragement.

Thanks also to my friends Professor and Mrs. Harvey S. H. Lam at Princeton University; Mr. K. P. Chu; Professor Z. Z. Gan at Beijing University; Dr. and Mrs. I. S. Cheng; and Dr. Y. F. Zhang.

Special thanks to my family, especially my brother, Ying, and my uncle and aunt, Professor and Mrs. Jack Y. K. Lou, for their unwavering support and unfailing love.

A GENERATION
LOST

I

Dear Professor Hu,

I am writing to you from the Boston airport.
About three hours ago, my brother, Chi-kai, and
I found your notebook on the floor by a display case
in the Hart Nautical Museum near the Massachusetts
Avenue end of the Infinite Corridor at MIT. The logo of
Shanghai Fu Dan University on it caught my eye. Since we wanted
to return the notebook to its owner as soon as possible, we went
through the pages and read the letter to your son tucked inside.

I hope that Chi-kai has already found you and returned your
property. He is studying in New York, so when I came to visit MIT two
days ago we met in Cambridge to talk. My brother is still young and
does not have much experience in life. If he has offended you in any
way, please forgive him.

Life is the most important thing. When God gave us this life, He
did not promise that every day would be sunny and peaceful. This is a
famous poem by Pushkin:

> We focus our thoughts on the brightness to come,
> Although the present is grim and black.
> But what now we feel with sadness and gloom,
> We will think of most fondly as we look back.

Professor Hu, I beg you to give up the idea of leaving the world in
this way. You teach in a first-class institution, Shanghai Fu Dan Uni-

versity, and have the opportunity to do research in a famous place like MIT. Since birth you have received the contributions of those who came before you. Their diligence and wisdom make your life what it is today. You have the responsibility, just as they did, to make contributions to future generations. You may be miserable, Professor Hu, but many are worse off and yet still live bravely. Your skin and hair are gifts from your parents; you do not have the right to destroy your life this way. Your wife, parents, and children are connected by flesh and blood. If you do anything to yourself, you will be hurting them deeply.

I have to board the plane for California now, so I cannot write any more. I will write to you again as soon as I arrive in California—I still have much more to tell you. Please do not take any drastic action.

My address is on the envelope so that you may reply, and my telephone number is in the Pasadena directory.

Sincerely,
Xi-ou Tan

2

Dear Professor Hu,

When I got home from the airport I called
my brother, who told me that he had already seen
you and returned your notebook. Immediately after
mailing the letter I sent you from the airport, I had some
regrets. Perhaps I talked too much about the meaning of life
and its responsibilities. It may be exactly these responsibilities
which make you feel trapped, unable to breathe.

You must have your reasons for despairing. I have had reasons at
times, too. I do not expect you to open up to me and tell me your
problems, so I will tell you my story instead. From now on, I will write
you one story a day for a month. I am confident that by then you will
think differently. You must be raising your eyebrows and laughing at
my naive self-assurance. However, if you have been miserable for so
long, it shouldn't make any difference to you if you leave this world
now or in thirty days. Please, give me a chance.

    △△ Let me start when I was born.

I rushed to meet the new world with the first rays of dawn in the
year 1950. The enormous midwife brought me to my exhausted
mother, saying cheerily, "Congratulations, Mrs. Tan! It looks like
you'll be buying another pink dress!"

My mother stared at me in disappointment. Since she already had
a daughter, she had wanted a boy; instead, she had a less-than-

appealing baby girl. The eyes were spaced too far apart and, although the head was round enough, the face had a distasteful flatness about it. While she couldn't make out the exact shape of the nose in the dim light, she could tell that it was not a pleasing one.

The midwife left the delivery room to inform the waiting family. After expressing his joy and relief that both mother and daughter were safe, my father turned to the little girl who sat next to him on the bench, dangling her legs playfully. "Rei-qing, you have a new sister! How do you feel about it? Are you happy?"

My sister, four years older than I, quickly nodded yes.

The midwife went back to check on my mother. Instead of finding the fatigued woman she had left only moments before, she saw that my mother was refreshed and strong.

"Look," my mother said. "She already knows how to smile!"

△△△   "We'll call her Xi-ou," said Chun-pu Chu, the most renowned artist of the age. As my father's mentor, the task of naming me fell to him. From a large red envelope that he had designed and painted, Chun-pu Chu produced a piece of silk twine strung with washer-shaped pieces of copper symbolizing ancient Chinese currency. The ornament was a traditional gift to wish the newborn long life and prosperity. "This way, she'll have two names. You can name her Xi-ou, but at home, she can be 'Shiou' Tan." When pronounced as one syllable, the word is Mandarin for "beautiful." "She was certainly born at the right time," he continued, "at the birth of the People's Republic of China. Xi-ou: the bird of hope, the dove of peace. She is the hope for the future, the fighter for freedom and equality."

My mother's wish for a boy came true three years later with my brother, Jian-nan. He was followed by another, Chi-kai, three years later. Still, every time I heard stories about my birth from my parents, I thought I heard my mother say, "Look, she already knows how to smile!"

But life did not smile back. In 1958, when I was seven, my father, the editor of an encyclopedia at a prestigious publishing house, was branded a Rightist during the Anti-Rightist Movement that began in

1957. Though he had spent most of his life working for the revolution, jealous colleagues manipulated him into a vulnerable position. He was exiled to the isolated province of Qin-hai, near Tibet. My mother, a journalist and novelist, also came under accusation. She was kept in Shanghai as a forced laborer so that she could take care of her four children. Two years later, when I was nine, my father returned. The high altitude of Qin-hai had taken its toll; he came home almost dead from anemia. I accompanied him on his visits to the Party chiefs to obtain the necessary papers allowing a permanent move back home from Qin-hai. These officials were often rude or belittling, so one of the first things I learned in life was endurance, whether it was for embarrassment in school, society's vicious discrimination, or the harsh poverty forced upon me.

On a cloudy May morning in 1966, when I was fourteen, my sister and I went to the courthouse to eavesdrop on a trial. A man named Ji-wang Bai allegedly had conspired with two other people to defect to Hong Kong. He had confided in his sister and brother-in-law, who strongly urged him against it, but, unheeding, he attempted to cross the border in secret. The friends with whom he had planned to escape betrayed him, and he was arrested before the train had left the outskirts of Shanghai. The sister and brother-in-law were charged with failure to report the incident. The trial had lasted a year and a half, and today, at last, the sentence would be handed down. Ji-wang Bai was my uncle, and my parents the sister and brother-in-law in question. Trials were not open to the public; only my uncle, mother, and father were present besides the magistrate, the court recorder, and two or three people from the Public Security Office.

Rei-qing kept guard while I climbed up the walls to find the room where the trial was being held. I grasped the bars on the window and pressed my ear to the wall to listen. The verdict was long, full of legal jargon and Communist Party propaganda. When the magistrate read that both of my parents were to be sentenced to seven years, I nearly lost my grip. My father was granted clemency to see doctors, but my mother was to be put into jail immediately. The words exploded in my brain: For 2,555 days I would be a child without a mother.

Although we waited in the lobby for a full hour after the verdict was read, Father did not appear. Already very late for school, I could wait no longer. I had missed all of my four morning classes. When I raced through the school gates, the clock read 1:10. I pushed through the door, perspiration beading my forehead. Teacher Peng was writing something on the blackboard. At the sound of the door opening, he turned, drawing his eyebrows together in disapproval.

"Xi-ou Tan, why are you so late?" he asked sternly.

"I, I . . ." Fifty-four pairs of eyes stared at me, and my stomach tightened.

"Very well, take your seat and explain it to me immediately after class."

Teacher Peng turned back to the blackboard and continued writing his three questions. His handwriting's slant to the right mirrored his body's slight disfigurement. First he wrote, "Why is Tan's paper so much better than the others?" The second comment was, "What made Tan's paper so much more vivid and touching than any other even though everyone was working with the same subject matter?" The third and final comment was, "What in particular demonstrates the superior writing quality of Tan's paper?"

I opened my notebook and started to copy the questions, but my mind was still a thousand miles away. The words did not make any sense to me, and Teacher Peng's handwriting did not help matters. Who was "Tanspaper?" I nudged my neighbor with my elbow and asked, "What is he talking about?"

My best friend and seatmate, Ah-di Chen, giggled and opened her mouth to speak, but before she could tell me, the teacher had already turned around to find the disturbance. Ah-di jotted down something on the corner of a piece of paper, quietly tore it off, and passed it to me. "Tanspaper means 'Tan's paper'—Xi-ou Tan's paper!"

In today's class, Teacher Peng would be commenting on the essays we wrote for the previous week's assignment, *People's Good Servant, Jiao Yu-lu.* Just as my mind began to reorient itself, the dismissal bell rang.

"Now," Teacher Peng said, "I have mimeographed Xi-ou Tan's paper and am giving each of you a copy. After break, we will divide into small groups and discuss it. For the last twenty minutes, I will give my own views on it." He walked over to my desk and fixed his small, penetrating eyes on me. "Xi-ou, this was an outstanding composition. I am going to recommend that this paper be entered in the Shanghai middle-school writing competition."

I managed a faint smile. Sweat had pasted my hair to my forehead and my cheeks still burned from the long run from the courthouse. My heart had not yet slowed to a normal pace, and I was petrified Teacher Peng would ask me why I was late. Luckily, I was rescued when Old Man Xue, a former faculty member who was doing forced physical labor after being denounced in the 1957 Anti-Rightist Movement, appeared at the door. He bowed subserviently to Teacher Peng.

"What's the matter with you?" Teacher Peng asked impatiently, making no move to invite the old man into the room.

"I would like to take some time off to go to the hospital to see an eye doctor." He raised his head, exposing a badly blackened right eye.

"What is it this time?" Teacher Peng asked in rage. "Today it's a black eye, last week it was a broken thumb, before that you broke three ribs. Tomorrow you'll probably come in with a gash on your check! Why do you always want to go to the hospital? Are you trying to avoid doing your share of manual labor?"

"No, no, Teacher Peng, I would never malinger! I was careless before; I promise I'll be more careful in the future." Teacher Peng grabbed the excuse form and quickly signed his name. He was the chairman of a committee appointed to make sure that Old Man Xue was not performing any anti-Revolutionary activities.

The bell rang, ending the afternoon break. The students filed in and took their seats, and the discussion began. The room buzzed with voices as all the students tried to make their points at once. My thoughts were lost in the morning's events and I became oblivious to what was going on around me.

I was startled back to my surroundings by a shout. Xiao-yi Wu now held the attention of the entire class. "Here in this composition, Xi-ou says, 'Anyone who has ever made a mistake but corrected it is a good comrade.' What does this mean? Is Chairman Mao a good comrade? Has Chairman Mao ever made a mistake?"

Teacher Peng patiently tried to explain. "Comrade Jiao Yu-lu was trying to unite all the comrades who had made mistakes in the past but had corrected them in order to further the cause of the Revolution."

"Don't try to avoid my question!" Xiao-yi Wu interrupted. "Answer me! Is Chairman Mao a good comrade? Has Chairman Mao ever made a mistake?"

The sensitive nature of the question terrified Teacher Peng, and he had difficulty formulating a response. "Well, of course, Chairman Mao is a good comrade, and he has always been great and wise."

"Don't beat around the bush! Tell me! Has he ever made a mistake?" Xiao-yi Wu demanded.

"Of course not, of course the Chairman has never made a mistake," Teacher Peng said automatically, as though he were raising his arm to block a blow to his face.

"Well, all right then. In that case, this composition is anti-Revolutionary," Xiao-yi Wu said confidently, and rose to his feet ready to leave. "I refuse to join this discussion!" The classroom was silent.

Teacher Peng, a master teacher and Party member for more than ten years, dispelled the controversy with a wave of his hand. "Well, class, Xiao-yi Wu has raised a very important question. Your discussion groups will now go over the question that he has brought up." He looked at his watch and continued, "There are only twenty minutes left, and I had planned to summarize the discussion, but now I think that it is better if all of you continue. Tomorrow, I will use the first twenty minutes of your Chinese composition class to summarize." He paused and asked, "Xiao-yi, what do you think of this arrangement?"

Xiao-yi Wu shrugged his shoulders nonchalantly and sat down, obviously satisfied with himself. Because his father was a high official in the Revolutionary government, Xiao-yi Wu was one of the young people honored by the title "Son of the Revolution." This automatically made him a leader and a powerful threat. He was popular with the girls in the class, and many of them tried to catch his eye. I found nothing attractive about him, and I despised the way he looked down on other people. I was not surprised by his behavior, but I was shocked by Teacher Peng's handling of the situation.

While Teacher Peng frequently humiliated people like the Rightist Old Man Xue, he was generally a good judge of character and did not base his opinions on people's backgrounds. My parents had been labeled Rightists just like Old Man Xue, yet he was still supportive of me. Why such a secure and intelligent man should back down rather than confront Xiao-yi Wu was hard to understand.

My temples throbbed as I raised my hand to speak. I had once been comfortable arguing a point in public, but after 1957, when my parents were branded as Rightists, I preferred to stay in the background. I feigned shyness to deflect the jealousy of two girls who were class president and chairman of the Youth League. When we began middle school together, we were on the same level, but within a few years, I had surpassed them academically. When I resigned my post as class vice president in charge of studies, I lost all of my opportunities to distinguish myself, which deflected the envy of the two girls for a while. However, since I had more time for study, my schoolwork improved even more.

The chairman of the Youth League sat behind me. Whenever she sharpened her pencil, she blew the graphite dust onto my spotless white shirt, chanting, "Let one half be white, let one half be black, let one half be clean, let one half be dirty." Ah-di would get angry, but I would laugh it off. For eight years I had been taunted by my classmates, and there was no more harm anyone could do me. Today, however, the controversy confronting me was far more serious, one I could not brush off as a prank. If I did not stand up now, I would be sealing my own political fate as well as that of my parents, who were already in trouble with the authorities. I decided to fight back.

"I disagree with Xiao-yi Wu's point of view. All I wanted to say in my essay was that it is a good thing to see a mistake and correct it. When I wrote this paper, I had no intention of saying anything critical about Chairman Mao. This has nothing to do with the Chairman, and I don't know why Xiao-yi Wu is bringing him into the picture."

"Let me ask *you*," Xiao-yi Wu interrupted. "Is Chairman Mao a good comrade?"

I ignored the question: "Those who make mistakes and correct them are good comrades, but this doesn't mean that good comrades necessarily make mistakes. If you understand the logic involved, then this statement is not wrong, even as it relates to Chairman Mao."

Before Xiao-yi Wu could respond, the chairman of the Youth League rose abruptly and burst out, "Xi-ou is trying to sneak out of this. There is a severe class struggle going on right now that everyone in the room should be aware of."

Teacher Peng obviously had lost control, and his sudden inability to deal with the situation in the classroom irritated him. The bell rang, signaling the end of the school day. "Very good, class, tomorrow in our Chinese composition class we will continue the discussion."

After class, I ran home at full speed to see if my father had actually been released. When I entered the house and found him and my sister sitting face-to-face, I burst into tears.

My father took out a handkerchief and handed it to me. "After the sentencing, I went to the judge's chambers to see if he would release your mother in my place on the grounds that she is more essential to raising you children than I am. I also pointed out that she was still recovering from a major operation that left her very weak. The judge rejected the request, but I'll submit a formal written request later."

I was furious. "Father, why do we have to accept this ruling? Can't we appeal?"

He shook his head. "No, if we ask for an appeal, things will only be worse. I remember back in 1957, the people who had asked for appeals after being convicted as Rightists were immediately condemned as enemies of the people. They were exiled to Mongolia or Qin-hai, as I was, where they died of hunger and exhaustion. Appealing would just be beating our heads against the wall."

I quietly put down my schoolbags and went into the kitchen. I was so hurt by the realization that we would be without my mother that, for the first time in my life, I did not relate the day's events over the dinner table. I did not want to add the terror of the class debate to the family's worries.

My two brothers were too young to understand what was happening. Father and Rei-qing were so absorbed in discussing the wording of the formal request for Mother's release, they did not notice my mood. After we finished eating, I cleared the table and asked permission to be excused to do my homework. When I finished, I browsed through the books of Marx, Engels, Lenin, and Mao Zedong to find ammunition for the debate.

I had trouble sleeping that night. If I could not prevail the next day, I would be branded as anti-Mao and most likely sent to reform school for my political heresies. My family would certainly suffer ostracism forever. It was late, and the world was quiet. I opened my eyes wide and stared at the dark sky outside my window. The hours slipped away and I heard my neighbor's white kitten knock over a windowbox. I jumped out of bed and scribbled in my notebook, "A cat has four legs, but everything with four legs is not necessarily a cat."

△△ The next morning, several girls avoided me in the schoolyard. My nervousness increased, but when I entered the classroom, Ah-di's bright smile helped calm me.

Ah-di was from a working-class family. Instead of doing homework, she preferred to spend her time at the opera, where one tragic scene could make her cry for hours. When she began sitting next to me in class, I realized that she was not stupid, as she would say, she had just never learned to study. I taught her a few of my tricks, and her grades improved. We became close friends, and I learned from her a way of life far different from my own.

"Three generations of my family made bricks in a kiln," she told me. "When my sister entered ninth grade, she took me to the examination center so I could take the test to get into school. She met a boy there and quit school to marry him. He catches fish in the lakes around Shanghai and brings them into the city to sell. He makes a lot of money that way. I'm the intellectual of my family."

How romantic, I thought, to bake bricks and catch fish and quit school and get married! For a moment, I longed for a life without complications.

"What about you? What's your family like?"

I looked away briefly. Ah-di knew that I came from a bad, intellectual family, but she never allowed her pure working-class blood to get in the way of our friendship. The sister who had quit school to get married had the privilege of returning whenever she wanted and could continue her studies as long as she did not fail. On the other hand, my sister, Rei-qing, who had won a citywide competition in mathematics, took the university entrance exam twice and was turned down. After the second refusal, she went to the Shanghai Office of Educational Testing and Admissions to find out her score. The administrator would not see her, but she later received the following letter:

> Comrade Rei-qing,
>   We have received your request for admission to the university. We are denying it.
>   It is clear that you either do not understand the concept of loyalty to the Party or are acting selfishly in seeking to advance your own goals rather than the goals of the Party. You should understand by now our concept of "one red heart, but two life paths." Our criteria for admissions are not based solely on scores. Regardless of this, you should be prepared to go where the Party tells you, to follow the life path the Party has chosen for you. Your duty is to go to the remote countryside and work there.
>   The Party has made its decision. Do not submit another request.
>
>   Revolutionarily yours,
>   The Committee

I felt sick. If I told Ah-di that my sister could not get into college because of her scholastic ability, she would know it was a lie. If I told her that it was because of a bad family background, that would lead to a series of embarrassing questions.

"Do you have a sister?" Ah-di asked.

"Yes, I do. I also have two brothers." I stood up quickly. "I'm going to the library," I said, and left the room. I went into the bathroom instead, closed the door, and cried. When I returned to my seat, Ah-di asked me why I was crying.

"I wasn't crying," I lied, blushing with shame. "I just had something caught in my eye."

△△△ When the bell rang to begin class, the principal entered, along with the Party secretary overseeing the operations of the school. As a loyal Party member, Teacher Peng had reported yesterday's incident to his superiors. His nervousness exaggerated the slant of his body as he wrote the "controversial" statement on the blackboard. At the class president's command, the entire class rose. Ah-di reached over and grasped my hand firmly.

Teacher Peng cleared his throat. "Secretary, Principal, students, yesterday we discussed Xi-ou's essay on *People's Good Servant, Jiao Yu-Lu*. Xiao-yi Wu has excellent political acumen. He made a deep interpretation of the statement referring to the man who corrects his mistakes, and he expressed his doubts as to its political acceptability. We appreciate such comments. I reported yesterday's events to the secretary and the principal, and they have chosen to attend our class today to observe our discussion. Everyone will have a chance to participate, as our visitors are interested in each individual's opinion on this matter. First, let us welcome our Party Secretary Zhang and Principal Chen and show our appreciation for their taking time out from their busy schedules to be with us today." Teacher Peng applauded and the class joined in.

Xiao-yi Wu repeated his statement that my essay was anti-Mao and the class president and chairman of the Youth League rose, belligerently parroting Revolutionary slogans. When the commotion subsided, I raised my hand.

"Very well," Teacher Peng said. "Now we listen to Xi-ou's opinion. I hope that after hearing the wisdom of her classmates, her understanding will have been elevated." His noncommittal opening remarks dashed my hopes. My sole comfort had been the knowledge that Teacher Peng was on my side—that of reason, not ignorant mob rule. Now I was on my own.

"I have read over my composition and feel that I have progressed in my understanding of the meaning of this particular sentence. I am glad to say that I can explain it more clearly. I stand by what I said yesterday, 'One who makes mistakes and corrects them is a good comrade, but a good comrade does not necessarily make mistakes.' This is an example of a converse statement. Comrades who make mistakes and correct them are only one type of good comrade. The other type of good comrade is one who never makes mistakes. There is no unique correspondence between 'good comrades' and 'those who make mistakes.' Therefore it does not follow that good comrades have necessarily made mistakes. Another example is a cat. All of us know that a cat has four legs, but we also know that many things have four legs, and yet are not cats, such as cows, sheep, and dogs. If we say, 'Tables have four legs' can we then also conclude that a table is a cat?"

The classroom was silent. Teacher Peng seemed to be thinking so hard that he forgot to ask me to sit down. Only when Ah-di raised her hand to ask permission to speak did his attention return to the class. Teacher Peng snapped uncharacteristically, "Ah-di, you also want to speak? Just stand up; Xi-ou, sit down."

I was surprised. Although Ah-di could be boisterous with her friends, she scarcely uttered a word in class, and then only when asked. For her to raise her hand was something novel indeed.

"Xiao-yi Wu infinitely extrapolated Xi-ou's remarks to extend to Chairman Mao, and it was unfair. I am angry with Xiao-yi Wu for doing this!" She sat down.

Xiao-yi Wu stood up, panting like a hungry wolf who has just seen its prey escape into an unseen hole. "You, you . . . ," he began. "You are subservers to the Revolution!"

He had actually meant to say "subversive," but Xiao-yi Wu's mastery of language left much to be desired. Teacher Peng was mortified by his pupil's incorrect usage of Chinese, especially in the presence of the principal and the Party secretary. He had no choice but to correct him.

"Xiao-yi Wu, you meant to use the word *subversives* to accuse them of being anti-Revolutionaries. What you actually said was that they are loyal followers of Chairman Mao!" The class laughed uproariously.

"You bourgeois intellectual!" Xiao-yi Wu shouted. "You are repressing Revolutionary students!"

Xiao-yi Wu had a sidekick named Zheng-gou Wang, who sometimes acted as his adviser. Zheng-gou was from a bourgeois family that was particularly looked down upon, so he sought every opportunity to ingratiate himself with the Revolutionaries in the class. He came from Canton and thus acquired the nickname of Canton Kiss Up. Canton Kiss Up rose, cleared his throat, adjusted his glasses, and drawled:

"Recently, all the important newspapers and magazines have begun a very serious discussion of our loyal comrade Yao Wen-yuan's exposé of the anti-Revolutionary conspiracy. Such anti-Revolutionaries use their novels and plays to falsely accuse Chairman Mao and the Party's Central Committee. Therefore, there are some people who wish to use literature for their own anti-Revolutionary ends. There are also some people who wish to protect these enemies of our Revolutionary society."

The class murmured in confusion. Canton Kiss Up surveyed the reaction to his address, smiled with malicious satisfaction, and sat down. Teacher Peng checked his watch. Forcing a smile, he addressed the secretary and the principal, who were seated in the last row of the classroom, and asked them deferentially, "Secretary Zhang and Principal Chen, do you have anything you wish to add?"

The administrators put down their notes and waved their hands to signify that they had nothing to say.

"Well, class, after these two in-depth discussions, we have clarified many issues in our minds. Such discussions are very healthy and beneficial to all pursuing the furthering of the Communist Revolutionary Ideal. . . ."

Xiao-yi Wu interrupted yet again. "Well, who is right?"

"Who is right is not what is important. What is important is the raising of consciousness brought about by this discussion."

"But, it's the difference between the Revolutionary and the anti-Revolutionary! How can you say it isn't important?"

"After class, I will be glad to discuss this further with you."

"A Communist is not afraid to openly express his point of view. Wen-shai Peng, we demand a direct answer."

Teacher Peng smiled and dismissed the class.

Professor Hu, I should end this letter here. I've been writing the whole night. It is morning now; the sun is shining brightly and I have to go to school—I am doing research at Cal Tech. Spring vacation begins tomorrow, so I will have an entire week to write to you. My story has just begun.

Take care of yourself, and wait for my next letter.

Sincerely yours,
Xi-ou Tan

 I had been working as a research associate at Cal Tech for the last year and a half. Since midterm exams were underway, most of the students were studying in the library and the computer room was empty. I should have been able to get more work done with the unusual quiet, but I spent most of the day thinking about the letter I had written to Professor Hu. I was sure his misery was linked to the Cultural Revolution and Chairman Mao, and I wanted to show him that although many lives were destroyed by the madness China had inflicted upon itself, there was still reason to live.

On May 25, 1966, Beijing University put up its first official "Marxist-Leninist" wall poster. Although many posters had been hung since the Anti-Rightist Movement in 1957, this was the first one that Chairman Mao declared Revolutionary. This marked the beginning of the Grand Cultural Revolution.

People's Daily, the mouthpiece of the Party, was criticized for being anti-Proletariat and underwent a change of management. In June, it was announced that all classes at the universities and middle schools would be halted to carry out the Revolution. Students were still required to go to the schools each day to read editorials in the newspapers and Chairman Mao's instructions, as well as to write wall posters criticizing the teachers. On August 5, 1966, Chairman Mao published his own wall poster. Three days later, the Central Committee circulated the Sixteen Principles, a guide for the Proletariat to institute the movement.

> *The Grand Cultural Revolution is a new stage of the Socialist Revolution.*
> *Keep in mind the real direction of the Revolution and do not be afraid of the inevitable difficulties.*
> *Be brave and mobilize the Revolutionary Mass.*
> *Let the Revolutionary Mass educate themselves during the Movement.*
> *Resolutely follow the Party line on class struggle.*
> *Fight your enemy with your tongue rather than your fists.*
> *Students are not allowed to chastise other students.*
> *The main objective of the Grand Cultural Revolution is to purge the Party of those powerful members who inwardly believe in capitalism and wish to lead China into it.*
> *Promote the Revolution and improve production.*
> *Neither the army nor prison officials can institute any activities of the Grand Cultural Revolution.*

3

Dear Professor Hu,

I think you see why I used a simple argument among middle-school students of twenty years ago to begin my story. Although naive, it was not without a point. Was Chairman Mao a good comrade? Had he ever made a mistake? History has already answered these questions. All contemporary Chinese, whether living in Mao's lifetime or born afterward, were affected by his actions.

I had fought my classroom battle bravely but never felt that I had won. The British philosopher David Hume said, "One who never errs in interpretation cannot be given any other compliment besides 'He has interpreted correctly.' However, one who errs but then corrects his mistake, of him can be said that not only has he found the right answer, but that he has had the courage and humility to question even his own judgment." Many nights I stared at the sky and imagined saying, "Yes, a good comrade must have made mistakes. I make mistakes. You make mistakes. Chairman Mao has also made mistakes. What is wrong with that? Don't people grow wiser by learning from their mistakes? Read what Hume said! The one who errs should not feel ashamed. It is he who errs but denies it who should feel shamed!"

Teacher Peng continued to devote class sessions to my paper. After a while, only a third of the class remained interested, about the same number listened with indifference, and the rest viewed it as a waste of time. Teacher Peng generally favored Xiao-yi Wu's position, but his halfhearted arguments indicated that these were not his true feelings.

By August, the classroom debates over my essay cooled down. One of the Sixteen Principles mandated that students not attack each other on political issues, so I was given a reprieve.

My father had always told me, "Your mother and I gave you your body, but your mind and everything in it come from your teachers. So, your teachers are your parents as much as we are." The lifelong friendship between my father and art professor Chun-pu Chu only proved this. My parents quoted Confucius: "If you learn a truth during the day and die that night, then it has been a profitable day." I saw truth as the ultimate good, and I believed that seeking it was the noblest ambition. Teachers, who had the responsibility to reveal truth to the young, deserved to be respected above members of any other profession, so Teacher Peng's behavior disappointed me. I ignored his greetings in the hallway, and when I passed his office, I stamped my foot in contempt.

△△△ National changes began occurring so rapidly and chaotically that even politically astute people could not understand the course of events. Teachers began exchanging political graffiti, accusing each other of being pro-American, pro-Taiwanese, anti-Revolutionary, Rightist, anti-Mao, Revisionist, or any other suitably derogatory label. Then the students attacked their teachers.

As could be expected, Old Man Xue was the first person to be criticized publicly at the newly instituted "Fight to the Death for Chairman Mao and the Central Committee" meetings. At one meeting, a laborer wearing heavy boots jumped onto the stage, rushed over to Old Man Xue, and savagely kicked him in the buttocks, knocking him down. When Xue stood up, blood was streaming down his face from a large cut on his forehead. "He is only pretending to be hurt! You see it all the time! Down with the Old Rightist! Down with Xue! Long live Chairman Mao!" During his monologue, the worker revealed his reason for despising Xue, his neighbor: The old teacher had an apartment two square meters larger than his. The worker shared an apartment with two other family members, but Old Man Xue shared his with six.

I thought of our own new neighbors. After my parents were

convicted in May, Mother was immediately put into jail, and the remaining five of us were chased into one of our four rooms. The other three rooms were now occupied by a worker's family of seven people. Upon moving in, the worker stood at the door to our room and beat his shoes together while singing, "Purge the bourgeois pollution, Join the Cultural Revolution!"

Eventually he switched to shouting, "It's justified to rebel! It's justified to rebel!"

When Xue had asked Teacher Peng for permission to go to the hospital, it must have been because his neighbor had beaten him up. The "noble working class" were nothing but a mob of Proletarian hooligans.

When I told my father what had happened, he said, "Do me a favor then. Each time you see Mr. Xue at school, it doesn't matter who is there with you or watching, you must smile at him. . . . No, every day, you have to go out of your way specifically to meet him, just to let him know that *someone* cares about him."

I arrived at school the next day to find that Secretary Zhang, who only the day before had presided over Old Man Xue's chastisement meeting, had been relieved of his position. Wall posters all over the school had such slogans as, "The secretary must open the pot of class struggle!" and "We must smash the cradle of Revisionism!" All of the names of the school administrators were written upside down with large red X's over them. Teacher Peng was a Party member as well as the secretary's right-hand man, so it was no surprise to see his name written upside down as well. The signature at the bottom of each slogan written against Teacher Peng was a name I had never heard: Robin. The posters accused him of having an affair with a former student who had relatives in the United States. "Robin's" wall poster had an eye-catching headline: "Look! A Communist Party Member Is Sleeping with a Bourgeois Wench!—A *Real* 'Class Struggle!' "

A crowd gathered to read what was directed at Teacher Peng. I tried to get close enough to see for myself but was forced to move along and read some of the others. The wall in front of the dining hall was specifically devoted to posters, and former Secretary Zhang and former Principal Chen, together with Old Man Xue, were busily sweeping the pavement in front of it. Now the two administrators were once again united with Xue on a platform, but both were hard-pressed to match his prowess with a broom. The old Rightist put them both to shame.

After hesitating before approaching the scene, I tried to get Old Man Xue's attention. Although the day had just begun, his shirt was drenched with sweat and he moved with obvious pain after the previous day's beating. Sweat, blood, and iodine on his forehead turned his head bandage into a hideous rainbow. Some of the younger students peppered him with pebbles, and I heard a tiny voice shout, "Get him in the eye! Make a Cyclops out of him!" I felt like vomiting, and tears came to my eyes. No one really remembered what he had done ten years earlier. A terrible feeling crept over me that I was witnessing my father's future.

Suddenly I felt a hand on my back. It was Ah-di, frantic. "Where have you been for so long? I looked everywhere for you! I stuck my head out of the third floor and called your name at least ten times. Didn't you hear me?"

"What's going on?"

"Have you seen Robin's poster?"

"Yes, but I haven't read it all. I couldn't get close enough."

"It makes me sick! That isn't what happened at all. I heard that this 'Robin' person was chasing after Teacher Peng, but he wouldn't even look at her. She's just using this to get back at him."

We were distracted by a disturbance in front of one of the wall posters. Xiao-yi Wu was dragging Teacher Peng by the arm, followed by Canton Kiss Up and other mindless students. Xiao-yi Wu pushed Teacher Peng up against the wall and shoved a megaphone in his face. "Read it, you scum! Tell us all about it!"

Xiao-yi Wu and his cohorts had drawn another wall poster about Teacher Peng earlier that morning, claiming that he had turned students against each other and caused everyone to fight with me. His alleged motivation was to show his scorn for the Revolution, to try to abolish the Central Committee, and to repeal the Party's Sixteen Principles. They wanted everyone in the class to sign it, especially Ah-di and me. Xiao-yi Wu was angry when we refused, but the thirty-eight signatures already collected were more than the two-thirds majority required to warrant hanging the poster.

Canton Kiss Up had another idea. On his advice, Xiao-yi Wu put a copy of the wall poster by Teacher Peng's desk in his office, and another near his bed in the dormitory. People paraded through his rooms to read the accusations and Teacher Peng lost all of his privacy.

The second day of the student takeover, there were three registration tables outside the front door, each manned by Red Guards. A large banner hung above them, reading, "Throughout the world, throughout eternity, this is the truth." Underneath, a smaller banner read, "Acknowledge your true identity or suffer the wrath of the Revolution." To the left, a vertical banner proclaimed, "The son of a hero, a hero shall be." At the far right, a similar banner read, "The son of a Rightist is our enemy." The table on the left had "Registration for Five Classes of Reds" written above it, and a list of the five types of Reds: working class, peasants, soldiers, sons of the Revolution, inner-city poor. Since those who were classed as Reds were supposed to fight for and protect the Revolution, they were also called Red Guards. The middle table was for the Whites: clerks, bureaucrats, and small business owners. The right-hand table had a sign that read, "Registration for the Six Classes of Blacks." Listed were the six types of Blacks: landlords, rich peasants, anti-Revolutionaries, criminals, Rightists, capitalists. I had to register as a Black, while Ah-di, a brickmaker's daughter, registered as a Red.

The new curriculum was now expanded beyond the mere reading of editorials and wall posters and the humiliation of the faculty. The Cultural Revolution was to be taken outside the safe walls of the school. That afternoon, a thousand upper-grade students gathered to tear down the Rong Hua Buddhist temple. A senior in charge of the Red Guards of the school made a speech. "Rong Hua Buddhist temple is the cradle of the Four Obsolete Vestiges: the Obsolete Culture, the Obsolete Morality, the Obsolete Traditions, and the Obsolete Habits! As the autumn wind sweeps away fallen leaves, so should we sweep away these vestiges!"

The Red Guards had been notified that the Revolutionary Headquarters would be unable to supply prefabricated banners that day. Although Blacks were supposed to stay in the classroom and study the

Sixteen Principles, I was pressed into service because I could draw large characters neatly and quickly. The banners had to be done by the time the other students were ready to march on the temple, so twelve of us rode bicycles to the temple with our drawing materials. Approximately fifty head Red Guards also rode bicycles so that they could maneuver more quickly in the crowd.

On the way, a conflict erupted between Xiao-yi Wu and a group led by another working-class student, Da Lu. Xiao-yi Wu's gang had sticks and belts to beat the Buddhist monks and nuns into submission. The rival group quoted the Sixteen Principles, which demanded persuasion over violence. Da Lu felt that it was more in the spirit of the principles verbally to convince the monastics to relinquish their religious beliefs. Xiao-yi Wu did not agree, and the two gangs almost came to blows. They decided to attack the temple separately.

The twelve of us in the writing groups were absorbed with copying the slogans received from City Hall when Xiao-yi Wu snatched most of the completed banners and started off. Before he could get far, Da Lu appeared. Both gangs claimed our services, whereas we professed autonomy. Xiao-yi Wu backed down, while Da Lu's group surrounded us to prevent him from taking more signs. Xiao-yi Wu's gang grabbed as much as possible of the sign-making materials and proceeded to the temple.

Now that I was no longer of any use to the gangs, I was frightened for my safety. Ah-di, wearing a red armband signifying membership in the Red Guards, led me by the hand into Da Lu's gang. I had avoided her all day, because I did not want other students to accuse her of being soft on anti-Revolutionaries.

I asked her timidly, "Can I come with you?"

"Of course, why not?" she answered. "Destroying the Four Obsolete Vestiges and replacing them with the Four Modern Ideals is a Revolutionary act, and everyone is involved. It's not just your right; it's your duty." My shy friend had been transformed quickly by the events of the previous two days.

At the temple, Xiao-yi Wu, Da Lu, and all of my classmates disappeared into a sea of people. Thousands of workers, peasants, and students had already surrounded the temple. In the center, a temporary platform had been set up and an impromptu "Fight to the Death for Chairman Mao and the Central Committee" meeting was being held. A worker was denouncing a dozen or so nuns who were on the platform.

"You sluts! Your mothers were whores and so are you! Don't put on those nuns' robes and pretend that you're virgins! We know what goes on during those rituals! Admit it! You've slept with so many monks you can hardly walk straight! Long live Chairman Mao! Now we're going to wash you parasitic scum into the Huang-pu!"

The crowd jeered and roared with laughter. The nuns stood with their heads bowed and their caps removed, revealing their shaved heads. The frail old mother superior stood with her head and feet bared, prayer beads missing. She trembled in the bright sun.

"Let's leave now," Ah-di whispered to me.

I silently agreed, and we walked to another part of the temple. Ah-di said sadly, "When my grandfather died, we asked the monks to come to our house and pray with us. I remember that they said the name of the Buddha over and over, chanting, 'Let the karma cycle be ended, may his body rest and be free from rebirth, may his spirit enter Nirvana, may he find peace and joy.' Now they are chastising these holy people! When these hoodlums die, they won't get into Nirvana."

We continued around the temple complex. When we passed a smaller building near the main hall, a voice called, "Hey, Red Guard! Come and help us! Do your share of the Revolutionary duty!"

We entered the building and found more than a hundred people attempting to topple a large statue of the Buddha. He had a fat belly, a smiling face, and thousands of arms. A massive rope was tied around his neck, waist, and hands. There were so many ropes around the Buddha that he looked as if he were caught in a fishnet. When the order was given, the crowd pulled with all its might. The statue wobbled for a few seconds before falling on its side. The crowd was jubilant. Even lying down, the Buddha still smiled.

I was telling Father about the experience over dinner when he cried, "Look! Outside! Do you see the fire?" I got up from the table and stepped onto the balcony, facing the playground of the Nan Yang Model Middle School. The Nan Yang Model schools were famous throughout China, and many families had relocated to this area just so their children could attend this one. Now this center of education had become the new frontier of the war that had been declared on civilization. On the playground, the road, the roof of the library, even under the grapevines in the school's vineyards, people were burning books. The sky turned red. Red Book, Red Commander, Red Guards, Red heart, Red flag, Red armband, Red billboard, Red bricks, Red wall, Red buildings. The anthem of the Liberation rang in my ears:

> East is red,
> Rises the sun.
> China has brought forth
> A Mao Zedong.
> For the People's happiness he works,
> He is the People's Great Savior.

The setting sun disappeared, but even the pure, white, cool rising moon turned red. To me, the "Red Sun" of Mao Zedong was more like a moon: As he rose, casting a lurid glow over the country, China sank into darkness, and my generation was lost.

△△△ In the following days of mid-August, life around me was transformed into a vast array of torture, violence, and madness. Wives spied on husbands. Children informed on parents. Brothers dragged each other to the police station. Students threw devoted teachers into prison. It was a society gone insane.

Because of Teacher Peng's former association with the Party secretary, and also because of Robin's wall poster, he received more than the usual amount of abuse. He was forced to work in a labor camp all day, and at night to write a confession of his anti-Revolutionary sins. At three o'clock one morning about a week after the temple ransacking, Xiao-yi Wu burst into Teacher Peng's room. Beside the pillow he found a picture of a woman, and he assumed it to be the "bourgeois wench" of the wall posters. He tore up the picture, forced Teacher Peng to his knees, and beat the screaming man for the rest of the night.

At 7:30, when the students began to arrive, Xiao-yi Wu dragged Teacher Peng into the classroom where a few weeks earlier he had been master. The room was now only a place for students to read posters. Xiao-yi Wu found a broken chair. Discarding the wooden seat, he took the intact iron frame and shoved the makeshift stocks over Teacher Peng's head, arms, and chest. Then he forced Teacher Peng to walk on his knees all around the room. Xiao-yi Wu's peers were fascinated by the invention and proceeded to break the other chairs.

The rest of the school poured in to see Teacher Peng's humiliation. Taking off his heavy leather belt, Xiao-yi Wu beat the helpless man about his body and face. Some students tried to dissuade him, referring to the Sixteen Principles and the ideal of nonviolence. But just as Xiao-yi Wu had not been turned back from his quest to "liberate" the Buddhist temple, he was not to be dissuaded now. As time went on, violence became the accepted form of political persuasion, and a heavy belt became a beloved Revolutionary symbol.

In my class, there were fifty-four students, of whom thirty-three were originally Reds. As the movement progressed, more Reds were reclassified as Blacks. Several students, who were called "Sons of the Revolution" because their parents were Revolutionary cadres, were reclassified when new information about their parents came to light, like one of my classmates whose father was found to have been a member of the Guomindang party before the Revolution drove it from the country. The number of Red students dropped to ten.

Toward the end of August, the headquarters of Shanghai Middle School Education announced that it would be giving away two free trips to Beijing to see Chairman Mao. This announcement spurred intense competition, and students investigated each other's backgrounds and actions in order to emerge as one of the true supporters of the Revolution. In the entire class, only two students had purely Revolutionary pedigrees going back three generations. One was Xiao-yi Wu. His father was a navy commissar, and it was specifically stated in the Sixteen Principles that soldiers should not carry out the Cultural Revolution. Simply by serving in the Navy, the father was considered loyal, and nothing else was expected. This made him and his family relatively immune to investigations or accusations.

The other purebred in the class was Ah-di, whose working-class lineage extended as far back as anyone could remember. To be fashionable, Ah-di changed her name to Hong-jie, which means "pure red." When she consulted me on the matter, I refrained from pointing out that she ought to abandon her surname, "Chen," which means "old" and therefore had anti-Revolutionary overtones.

The Red Guards of my class joined with those of other schools and went into the streets to remove the Four Obsolete Vestiges. They each wore an army hat and uniform, a red armband, and a leather belt. They checked the attire of each passerby to make sure that his or her clothes were in Revolutionary accord. The Red Guards were on a constant lookout for clothes that clung tightly to the legs or revealed the shape of the buttocks or breasts. They even watched for pointed shoes. Hairstyles were monitored for deviation from the standard ear-length, perfectly straight, official style. The Red Guards climbed ladders to destroy shop signs that did not properly reflect the Revolution and to replace them with ones that did. "Red East," "Red Guards," and "Four New Beginnings" were the most popular. Our school was renamed the Revolutionary Rebelling Middle School.

By the end of August, the Red Guards began searching houses. At first, they merely confiscated antiques, Bibles, and clothes not meeting Revolutionary standards. After each search, they hung three banners. To one side of the door, a banner read, "The temple is small, but thousands of demons come and go as they please." On the other side was written, "The garden is small, but thousands of serpents slither with ease." Over the door hung the Red Guard's overall judgment of the home: "Inside is a nest of rotten lizard eggs."

When the Red Guards returned to the school from their street jobs, they bragged about cutting the seat out of a young girl's pants or changing the menu in Muslim diners by substituting the forbidden pork for beef. They boasted of searching more than ten bourgeois families' homes in one night and told how their leader could hardly lift his arms when he put on all the confiscated watches. Unlike most of my classmates, I was not permitted to join the Red Guards, put on their uniform, go into the streets to remove the Four Obsolete Vestiges, search people's houses, or go to Beijing to see Chairman Mao. Eventually, sympathy for the victims and love for my family subdued my jealousy.

Two spinsters and their eighty-year-old mother lived next to the

Nan Yang Model Elementary School, which had been renamed the East Is Red Elementary School. They lived in a beautiful Spanish house with a garden nearly as large as the elementary school's playground. When I was in elementary school, I skipped rope by the fence that separated the playground from the women's house, and when I was tired, I leaned against it. Sometimes I could hear music coming from inside. Through the fence, I could see trees in the yard and smell the flowers. It seemed like something out of a pleasant dream.

The spinsters were attentive and respectful to their old mother, who was confined to a wheelchair. They had reconstructed the city of Shanghai in their home and would wheel their mother through the house, saying, "Look, Mother, here is South San Xi Road. Do you want to go down this way? Do we need anything in the stores down there? Nan Jin Road is coming up. Do you want to turn here? Remember that dim-sum place over there? Are you hungry?" These stories always touched my heart and made me think of how I loved my own mother.

It was still late August, when one day the door to the Spanish house was flung open and the two spinsters were forced to kneel in front of it. Dragged from her wheelchair, the old mother was told to join them, but she was so feeble that she collapsed into a heap on the terrace. A mob yelled and screamed, banging their fists on every available surface. The old women were called "bloodsucking leeches," "maggots," and "intestinal parasites." Outraged that the women possessed such a large house, the mob called them "real estate imperialists." The schoolchildren followed the example of their elders and the unwritten rule of the Revolution: When in doubt, break something. They climbed over the fence and tore the garden to shreds, then kicked and spat on the women, whom they should have revered as grandmothers. Instead, they shouted, "Whores!"

The old mother was the widow of one of the great heroes of the Xing Hai Revolution in 1911. She and Madame Sheng-ye Xian had helped hide many of the revolutionaries of the period from the emperor's death squads. It made no difference to the Revolutionary mob. Madame Sheng-ye Xian came from a Black family and had numerous connections with the West. "So why should we care about this Xing Hai Revolution, where the power was wrested from the emperor only to be handed over to the bourgeoisie? And this notice from the State Department, what is that to us? After all, we don't know whether they are Revolutionary or anti-Revolutionary, so why should we obey them? We take our orders from Chairman Mao!"

Much later that night, I went into the empty garden to look for signs of life. No friendly lights or familiar music came from the house. A few lonely crickets chirping sadly in the ruins of the garden were the only things that had survived the raid. The mother died before the public chastisement had even finished. As for the sisters, I heard that the elder was suffering from a fever, but no one knew where they had gone.

The next day, the door to the garden was shut and a notice hung on the gate: BY ORDER OF THE STATE DEPARTMENT: ALL ENTRY IS FORBIDDEN UNLESS DIRECTLY AUTHORIZED BY THIS OFFICE.

The house became the Red Guard headquarters for performing their administrative duties—drinking bouts, lewd parties, endless gluttony. The garden became a sandpit for wrestling matches, and the ancient tree in the front of the house was used for target practice.

△△△ During the months of August and September 1966, which later became known as the "Red Terror," Father left the house only to do his forced labor. One day I told him a story I heard in school. "Do you know what one lazy person did? He stayed home all the time and collected sick pay, taking advantage of our commitment to the infirm. But when the Red Guards searched his home, they found that the quilts on his bed were stuffed with sixty-seven bankbooks, from every bank in Shanghai. He had pasted them to the linings. There must have been seventy thousand yuan in deposits! Under his bed they found fourteen five-liter containers of cooking oil. All we get is two hundred grams for a whole month! And I don't know how he got them, but he also had ration coupons for 250 kilograms of rice. How much rice can one person eat? Yesterday he jumped from the ninth story of the Wu-kong building. They said that everybody in the stores on the ground floor heard his body hitting the pavement. His bones shattered and all his muscles splattered into such a mess that you couldn't tell it had been a person. But his watch was still ticking! Why should I care about someone who felt that, after his precious money and oil and rice coupons were seized, life was not worth living anymore? A death like that is meaningless! All this filthy miser ever cared about was his money. He never had any intention of sharing with the poor all those things he hoarded. They were only for his precious self. Now, at least, these things are back in the hands of society where they may do somebody some good!"

Father was shocked. "How can you judge so quickly? What do you know about this, really? You said that he pretended to be sick. How do you know that he really wasn't? Are you sure that he wasn't saving the money for his old age? What about his family! Did he have a family? You can't blame a man for wanting the best for his family! And anyway, if he got his money honestly, what business is it of yours or mine or anybody's what he did with it? It was his to do with as he pleased. To save, or spend, or give away, or throw away was his basic human right, and these Red Guards have taken away that right. Not only are you not angry about someone losing his rights, you approve, you even admire these actions! How can you feel this way?"

The values Father had tried to instill in us were in danger of giving way in the Revolution. My brothers were still very young, but Rei-qing and I were growing up, our minds expanding, bodies growing, sexuality awakening. Shaking off our youthful innocence, we were taking a look outside to see what the world had to offer. We were fledglings whose wings, while still not totally developed, were ready to be tried. Father wondered if, when we saw an insane, cruel world, we would use its model rather than that of our family.

Father was not alone in his worries; many parents shared them. Boys whose voices were changing would use them to shout at the teachers or try their muscles by untying their belts and beating them. The Red Guards who went to Beijing brought back advanced techniques for tormenting Blacks. The most common form of torture was to darken the faces of the Blacks, either with coal or black paint, and to make them kneel bare-kneed on ground strewn with broken glass or sharp rocks for the hottest part of the day. They also had a new label for teachers and similar anti-Revolutionary indoctrinators: "Ox Ghost," since the guardian of hell in Chinese mythology had the head of an ox. People so labeled were forced to crawl around and eat grass. Xiao-yi Wu's favorite torments were sticking knives in a chair and compelling a person to sit down, forcing people to take a bath in boiling water, and burning people's hair. He could not wait to try them on Teacher Peng.

Every day I heard of more suicides. A famous pianist, Gu, had killed herself with the gas from her stove. The writer Lao She drowned himself in the Tai Ping Lake in Beijing. I thought they were wrong to do this; only by living through such experiences could they reveal to others the beauty as well as the ugliness of life. In early September, Mr. and Mrs. Fu Rei hanged themselves in their apartment. My father and Fu Rei had belonged to a minor party called "93," which had been formed by the intelligentsia of China. They often would study together. Father told me that because of Fu Rei's diligent translating, the sales of Balzac's works in China far exceeded those in France. He did the first translation of a biography of Beethoven and also introduced China to Mozart, whose mind was as bright and romantic as the beloved poet Li Bai. Li Bai had once written:

> You can almost reach and touch a star
> From a wobbling tower a thousand miles high,
> And there remain so very quiet,
> For angels are sleeping in the sky.

This poem had touched the Chinese people in the same way that Mozart's music had touched the West. Although survival for both Mozart and Li Bai was a living hell, they continued to create. The suicides I was hearing about troubled me. When I told Father, he said, "Don't ask yourself too many questions, daughter. They would rather be broken emeralds than perfect bricks."

Every day on the way to school, I passed a Nan Yang Model Middle School teacher. Unmarried, she was from a family of wealthy bureaucrats and spoke with a distinct Beijing accent. Although she was in her fifties, she was still full of energy and always meticulously dressed. One day in late August, I noticed that her white shirt had large blue and red ink spots on the back. The next day, she wore a sign around her neck. Written in white letters on a black field was the word "Anti-Revolutionary." Her name was written upside down with a large red X on it. The third day, the right side of her head was shaved in another invention of the Red Guards, the "yin-yang haircut." She walked undeterred even as children followed, spitting on her and throwing pebbles.

I thought, "I don't like this philosophy of 'Better a broken emerald than a perfect brick.' This woman has true wisdom. If you aren't a slave to flesh and the world, then no violence can take away your spirit and will to live. Life was given to me at birth, and as long as there is life in my body and just the faintest hope, I'll continue to fight."

Depending on the post office, I think that by tomorrow you should receive my second letter. Please take care of yourself.

Sincerely yours,
Xi-ou Tan

The first time I had sat down to write to Professor Hu and faced a blank sheet of paper, I froze for a moment. Thoughts of the cruelty I had seen began to trickle into my consciousness. Soon a dam burst in my soul, and all the memories and repressed emotions flooded out.

When I walked to Cal Tech to mail the letter, everything I saw reminded me of the Red Terror. A traffic light I passed on the way reminded me that the Red Guards had once suggested that since red was the color of the Revolution, the meanings of the red and green of the traffic lights should be reversed. At the sight of an Indian woman wearing a sari, I recalled how the Red Guards ripped off women's veils, urging them to listen to Chairman Mao and his views on women's liberation. Crossing the campus, I passed the faculty lounge. The waiter, wearing a red uniform with a black bow tie, was busily serving patrons in the open-air restaurant. Twenty years ago, the ambassadors at Chinese embassies were forced to don aprons and serve the people, while the janitors and washroom attendants sat and discussed the issues of the day with the guests. As I stood in front of the newly built organic-synthesis laboratory decorated with the Greek personifications of Imagination and Law, I remembered how any piece of art, no matter how old or intricate, was destroyed if it was even remotely related to "foreigners, mummified people, the emperor, or mythological figures." "Mummified people" referred to dead famous persons who had not lived during Mao Zedong's time.

I crossed a crisp, green lawn where a mother was proudly helping her child learn to walk. The mother's long brown hair and white teeth caught the sunset's glow. I remembered when Chinese women were only allowed to have ear-length hair and the beauty salons stopped offering permanents and manicures, since only "bourgeois snobs" would want them. For the same reason, the dentists in the hospitals would not clean teeth or provide braces.

I walked up the steps to the auditorium. The public bulletin board was full of colorful announcements for concerts, seminars, and other activities. Twenty years ago, all of China looked like a bulletin board: The walls of schools, the shop windows, the sides of the buses, the staircases, and public restrooms, any blank space was quickly filled by Revolutionary slogans and announcements of chastisement meetings. Pamphlets full of sensational news rained like confetti.

It was growing dark and the lights in front of the auditorium came on. For several months in the late summer and early fall of 1966, the theaters in China showed only documentaries of Chairman Mao receiving the Red Guards in Tiananmen Square in Beijing, where he lived. Altogether, he received a million of them in eighteen trips. The Beijing post offices were so full of Red Guards sending telegrams to their "fellow fighters" that other messages, such as "Mother is critically ill. Come home at once!" often didn't get through.

It suddenly seemed as if I were walking into the Shanghai movie theater on the late August day of 1966 when I learned that my home would be searched by Red Guards for the first time. I decided to write about the search to Professor Hu.

4

Dear Professor Hu,

Everyone experiences profound misery in
life. However, no matter how cruel the hurt is, if
one can analyze it with a cool eye, it has already
begun to heal. For instance, I still feel pain over the story
I am going to relate to you today, about when my home was
searched for the first time, but I have not let it diminish my joy in
life.

One late August afternoon in 1966, I went to a theater
near my school to see one of the documentaries on Chairman Mao
receiving the Red Guards. Since seat assignments were based on the
theatergoer's political classification, I found myself in a corner in the
very last row. The lights dimmed and the "East Is Red" anthem began.
On the screen, nature's red sun rose over Tiananmen and then was
replaced by Chairman Mao. Everyone in the theater rose. I was so
nervous my entire body broke out with goosebumps. Chairman Mao
stood in his Jeep, his bright green military uniform glowing in the
sunlight. Slowly, almost shyly, he waved to the crowd of Red Guards.
The camera focused on the throng, many of whom were crying with
joy. Although I found the scene repulsive, I began to cry as well, but for
decidedly different reasons.

Someone grasped my arm in the dark and a deep voice ordered me
to make room for a latecomer. Ah-di, the purest Red of the Red Guards,

sat down quickly and whispered, "Listen, after the movie, go straight home and hide anything you don't want the Red Guards to find. We just had a meeting, and they're going to search your home. I tried to tell them not to, but they're going to do it anyway. I did manage to convince them not to go tonight, so you're safe at least until tomorrow." Ah-di caught her breath and continued, "Every night there's something going on. I'm doing my best to protect you, but I think you'd better be careful."

Tears again blurred my vision. Whenever Ah-di had asked about my family, I had evaded the inquiry, and now I felt guilty that I had not taken her into my confidence. We gripped each other's hands tightly for a moment. Hers were warm and alive, but she must have found mine cold and lifeless.

When the movie was over, I left the theater and followed the crowd along Hen Shan Street. A wall poster described "the ten evils of pigtails." Pigtails, it said, were a decadent symbol of feudalism and a link to the Four Obsolete Vestiges and so should be wiped off the face of the earth. A group composed mostly of workers read it under the hot afternoon sun. There were several factories on this road running on three shifts, and the afternoon shift was just arriving. A middle-aged worker read aloud the evils one at a time:

"First, they are a residue of feudalism and a symbol of the subjugation of women, which suggests a society straitjacketed by class distinctions. Second, through pigtails, the bourgeoisie are able to distinguish themselves by enhancing their appearance. This will undermine the authority of the Proletarian Dictatorship. Third, pigtails make washing and arranging the hair more time-consuming. This wasted time could be much better spent performing manual labor. Pigtails, then, represent the bourgeoisie, who exploit the working class and do not labor, leaving themselves time to waste on trivial matters. Fourth, money spent on pigtail maintenance items such as soap and shampoo is a wanton waste of the wealth of the nation. . . ."

He snorted in disgust and spat on the ground.

An older worker said, melodramatically, "My mother has bound feet! Certainly bound feet are part of the Four Obsolete Vestiges! I guess we'd better cut them off!" The crowd laughed. From the corner

of Yu Qin Road and Hen Shan Street marched a group of Beijing Red
Guards in uniforms with rolled-up sleeves, singing the Revolutionary
anthem:

> Our rifle and pen are one and the same,
> The Communist Party is my parents and blood.
> He who insults the Party's great name,
> We will kill and leave to rot in the mud!

The crowd exhibited mixed feelings toward the Beijing Red Guards, the
favorites of Chairman Mao. It was rumored that these model Revolutionaries had killed more than three hundred so-called anti-
Revolutionaries in a single county. In order to get to the root of the
"anti-Revolutionary weed," even babies too small to lift their heads
were slaughtered.

   At daybreak Sunday morning, Rei-qing and I spent an hour hiding
everything the Red Guards might interpret as anti-Revolutionary. We
were afraid to do this at night, because Red Guards preferred to
perform their duties after dark, and it would be worse if we were caught
hiding things.

   Rei-qing picked up my mother's gold necklace—with its heart-
shaped locket containing a photograph of our parents taken when they
were engaged—sewed it into a small piece of cloth, and put it in my
schoolbag. I had a secret notebook containing the thoughts of more
than one hundred people from all periods in history and all parts of the
world. I was desperate to keep it. It was a mirror of my mind, from
Vladimir Mayakovsky's "Live so that others will benefit from your
life" to Napoleon's "The soldier who lacks the ambition to command
is not a good soldier." From Hu Shi's "History is a serving-girl whom
you can make up to look any way that you wish" to Patrick Henry's
"Give me liberty or give me death!" My parents had long ago given up
keeping diaries, and they had destroyed important letters from friends
as soon as they had read them. Despite the political climate, I had been
allowed to keep this notebook. I scanned it as fast as I could, trying to
remember every single one of the quotations I had loved so much.

   My eleven-year-old brother, Jian-nan, had developed asthma

when he was two. People say that a child with a weak body develops a superior brain, and this was true of Jian-nan. He came to me with a picture of his idol, Albert Einstein. A year earlier, he had ripped a page out of a library book and tried to make it look as if it were a copy of a photograph. When Mother found the ruined book, she made him kneel in a dark closet under the stairs until he confessed, and then she made him go to the library to pay for it. Rei-qing wanted to go with him, but Mother refused, saying, "No! If he knows how to destroy a book, he should know how to pay for it, too." The librarian, moved by the story, did not ask Jian-nan to pay for the book. Instead, she gave him a photograph of Einstein from her own collection. He made an envelope for it and gave it to me to hide.

My other brother, Chi-kai, was eight. He handed me an old doll with a duckling under its arm. "What do you want to hide this for?" Rei-qing said, annoyed.

"He's got blue eyes and yellow hair. He's a foreigner," my small brother protested. He was right; we took it from him.

The only controversial items in Father's possession were his collection of books and artwork. Hiding all of them would be impossible. His books, from the cheapest paperback to the rarest first edition, and every piece of art, from the least expensive reproduction to the most treasured original, were of equal value to him, so he left them all in the open. Rei-qing was more practical. "Shouldn't we at least do something about Grandfather Chun-pu's works?" she asked.

When Chun-pu Chu released paintings for publications, he sent the originals to the publishing house and had the publishers send them to Father, his good friend and former student, after the books had been printed. Thus, over the years, Father had built up a fine collection. With the onset of the Anti-Rightist Movement, artists fell out of favor and Chun-pu released fewer and fewer paintings, making the works we already owned more precious to us. Father had considered Rei-qing's suggestion much earlier, but he could not think of any place outside the house to keep nearly 140 paintings. He also could not decide which paintings should "live" or "die." Above everything else, he felt they should not even be considered anti-Revolutionary. They were simply Chun-pu's expressions of himself, a sincere combination of humanism and patriotism. If humanism and patriotism were anti-Revolutionary, then what was not?

We also had three of Father's manuscripts. Although the books in the house could conceivably be replaced, his work would be lost forever if the manuscripts were destroyed. We did not think of this. It was hard to believe that Father, a brilliant economist and editor, could be more naive than one of us. We had cleverly hidden a notebook, a small necklace, a doll, and a photograph, objects that could never compare in value with the precious manuscripts that were left lying on a desk.

At eight the next morning, I left the house with the book bag full of items to be hidden. I walked toward the Artists' Hospital, passing the bus stop where people met their dates when they did not want to be watched by their neighbors. People assumed that one was merely waiting for a bus, not for someone special. My father's best friend, whom we called Uncle Xiong, had a son, Tao-ran, who suddenly jumped off a bus and came toward me. (He was later to become my brother-in-law, but of course we did not know this at the time.)

Tao-ran appeared not to notice me, so I had no choice but to keep walking to avoid suspicion. I stopped at a newsstand not far from the station and was browsing through a book of Chairman Mao's poems when Tao-ran came up behind me. "Xi-ou, is that you?"

"Oh, Tao-ran!" I answered, pretending to be surprised.

"I didn't know you came here to buy books, too!" he said, coming closer. We left the shop, chatting. By the time we had gone a few steps down West Huai Hai Road, I had slipped the book bag with its incriminating contents into his briefcase. After several more worry-filled days, the dreaded event came to pass.

△△△ Professor Hu, when I arrived in the United States in 1980, people asked me if there was a word for "privacy" in Chinese. Only recently has this word begun to appear in our newspapers. For thirty years, Neighborhood Committees paid people to unearth every family's secrets; a committee would stand or fall by the quality of its gossip network. It was of utmost importance to know whose daughters were pregnant, who was having an affair with someone's spouse, which families were buying fancy dishes, who violated the local zoning restrictions by raising poultry for consumption.

When regular workers finished their shifts and were ready to settle down for an evening of food and rest, the Neighborhood Committee members were just beginning. As workers arrived at their homes, Neighborhood Committee members would slither out to make "friendly inquiries" about people's health. If a family had a visitor, the Neighborhood Committee arrived to make sure that the accommodations were suitably clean. Just so they would not miss any cockroaches or mice, they checked all the drawers, cabinets, closets, and any other place a pest could hide. In their infinite consideration, they would inquire about the reason for the guest's visit to Shanghai. A large crowd of people would quickly form what Chairman Mao dubbed the "People's Wall" around the house, to make sure the guest did not leave before he was ready to go and therefore feel unwelcome. After the guest and the Neighborhood Committee—or "Big Sisters," as they were often affectionately called—left, a security force arrived to make sure that no details had been forgotten.

Since the secretary of our Neighborhood Committee was one of the ugliest women I had ever seen, I nicknamed her Madame Couvre, after a character in one of Balzac's novels. Although subhuman, she wore a most honored crown: the title of Representative of the Revolutionary Mass. She wielded a great deal of power, and her slightest whims had far-reaching consequences. If a neighborhood child had a fight with one of her children, a simple "That boy should be taught a lesson" was enough to send him to a reform school for years.

Several days after meeting Tao-ran, I returned from school to find a large crowd assembled outside my house. Terrified, I ran, realizing that the Red Guards were there. A group of tables had been pushed together to form a stage. Madame Couvre stood on them, screaming Revolutionary slogans into a microphone. Two men being restrained by the Red Guards were on the stage with her. Both were wearing tall dunce caps, their heads forced downward by poles jammed into the backs of their necks. One of them was my father. Closing my eyes, I silently called to him.

Rei-qing had been summoned to do manual labor that day and had not yet returned home. My two brothers were standing in front of the stage, their heads barely reaching the top of it. Trembling, they leaned against each other for support.

"Now let the son of anti-Revolutionary Jin-ren Tan come up on the stage and reveal his father's anti-Revolutionary atrocities!" Madame Couvre bellowed. My heart sank at the sight of my brother's predicament. I tried to push through the crowd but could not get close enough to do anything. Jian-nan took the microphone from Madame Couvre and launched into a mildly Revolutionary speech:

"My father always told us that the only noble pursuit in the world was that of academics, that books were the most valuable treasures on earth, but now I know that he was lying! Intellectual dinosaurs like my father are only in the way and will have to step—or be pushed—aside to make way for the Revolution! Long live Chairman Mao! Only after such Obsolete Vestiges like my father are removed can the nation move forward and wipe the filth of Western pollution from the face of the New China!" Madame Couvre grew impatient with the moderate nature of his speech and grabbed the microphone from Jian-nan, pushing him off the stage.

Since I had cut my hair in accordance with the Red Guards' position on pigtails, no one recognized me. I could see the gray hairs on the back of my father's bowed head peeping out from beneath the dunce cap. In the horror of seeing my father treated that way, I thought of the ancient Tibetan proverb, "Even if a torch is held upside down, the flame still points upward."

△△△ While my mother was giving birth to me, my father was going through a painful delivery himself, the birth of his Chinese economic model. This model for socialism was highly criticized in the early 1950s for being too liberal. He was ostracized from the academic community and assigned to an editorial job for the Chinese Encyclopedia Publishing House. As the Anti-Rightist Movement gained momentum, the Party exiled him to Qin-hai. Eventually, even this was not enough to satisfy the Party, and with the onset of the Cultural Revolution, he was branded as an anti-Revolutionary, given a suspended prison sentence, and forbidden to undertaken any form of work for pay.

My father's position, lifestyle, and political environment had changed, but one aspect of his life was immutable: the little green reading light burning continuously in our home from dusk to midnight. Every night at bedtime, I went to my father's desk to say goodnight. Turning from his work, he would look at me kindly and bid me goodnight with a smile. Then he would return to work. Until she was imprisoned, Mother stayed up with him. One night, after her imprisonment, Father was composing a letter to the judge, repeating his request that he be allowed to serve the sentence in place of his wife. My own work was disturbed by his coughing, which was not a simple clearing of the throat, but a painful, deep hack that signaled severe infirmity. Alarmed, I looked up at him. His misshapen back indicated stress and age. I wept, realizing that the experiences of the last few years had done this to him. Wiping the tears away with the back of my hand, I thought, "Father is a strong man. A strong man has no need of tears."

△△△ Remembering his strength, I felt my courage renew itself as I watched my father on the platform. The meeting was over, but the frenzied crowd demanded further retribution from the accused. They shouted that the men should be paraded through the neighborhood as an example of Revolutionary justice. Madame Couvre traded her microphone for a tin megaphone and led the mob through Tianping Road—megaphone in one hand, a rope attached to the two accused men in the other—showering the spectators with slogans and spittle. I desperately wanted to be close to Father to protect him from physical harm, but there was only one way to remain nearby without becoming a target myself: to follow the Red Guards and delinquent children, repeating their slogans and insults. I was afraid, but if anyone dared to hurt him, I would stand up and fight. Not to interfere was one of the most difficult decisions of my life.

In Shanghai, September is called the "autumn tiger," because the heat and humidity make it the most uncomfortable time of the year. At three or four in the afternoon, the weather is so oppressive that one's skin feels as if it were being roasted over a slow fire. The still air was filled with the loud call of millions of locusts. It was difficult to breathe, and even the Red Guards showed signs of tiring, but Madame Couvre was as fresh as ever. People marveled at her stamina as she drowned out the locusts.

My father's codefendant was accused of being a closet slumlord, though of what slum no one knew. He suddenly fainted in the middle of the street, throwing the mob into confusion. Neither the stupid Madame Couvre nor the inexperienced Red Guards knew how to handle the situation. Meanwhile, a bus pulled away from a stop, scattering the crowd. Only the unconscious "closet slumlord" remained in its path.

With a burst of adrenaline, Father ran to his codefendant. As he lifted him from the street, the man's dunce cap fell off, revealing a head of almost entirely white hair. The bus continued on its course, crushing the cap. The passersby, seeing this close call, applauded.

Father gently put the man down and begged the crowd to get a stretcher. Madame Couvre regained her composure and kicked the unconscious form. "Parasitic, lowlife slumlord! You're always trying to get out of work any way you can! Even now you're trying to avoid justice by playing dead! Get up, you pig-dog! Do you think the Revolution will wait while you sleep? And you," she said as she turned to my father, "isn't it enough for you to be punished for being the lazy, anti-Revolutionary intellectual that you are? Now you're showing your sympathies to the bourgeoisie right in front of us! If you want to save a slumlord from punishment, you must be a closet slumlord yourself! Chairman Mao spoke wisely when he said that the anti-Revolutionaries and the landlords share the same pants!"

A worker from the crowd stepped forward. "Hey, Big Sister, don't be so dogmatic! Chairman Mao said that we should be like doctors and devote ourselves to curing those with political diseases. He said that Revolutionary justice should be tempered with Revolutionary mercy. If it were not for this venerable man," he shouted, and then continued in a melodramatic whisper, "you would be tried for murder!" Enjoying the show, the crowd cheered in approval. I crept near Father and escorted him home. I was glad to see that although he was shaken, he was not otherwise injured.

During the demonstration, a joint team of Neighborhood Committee members and Red Guards were searching our home. They knocked a hole in the ceiling and took Father's entire art collection, including the precious originals by Chun-pu, and all of his reference books, with the exception of one entitled *A Modern Interpretation of 305 Classic Poems*. Since it was of old-fashioned workmanship and origin, the Red Guards would have been expected to seize it, but they had reverently dusted it off and carefully placed it in the center of the desk. The faithful green reading lamp was smashed.

It was so late by the time the Red Guards left that we went to bed in the room as it was. My mind raced with the prospect of the imminent changes in my family, for Rei-qing had decided that it would be better for her to volunteer to work in the Shanghai countryside than to wait for an order to do so. She was to start as a farmhand in two days. She had taken care of all the household necessities since Mother was imprisoned, and now the entire burden would fall to me. From my window, I stared at the midnight sky dimly lit by the Red Guards' fires. In the distance, I could make out the sounds of slogans shouted through a public-address system. Father sat in front of the open window by the balcony and lit a cigarette. Its glow illuminated his stoic expression.

Realizing why the Red Guards had not taken the book of poetry, I jumped out of bed and tiptoed over to Father. Letters and hundreds of pages torn from books and manuscripts were strewn across the floor. "Your cigarette reminded me of Mao Zedong's quotation, 'A spark is enough to burn a prairie.' The 305 poems were interpreted by Hung Mao. Even though Hung Mao has been dead for a thousand years, isn't it possible that the Red Guards thought this was an interpretation of Chairman Mao's poems?"

Father smiled mirthlessly. "Anything with 'Mao' associated with it is safe in this country." He thought deeply for a while and continued, "A spark is enough to burn a prairie. Yes, definitely, a spark *is* enough."

"What do you mean by that?"

"Well, as long as there is something left, I can work. These poems are my spark. I will interpret them. My next book will be *A Contem-*

porary Interpretation of 305 Classic Poems. My work has only just begun."

△△△   At dawn two days later, my brothers and I walked Rei-qing to the truck that would take her to the countryside. All along the street, other young people were also leaving their homes for the same reason. Some Neighborhood Committee members were playing drums and cymbals, lending an air of pomp to the otherwise dreary occasion. Most of the youths had large trunks, but Rei-qing's luggage consisted of a secondhand army blanket that was older than she, a bowl to be used for both meals and washing, a few hygiene items, her handwritten copy of Chairman Mao's thirty-nine poems, and a four-volume set of Chairman Mao's works—the standard gift from the Neighborhood Committee to the people being sent to the countryside.

The gloomy parade terminated at the truck. As it drove off, many of the young people began crying. Rei-qing grabbed the chain connecting the sides of the truck to its gate, leaned out, and yelled back to us, "Take good care of—" and with her index finger she made the traditional sign for the now-taboo and anti-Revolutionary word *father.* Our family had made a pact to correspond at least twice a week. Since anyone could read a Black's mail, we invented the code name "Brother Ying" to avoid using the word *father* or Father's proper name. Oh, Professor Hu, whenever I hear someone freely shouting "Father," even on TV or in a movie, my heart aches.

For ten years I could not openly say "Father" or tell him that I loved him. Now think of your son! You would not want him to have this regret, but if you commit suicide, he will feel the same loss I felt. Please do not do this to him, Professor Hu! Please take care of yourself, and think about this. I will write to you again tomorrow.

> Sincerely,
> Xi-ou Tan

5

Dear Professor Hu,

Bidding my sister farewell was like losing a part of myself. I went to school with a heavy heart, but did not count on something worse happening that same day.

As I entered the gates to the schoolyard, Xiao-wei, a boy from a working-class family, called to me. I barely knew him, but Ah-di had told me that he was quite militant and often beat people. "Comrade Xi-ou Tan," he said in a halting but firm voice, "we must talk."

I sensed a catastrophe. We walked past the playground, which had been converted into an outdoor indoctrination center. A large group of Blacks being lectured on Chairman Mao's philosophy stood near a bamboo wall erected for displaying wall posters. Among the Blacks were a number of former teachers, forced to remain bent over with their legs straight. They had been in this position for at least an hour. The chief Red Guard of the twelfth-grade class, now the highest-ranking person associated with the school, presided. His mechanical voice matched the cold, unfeeling expression on his face. A strong but dull-looking student stood on his right, obviously the chief's underling, while to his left, an attractive girl took the minutes.

Xiao-wei pulled me over to a quiet corner of the yard. Trembling, he drew a mimeographed leaflet from his pocket and clumsily thrust it into my hand. "Read this for yourself," he said, avoiding my eyes.

I smoothed the crumpled piece of paper and read the poem:

To my parents,
The morning sun lights up the skies,
And chases the sleep from my just-opened eyes.
I rise and look on the world that it graces,
Foremost of all my parents' bright faces.
I give thanks to you, God, mighty and pure,
You kept me this night, so safe and secure.
Oh, Mother and Father, please be assured,
To me you are the light of the world.
When illness attacked me and clawed like a hawk,
You took care of me, as a shepherd his flock.
Not the doctors or nurses, nor injections or pills,
'Twas the love of my parents that banished my ills.

With horror I recognized the poem I had written when I was ten years old, after recovering from pneumonia. I had been delirious much of the time, seeing myself already dead and my parents, friends, and neighbors in mourning. But the crises always passed, and each time I opened my eyes, I was surprised to find myself alive, my parents smiling down at me, concerned but grateful. Their warm faces were enough to make me want to live. I opened my arms and asked them to hold me. I was discharged from the hospital after ten days, on my parents' anniversary. Rei-qing had made paper flowers and dragons as a gift for them, and my two brothers drew a picture. This poem had been my present. Mother had carefully put away these gifts, keeping them in her dresser drawer. How had we forgotten to hide these items?

The Red Guards must have found the poem during the search. The leaflet was titled "What Could Be Worse Than This?" Underneath was written, "Look! The anti-Revolutionary whelp regards her anti-Revolutionary dog parents as the Red Sun!" Xiao-wei kicked at the gravel at his feet.

"The Red Guards from the Nan Yang Model Middle School were trying to find Xiao-yi Wu to settle this matter. He's out of town, so it's my job. They're organizing a meeting to criticize you for writing this anti-Revolutionary poem. Three thousand people will be present, so you should be well prepared."

I bowed my head, unable to respond.

He continued, "Don't worry. I'm in charge of this. Remember what happened with your composition. You can argue very well. You shouldn't be afraid."

"You and Xiao-yi Wu don't belong to the same faction, and the Nan Yang Model Middle School Red Guards have been looking for him. If you don't tell them about this incident, people might accuse you of trying to protect an anti-Revolutionary whelp."

He looked down silently. Finally, he said, "Who cares?"

△△△ At 8:25 that night, the Red Guards came looking for me, led by a girl about my age. She slapped the table with her broad leather belt and said, "You will submit a written statement of contrition to our headquarters absolutely no later than 9:15 tonight. In addition, you must make a wall poster of your statement and hang it outside the door of your house so that all may criticize your anti-Revolutionary crimes against the state."

Writing such a confession was not difficult, nor did the time constraint bother me. The painful part was the poster in front of my house for all the gawking neighbors to see. My confession began with a mindless, standard introduction:

A SCATHING DENUNCIATION OF A POEM I WROTE IN FIFTH GRADE

First, let me salute and wish a long, long life to our Great Leader, Great Teacher, Great Commander, and Great Helmsman, the Reddest Sun burning in our hearts, Chairman Mao. I wish Vice Chairman Lin Biao eternal health! Everlasting health to Lin Biao!

This great, unprecedented Proletarian Cultural Revolution has washed the concealed filth and scum off the streets and into the sewer like a spring torrent. Just as the harsh, autumn wind blows away the dead and useless leaves, so has the Cultural Revolution dispersed the Four Obsolete Vestiges and the Ox Ghosts and Snake Devils. The Red Guards came to my house and helped me. Such actions are both just and Revolutionary, and I welcome them. . . .

I finished early but waited until precisely 9:15 to hand it in, since a confession handed in with time to spare would be viewed as a halfhearted effort. I was told that the meeting would be held October 4, which gave me two weeks to prepare.

I also needed to paste a wall poster, but we were out of flour to make the glue. I went downstairs and timidly tapped at the door of "Aunt Zhou." "Uncle Zhu" let me in. Uncle Zhu was one of the relatively few members of the Communist Party and had been promoted to cadre at his factory.

Aunt Zhou, six months pregnant with her second child, was sewing as usual. When I told them what I needed, Uncle Zhu asked no questions but brought some flour from the kitchen. Aunt Zhou asked about my father, and I began to cry.

"Mr. Tan is a fine person," she said, sighing. "If it were not for him, our daughter would not be alive." During Aunt Zhou's first pregnancy, a tumor was diagnosed in her throat. Although the doctors had recommended that the tumor be surgically removed and the pregnancy aborted, Father had taken her to a doctor friend of his who specialized in traditional Chinese holistic medicine. After a few weeks, the tumor disappeared, and Aunt Zhou later gave birth to a healthy baby girl.

They did not have much money themselves, but she handed me two yuan. "Take this and buy some meat for your father so he can get his strength back. It isn't much; just take it as a token of our affection."

For the next few days, I felt like a porcupine with all its quills raised. Buoyed by my successful defense of my composition, I carefully set my plans for the meeting. My posted confession attracted many people's attention, because, at the time, few people in my age group were forced to write such self-denunciations.

One day, as I was leaving for school, I saw several Red Guards gathered around the wall poster. One said, "This makes me sick! It's disgusting! What a pathetic anti-Revolutionary bourgeois view this brat has, clinging to being a 'dutiful daughter' instead of pledging her loyalty to the only person worthy of loyalty, Chairman Mao!" Another night, when I was in the bathroom, I heard loud voices below. Peering out the window, I saw several figures reading the wall poster by flashlight. In panic, I ran to my father, telling him to prepare for a possible spot inspection. Returning to the bathroom, I put out the light and stood in the dark, monitoring the movements of the shapes below. I had been afraid of the dark from childhood, and even negotiating the six steps between the bathroom and the living room was terrifying. Now I was alone in the dark but did not fear the distorted shadows cast by the streetlights. Every nerve in my body was stimulated by a new anxiety: that the Red Guards below would enter the house and harass my family. I fixed my concentration on every sound, each time expecting to hear the dreaded footsteps ascending the stairs. Not until I heard them receding did I breathe freely again.

I rose before sunrise the next morning and rushed downstairs to read the comments that the Red Guards had written the night before. Straining my eyes to read their nearly illegible characters in the dim light, I shivered in the chill of the autumn air. "This Black brat should be sent to the guillotine!" "This anti-Revolutionary bourgeois scum should be drawn and quartered!" "Long live the Red Terror!" The harsh comments rang in my ears. I felt abandoned by every soul in the world. Grateful that the Red Guards had not invaded my house, I thought, "Sooner or later, all this suffering will end."

It was the last week of September and there was only one week before the meeting. I was reviewing my argument as I walked home through the crowded streets for lunch. A leaflet nailed to an electricity pole attracted my attention. It looked much like the one Xiao-wei had given me, but when I found that it was different, I did not want to stop and read it. Someone shouted, "Anti-Revolutionary brat! That's the one who wrote the anti-Revolutionary poem! Look!"

Turning, I saw the girl who had led the group of Red Guards to my house the week before. She had carefully tied pigtails under her cap and, despite her baggy uniform, her slim, attractive figure was clearly visible. Instead of simple shoes, she wore new, white sandals. All that spoiled her outfit was the heavy leather belt.

"It's her! It's her! Do you see her?" The shouts sprang up all around me and I found myself encircled by a frenzied, furious crowd. Instinctively, I ran, but in the opposite direction from my house. Besides a few Red Guards fanatically loyal to Chairman Mao, some young adults who just wanted to see a fight, and several retired workers who had nothing better to do, the crowd consisted mostly of malicious teenagers who were constantly in trouble. Shouting, "Catch her, catch her!" they threw stones at me. I felt my strength dissipating, but I kept saying to myself, "I'm almost there, I'm almost there," though where, I did not know. My legs began to wobble and my body stiffened. I saw a hotel in front of me. Although the hotel was on my regular route to school, I had never even looked into the windows. Without hesitating, I ducked into the doorway.

I stood in front of the registration desk, panting and dripping with sweat. The clerk was a tiny man in his fifties with a stern countenance. He drew his brows together.

"Please, help me! A mob is after me. . . ."

The crowd was at the door. The little old man jumped nimbly from behind the desk and quickly closed the door to the hotel. The mob pounded and kicked the door, shouting "You dare to harbor an anti-Revolutionary fugitive? You deserve to die for your crime!"

The left side of the lobby was illuminated by a dim light, and I could make out a stairway. The old man spoke in a pained, broken voice, "Pumpkin, come down here." A young girl in a spotless white maid's uniform appeared at the top of the stairs. She had been watching from the window upstairs and quickly took in the situation. There was no sign of surprise or alarm on her pretty, innocent young face.

"Take her out the back door and walk a little way with her," he ordered curtly. The back door of the hotel led to a small alley with many egresses. It was in this very alley that I had played hide-and-seek with my friends in elementary school.

The crowd was getting out of control, and I had no time to thank him properly. I flashed a smile in his direction and followed the maid through the back door. I was lucky to escape with my life.

Two days later, September 27, 1966, my whole family was awakened at eleven at night by shouts and pounding. "Open this door or we'll break it down!" The echoes had not even died down when I heard a thud. I put on a coat and turned on the light. After exchanging looks with my father and two brothers who remained in bed, I opened the door. Ten Red Guards poured in, shouting, "Where is the stinking old anti-Revolutionary?" The Red Guards pulled out several flashlights, shining them all into my father's face. Momentarily blinded, he turned away.

"What took you so long? I suppose with your trashy anti-Revolutionary wife in jail, you were messing with your daughter!" The speaker was the chief of the group, a Red Guard named Da-wei. Very tall and thin, he wore thick glasses and was at most one or two years older than I. He was more like a wild animal than a young man. I burned with anger and hatred, wishing to tear out their throats with my teeth. Recent experiences, however, had taught me control, so I said, calmly, but firmly, "He has a severe heart condition," avoiding the word *father*.

"If he dies, that's one less anti-Revolutionary scum that I have to keep an eye on!" Da-wei said. Before he finished speaking, he moved the flashlight beam from Father's face to a hole in the ceiling and shouted, "Search this place! Look sharp!"

The violence of this search made the previous one look like an Easter-egg hunt. The Red Guards emptied every drawer onto the floor and tore up all photographs. They opened the pantry and dumped all the food into the spittoon. Red and black ink was poured into a large bowl of leftover rice gruel. One Red Guard took Father's sweater, set it on fire, and threw it off the balcony. The noise roused the neighboring laborer, who had been banging his shoes in front of our door singing Revolutionary jingles several months earlier. He brought his wife and four children with him to join in the fun and acquire some souvenirs in the confusion. Around midnight, Da-wei abruptly waved his hand and ordered the Red Guards downstairs. Two strong men yanked Father from the bed and dragged him from the house while two female Red Guards kicked my brothers and me from behind. The Red Guards grouped several benches together and made a temporary stage under the dim streetlights. Da-wei shouted, "Put him on the stage!" My brothers and I were ordered to use a hold on Father called "the

airplane," the Cultural Revolution's contribution to the art of wrestling. Father's head was forced downward, while his arms were pulled
straight back with a cruel twisting of the wrists. The Red Guards were
adept at determining a weak hold and were quick to point it out. We
were warned that we would be beaten and further denounced if we
did not put as strong a hold on him as possible. We obeyed mechanically, trying to cause him as little pain as possible while appearing to
exert ourselves fully. Was I wise in appeasing the Red Guards, banking
on the fact that they would eventually get bored and leave us alone, or
was I simply weak and easily manipulated? Time stopped for a moment.

"Old stinking anti-Revolutionary, confess your heinous deeds!"

One of the Red Guards had stuffed something into Father's mouth,
and he gagged violently as he tried to remove it. It seemed as if a string
had wrapped itself around his tongue, garbling his speech. It amused
the Red Guards no end.

My brothers and I bowed our heads in sorrow, still keeping a tight
grip. We saw a short, scrawny Red Guard standing near us, completely
emotionless, occasionally stamping on Father's feet with his heavy
boots. No one had ordered him to do this, nor did anyone notice him
doing it; his movements were unobtrusive. Every few seconds, he let out
a mirthless giggle.

The night shift was about to relieve the evening one at the factories,
so there were many witnesses to the spectacle. A middle-aged woman
with a sad face, just visible under the dim light, said to my father quietly
and sincerely, "Just tell them what they want to hear, not just to make
it easy for you, but so it will be easier for these poor children." The
woman's eyes told of her long, strenuous day of work, yet her gentle
nature came through even in the midst of a lawless mob.

Father was carried off that night by the Red Guards. After the
demonstration ended, my brothers and I were interrogated until three
in the morning. The night's ordeal gave Jian-nan a severe asthma
attack, and he could not sleep. His special preparation imported from
the United States was declared by the Red Guards to be "an illicit
Imperialist drug," so they urinated in the bottle to show their disapproval. Lying on a carpet of Father's manuscripts, Jian-nan gasped for

air. I watched, helpless. For the first time in my life, I prayed for my family's safety.

⚠⚠⚠ For five days, there was no news of Father. On the morning of October 2, my brothers and I were summoned to the Nan Yang Model Middle School to retrieve him. We found him beneath the grapevines in the middle of the campus, tied to a stone bench, his hands and feet bound together behind him. We were forced to watch Da-wei and the other Red Guards beat him with their belts, although he already appeared to be severely injured from previous beatings. Sitting between my brothers, I pretended to be calm, though I felt every one of his blows on my back. Father winced in pain each time he was struck, but he did not cry out. I found no anger in my father's eyes, only the grief of a suffering martyr.

Professor Hu, do you remember Lu Xuin's novel, *Medicine*? The story was about a working-class family with a teenage boy who was dying from tuberculosis. A local folk cure called for dipping steamed bread into the blood of a healthy man and feeding it to the sick one. To get the blood, the family attended the public beheadings of the Revolutionaries who were fighting to topple the emperor. The poor would feed their children the blood of the brave men in return for their sacrifice. I did not then understand the symbolism of the workers drinking the martyrs' blood, but watching the scene in front of me made it clear. The working class felt no obligation to those who labored for their freedom, prosperity, and happiness. Father was not really a martyr, I thought, since he had not literally sacrificed his body or blood for the Revolution. Yet all his life, he selflessly gave of his intellect to improve the scientific and literary understanding of the Chinese people. There were far more men who gave their blood for the country than there were men like Father, who gave his mind and learning. If it were otherwise, how could the Cultural Revolution ever have happened?

⚠⚠⚠ Da-wei ordered our whole family to march single file. Jian-nan was first and Chi-kai second, followed by Father. I went last.

In front of and behind us were files of Red Guards armed with heavy sticks. We marched as the Red Guards bombarded us with slogans, insults, and blows. The people living on Tien-ping Road had already heard about our family and needed no encouragement to mock us. Some of the younger children jumped in front of Chi-kai, brandishing sticks. He had once been president of his second-grade class, so they shouted, "Anti-Revolutionary bourgeois authoritarian trash! You tried to take us over, but now we have the upper hand! Next time you'll think twice about competing with Chairman Mao! Long live Chairman Mao!"

Even the Red Guards laughed at this. The children did not realize how ridiculous their accusations were, but they began beating Chi-kai with their sticks. Father refused to go any farther. "Release my children!" he shouted. "They are innocent."

Da-wei beat Father with redoubled efforts until he fell to the ground, too weak to rise. Da-wei then ordered us to carry Father home. When we reached our street, all of the neighbors were gawking. It was as if the curtain had just risen on a play they had waited months to see. Some shook their heads and went home. Even this action could be construed as a sign of sympathy for anti-Revolutionary elements, so it required courage. I heard two middle-aged women commenting, "Such a big girl still wears such old clothes. She looks like a walking rag doll!" Another woman said, "She must have been the empress dowager in her last life, and now she's paying for it." Once, such words would have made me cry for days, but now they ran like the proverbial water off a duck's back.

Halfway home, we met Uncle Zhu, the last of our friendly neighbors. He was carrying a chair and helped us put Father onto it. Father's back had been injured during the beatings, and he could not sit straight.

Da-wei still followed. Outraged by Uncle Zhu's assistance, he yelled, "You anti-Revolutionary scum! What do you think you're doing? Can't you wait till you get inside to get cozy with your boyfriend?" People in the group behind began shouting rebukes of their own.

Uncle Zhu answered sternly, "I belong to the working class. I am a Communist Party member. We have to keep this anti-Revolutionary alive so we can find out his plans to destroy the Communist Party! If he dies, we will not learn of the conspiracies going on to undermine the Proletarian Dictatorship. You want to kill him? You must want to silence him, to protect these conspirators! Right now you're aiding the bourgeois capitalist subverters of our nation!"

Thrown off balance, Da-wei stammered. Uncle Zhu took the offensive: "What are you waiting for? Do I have to do all of your thinking for you? Get your tails over here and carry him upstairs! Now!"

Da-wei could do nothing but follow Uncle Zhu's orders. He relayed the orders to his platoon: "You heard the man! Chairman Mao isn't paying us by the hour!"

The Red Guards rushed Father up to the apartment. Intimidated by Uncle Zhu's authority, they dispensed with the standard lecture and left in a hurry, drawing the curtain on the skit.

Hours later, as the sky was darkening, Father regained consciousness. Overjoyed to see him awake, we tripped over each other trying to serve him. The three of us tucked him in, brought him water, and cooked gruel for him. By then, we had come to the decision that in order for Father to continue his work, he would have to pretend that the beatings of the Red Guards had left him paralyzed. He would have to stay in bed permanently.

It was not a naive game of "house" that my brothers and I proposed but a carefully deliberated course of action. Its advantages were obvious enough; it was the sacrifices involved that we had to consider. Father's entire world would be less than twenty square meters, and most of the time only his bed. He would be little better off than a prisoner, except for the luxury of having some of his children around him. The plan also meant that we would have to do much more menial labor to make up for his impairment, attend the lectures required for the Blacks, and hand in the regularly assigned confessions to the Public Security Office. However, if it meant keeping Father from further brutality, it was worth it.

Father eventually agreed. The seventeen hopeless years since China's "Liberation" had been a nightmarish betrayal of his ideals. The dream was over now, but in his children he saw hope. For the next twelve years, Father continued writing in secret.

△△△ Now that everyone knew where we lived, we had even less peace. Rocks from a slingshot came through our window as I carried soup from the kitchen. Broken glass fell into the soup and the pellet hit me on the cheek. From that day onward, the room became a battlefield, and we covered ourselves with blankets for protection. All thirty-four panes of glass were broken within a few days. A neighbor suggested transparent plastic curtains to seal the window, but I thought that if the Red Guards knew that slingshots were ineffectual, they would do something worse. One day at noon, ten Red Guards lined up outside the house. They held a target contest and threw stones at the few pieces of glass that were left in the windows. Two hours later, not a single shard was left.

△△△ October 4, the day of my chastisement meeting, neared. However, October 3 passed with no malicious visitors. So did the morning of the 4th, and the terror building in my family peaked. The meeting was set for two o'clock, so at 1:30, I stood ready at the door to the auditorium. Red Guards traversed the school grounds, but no one seemed to notice me. At 1:45, the auditorium was still completely empty. I once more read the announcement on the entrance:

COMING ATTRACTIONS!

October 4th, 2:00 P.M., 1966
Right here in the Nan Yang Model Auditorium
A public debate! The Red Guards vs.
The anti-Revolutionary whelp Xi-ou Tan!
The topics: Is it wrong to revere anti-Revolutionary
scum more than our beloved Chairman Mao?
Is Western poetry praising the Four Obsolete
Vestiges a threat to the Proletarian Dictatorship?
Share your views! Use your actions
to express your loyalty to our Red Sun!

It was two o'clock, October 4, 1966, and I was in the right place. I wanted to run home and tell my family, but I dared not leave. If the Red Guards came later and did not find me at the appointed place, there would be more trouble. So I waited. Finally I saw an old friend from elementary school. "Ying-hui!" I called excitedly.

The girl looked at me as if I were a stranger. She squinted, and after looking around cautiously to make sure that no one was watching, she stepped forward. "What are you doing here?" she asked flatly. Before I could respond, she scanned the notice and said, "Yes. I remember now."

My initial friendliness dissipated at her tone of voice. I turned my back on her, but she was undaunted: "Xi-ou, you're doing it all wrong! Just break with your family and join the Revolutionary melting pot. I reported that my parents had money hidden, and I led the Red Guards to our home. I joined the Red Guards and things are much easier for me now. When I pass your house, I always think, 'Why is she being so stupid?' You can't choose your family, but you can choose to follow the Revolutionary path!" I said nothing, and Ying-hui continued: "You know where I'm going tomorrow? Beijing! To see Chairman Mao! They posted the invitation yesterday!"

I threw a final glance at the banner. Realizing that the meeting would not be that day, I left. The Red Guards found that condemning an already denounced person paled in comparison to an audience with Chairman Mao and a free trip through China. Their acts of corruption filled my mind: the Red Guard leader with more than twenty watches on his arm; Da-wei's stuffed money belt; the heavy boots used to crush my father's tocs. I was deeply insulted that the Red Guards thought more of a free trip than of me. The cancellation of the meeting was a great relief for my family, but I was appalled that the Red Guards cared nothing for the ideology of the Revolution that they represented. However, I was most angry with myself for thinking like the Reddest of the Red Guards at that moment.

△△ I was very much an idealist then, Professor Hu. In many ways, I still am. When you are young, dreams, even if they are impractical, help you to survive, or to achieve. When you are older, you develop other reasons. I hope that you have used these reasons to reconsider your decision. It was really my parents' strength that held our family together during those terrible times. In my next letter, I will tell you more about them. In the meantime, take care of yourself.

Sincerely,
Xi-ou Tan

 My father, Jin-ren Tan, was born in 1913 to a long line of poor peasants in rural Cha Ling county in the province of Hunan. At seventeen, he arrived barefoot in Chang Sha, the capital of Hunan, with one yuan sewed into the lining of his belt by his widowed mother. After working for several months at menial jobs, he passed the entrance examination for aviation school. Two weeks into the program, he met Professor Yung-shan Tan, a famous scholar who had helped to found a liberal university in Shanghai. Professor Tan told him, "Right now there are two battlefields. China has no lack of brave young men who are willing to fight for glory, but she also needs brilliant minds and strong spirits to break the unreasonable, feudalistic traditions that have chained this nation to a darker age. Through education, we can set up a China of freedom, equality, and prosperity. You would be better to take off your aviator's uniform and go to Shanghai to study."

With money and recommendations from Professor Tan, Father left for Shanghai. He graduated from the university in 1934 and then worked in Beijing for three years on the first Chinese-Japanese dictionary. The anti-Japanese war broke out in 1937, so Father organized a group of young people to go through the countryside to instruct the citizens on the benefits of rising up against the Japanese imperialists. He set up workshops to teach basic economic principles to those students whose education had been interrupted by the war. These principles were designed to help them better produce and distribute commodities.

He was also in charge of farm loans for Zhe Jiang and Jiang Su provinces.

His activities brought him to the attention of the Guomindang government. Because of his criticism of the corruption in government, he was suspected of being a Communist. In late 1940, the local Guomindang secretary arranged to have his house searched, but a pretty young woman who was attracted to Father had Guomindang connections and warned him. Within a year, that woman and he were married.

My mother, Y-yao Bai, was born into a highly respected family in Zhe Jiang province. Having served as high-level bureaucrats for generations, they adhered to a strict, feudalistic philosophy. Y-yao's father and three uncles broke the tradition with their involvement in the May Fourth Movement of 1919, which introduced many Western ideas to China.

Mother grew up as a pretty, spoiled, dreamy daughter of a government official. Her mother died several hours after giving birth to her, so she was sent to boarding school when she was ten, about five years earlier than most children. She and her classmates encouraged people to rise up against the Japanese by putting on plays and distributing pamphlets urging people to boycott Japanese products.

She was sixteen when the war broke out in 1937. She went back home to her father, who got her a temporary job in the Zhe Jiang government as a secretary. It was during this time that she met my father. The nation's suffering had quickly changed my mother: The war with Japan took a heavy toll and touched everyone's life. Bombs exploded everywhere, and she watched as several of her colleagues were killed running to shelters when the alarm sounded. One Japanese air raid almost hit my parents' home; the explosion threw them to the floor. Father covered Mother's body with his own to protect her and was knocked unconscious. When he did not move for long seconds after the air raid was over, Mother thought he was dead.

My mother's dream was to write. In her thirties, she became a journalist and eventually wrote two books. Her first novel was unsuccessful, but the second one was a huge success. It was written as the diary of a woman journalist and owed its raw material to Father, who traveled and sent Mother reams of letters. When Rei-qing was born,

Mother found that the education of children in China was as barren as the tundra. To compensate, she invented many stories, but in October of 1949, before she could write them all down in her third book, Mao Zedong took over China.

In early 1949, my grandfather urged my mother to take her family and go to Taiwan with him. By then, he was a Guomindang Navy judge, and the political situation was dangerous for him. In March, she received a message from him stating that a ship was waiting in Ding-hai to carry her stepmother, her brothers, and himself to Taiwan. This would be her last chance to leave.

Mother and Father hated the corruption of the Guomindang government, and they believed that China would have a new chance with the Communist Party. But mother was close to her father, and it was impossible for her to imagine a life in Shanghai with him exiled in Taiwan. The conflict in her heart—to stay with her husband and daughter in Shanghai or to leave with her father—was intensified because of a new life growing inside her. She finally decided to stay in Shanghai so that the unborn child would not grow up without a father. The thought that the Communist Party might eventually persecute the relatives of Guomindang party members never crossed her mind.

6

Dear Professor Hu,

I cannot express the pain my family felt,
after the trial in May of 1966, when Mother was
taken to the Basket Bridge, the Shanghai prison on
the banks of the Huang-pu River. While we fought our
battles at home, Mother had her own. I would like to share
some of her experiences with you.

When she was first put into the Basket Bridge, we mailed her two
blankets and some clothes. Worried that we would need them during
the coming winter, she fought hard with the guards to let her give the
blankets back to us. Losing the fight, she was put into solitary confinement for her breach of discipline.

Because of the turmoil caused by the Grand Cultural Revolution,
the normal jail sentence was abandoned. Prisoners were no longer
allowed to send or receive letters, and visiting days were canceled. Her
fellow inmates told her that visiting days were usually held every two
or three months.

According to the Sixteen Principles, the prison system was not to
take part in the Revolution outside its own walls. Whenever important
articles were published, the wardens organized mass study and discussion sessions whereby the prisoners could connect the wisdom of the
publications with the horror of their past anti-Revolutionary deeds.
Most of the female prisoners were illiterate, so Mother was appointed
the group reader shortly after she arrived.

Mother sank into a deep depression, thinking of nothing but the persecution of her husband and young children, and her long and hopeless prison life. At night, she wrapped herself in a blanket and cried until dawn. During the day, she could barely move from lack of sleep. During her readings, she occasionally broke down after only half an article. Her group monitor, a semiliterate prostitute, was desperately afraid of losing her position, so, to protect it, she reported Mother's inability to read a complete article aloud, and a denunciation was organized. Mother, fortunately, never misread a sentence; if she had, it could have resulted in her being found guilty of "twisting the tongue of Chairman Mao." Instead, she was accused of shedding tears for the Ox Ghosts outside the jail who were losing the privileges that they had relished for years.

Prison left her despondent. In her occasional periods of lucidity, she decided that strength and determination were not gifts given at birth, but virtues that had to be developed. Within three months, she had become an infamous example of the Revolution's failure to rehabilitate. Instead of becoming more Red, she lost all drive to do anything.

The prison authorities periodically rotated the prisoners so that they would not form strong bonds with each other and conspire against the guards. After about three months of her sentence, Mother received two new cellmates. One was a severely mentally retarded woman who did not even know her own name or age. Jail was a blessing for her; she had a place to sleep and more food than she could possibly scrounge on the street. Mother was touched by this pitiful woman's condition, and, for the first time in months, she was drawn out of her self-pity.

The dim light of the jail burned all night. Staring at the distant light, Mother turned her attention from the retarded woman's snores to her other cellmate. She, too, had been tossing, unable to sleep. The woman had elongated eyes, thin eyebrows, a long, straight nose, and a chin that jutted slightly from her face. Quiet and simple, her general physiognomy suggested a highly educated woman. She was a Roman Catholic nun who had been jailed shortly after the Liberation when the Communist Party ruled that all religions were anti-Revolutionary. The nun had been there so long that people joked that she owned the place. She would be released if she would state that there was no God, but she refused.

When the nun rose from the floor, Mother assumed that she was going to use the toilet. Instead, she stepped over the retarded woman's sleeping form and crouched down beside Mother. Mother made as much room as possible in the tiny cell, pressing herself against the wall, and the nun lay down beside her. Glancing at the spot the nun had abandoned, Mother noticed that the blanket had been bunched up to look like a body.

"My name is Y-jin," she said quickly. "I've often heard you cry and have wondered about you. Could you show me a picture of your children?"

That one friendly remark brought the two close together, and tears streamed from Mother's eyes into her ears. She pulled out a picture that had been hidden beneath her undershirt and showed it to the nun. "The oldest girl is very quiet and gentle, but the younger one is stubborn and naughty. After them comes this one. He's shy and obedient. The youngest boy is very sensitive. I was far too strict with them," Mother murmured to her new friend. "I feel so guilty now."

"I'll pray for them," Y-jin said. In the dim light, Y-jin scrutinized the picture, committing all the faces to memory. She returned it, saying, "You're not alone. I'm praying for you."

Then she agilely went back to her own spot on the floor.

Mother gradually returned to her earlier energetic and hopeful state, greatly comforted by Y-jin's prayers, even though she knew very little about religion. She vaguely remembered her grandmother burning incense and praying before a statue of the Buddha as her father stood by, snickering to himself. After their marriage, my parents divorced themselves from all forms of faith, although they respected others' beliefs. Mother had never thought that she would believe in any form of a god, but the simple, sincere prayer of a devout Catholic nun brought her not only faith, but also the courage to continue living. Spies were everywhere, but even under these conditions, this nun, who knew nothing of Mother, had taken the risk of offering her friendship. Had Mother cried out, Y-jin would have been punished and Mother commended for her loyalty. If Mother had told the guards that Y-jin gave her some of her soap and toilet paper, the nun would have been accused of attempting to buy off fellow prisoners, while Mother would have been praised. Why, then, did Y-jin selflessly offer her friendship? If it was only simple human decency, why did everyone, including Mother herself, not act so bravely?

Night after night, as the retarded woman snored loudly on the floor beside them, Y-jin quietly explained the Bible and the Christian faith. The snoring made conversation difficult, but it also concealed their voices from the guards and other prisoners. The nun's stability and tenderness brought Mother back to her cheerful nature.

In December 1966, the prisoners were informed that there would be a visiting day the following week. When asked to fill out a form stating who would be coming to visit, Mother included Father's name, but since they had been codefendants, they could not see each other. For the first time in seven months, she received a letter from us with all the news of Father cloaked in Revolutionary language.

The visiting day finally arrived, and we children were part of the second round of visitors. Rei-qing had returned temporarily from her farm. When the whistle blew summoning the inmates, Mother stood in the middle of the confusion. It seemed an eternity before she heard our voices and found us. She looked at us hungrily.

"Prisoner 107, watch yourself!" the guard shouted. We had only ten minutes and much to communicate.

Happy to see that we were healthy and growing, and that we loved and took care of each other, Mother felt that things were not as bad as she had feared. We had each rehearsed short speeches and arranged them in a proper order for her benefit. "Brother Ying's asthma is very bad these days. It's because the weather is abnormally cold," Rei-qing said, twice for emphasis. Mother correctly interpreted this to mean, "The political situation is still bad, Father's in particular." Rei-qing and I recounted the situation in the schools and in society, along with some general remarks about the household. Chi-kai excitedly told Mother all he had learned in the previous few months. "I already know how to cook rice!" he exclaimed.

All four of us mentioned the tale of "The Lily Lantern," now "A Poisonous Weed in the Revolutionary Garden." In the story, a woman was imprisoned in a mountain by a god. Her brave young son journeyed through many dangers and finally split open the mountain with his ax, freeing his mother. Because he carried a lantern everywhere to light his way, it became his symbol.

Mother did not understand what we meant, but before she could ask us to elaborate, the whistle blew. We took advantage of the confusion to tell her that Rei-qing had just arrived from the farm the day before and had sewed the clothes in a hurry. If Mother did not like them, they could be resewn, we said. The guard silenced us, and we and Mother backed out toward our respective doors with tears in our eyes.

That night, with Y-jin's help, Mother opened the cuff of one of the shirts we had brought. She found a tiny piece of paper with "The Lily Lantern" written on it, although they could barely read the characters in the dim light. Y-jin did not understand, but Mother finally did.

"This is the 'The Lily Lantern.' There was a children's play with that name. When my third child, Jian-nan, was still an infant, my husband and I took them all to see it."

"Your children are very clever. Even if the guards found this in your shirt, what could they say? It's only a children's story. But what better way could there be to express their feelings to you?" The nun paused a moment, then added, "Filial love is also a gift."

Mother and "Aunt" Y-jin did not know that "The Lily Lantern" had another meaning. I will explain this further in my next letter. Please take care, Professor Hu. I hope you are enjoying my stories.

> Sincerely,
> Xi-ou Tan

 Ah-di returned from Beijing in November 1966. I filled her in on what happened while she was away and told her about the attack on my home and the beating of my father by the Nan Yang Model Middle School Red Guards on September 27.

"September 27?" she queried. "That's strange. The Red Guards from other schools did similar things, too. I wonder what was so special about it."

Soon after, she discovered that the Red Guards had made a concerted effort throughout Shanghai on that day to attack all anti-Revolutionaries. " 'The joyous triumph for the Revolutionary masses is painful defeat for our anti-Revolutionary enemies,' " quoted Ah-di. "October 1 is National Day, the most important day of the year," she continued. "On September 27, they decided to imprison all known anti-Revolutionaries so they could be assured of celebrating the triumphs of the Cultural Revolution in safety." When I looked alarmed, she quickly added, "I didn't say I thought they were right."

She had misunderstood my fright. I was afraid that on every national holiday like May Day, National Day, or New Year's Day, our home would be ransacked and my family tormented.

Friends of the family suggested that we turn Father in to the authorities for our own and his safety. At least in jail, wardens would not beat him as the Red Guards had. I appreciated their candor but found their solution unacceptable. Rei-qing and I had always believed that our parents were wrongly accused, and we decided, though Rei-qing was not often in Shanghai, to fight the system and have them exonerated. We would be the heroes of our own "Lily Lantern."

7

Dear Professor Hu,

The suppression we experienced in our youth made us fight harder. The young have more to lose, and thus more reasons to fight. Where others saw a hopeless, universal, slow death, naïveté was our shield: We saw only a temporary phenomenon.

At the beginning of the Revolution, the "dead tigers"—politically weak people like my father—had been attacked first. Next, people were investigated and their political classifications changed, like some of my classmates at school. Now, Chairman Mao declared that the power of the Communist Party had been usurped by class enemies who wished to return to the "paradise of the Guomindang and the imperialists." When I went to the General Publishing House in late November to look at the wall posters, I found that Q. Zhang and S. Jiang, the former heads of the publishing houses and the ones who had originally persecuted Father in the anti-Rightist purge of 1957, had been ousted. They were accused of crimes against the Party, socialism, and Mao Zedong's philosophy. Now they swept floors and cleaned toilets.

I did not understand the latest turns of events. People who had been considered loyal to the Communist Party were now treated worse than we were. Simple logic dictated that, if these people who had once accused us were anti-Revolutionaries, then we ourselves should be the true Revolutionaries. For years, there had been so many inexplicable events, such as Father being labeled a Rightist. We had never doubted our parents' innocence, and now we learned that the people doing the labeling were the real enemies of the state.

When Rei-qing came home for vacation that December, she and I formulated a plan. Because those who had made the accusations against our parents were now discredited, we felt that we had a real chance of getting our parents' names exonerated. Instead of hiding our affection for our parents, we might now be able to show our love openly and proudly. Mother and Father might once again be honored citizens of the People's Republic of China.

"Some of Father's friends who are still in publishing might give us some information on the current feelings about the Cultural Revolution in the Chinese Encyclopedia Publishing House," Rei-qing suggested. "The first injustice the Communist Party dealt our parents was labeling them Rightists. The newspaper is the tongue of the Party, so it would be difficult to work with them on Mother's account, but the publishing house is accessible. Whatever happens to one person happens to the spouse, so solving Father's problem also solves Mother's. Also, Father can give us information whenever we need it."

"Sounds good!" I said enthusiastically. "I'll go ask Father what we should do first!"

"No," Rei-qing said resolutely. "Don't tell Father. Until his name is cleared, he can't do anything except pretend he's sick. He'll only worry if we tell him. Besides, it's not right to waste Father's superior intellect on mundane matters like this."

We decided on four steps. First, investigation: to speak with everyone, including Father, who had knowledge of the events of the spring of 1957. For this phase of the operation, we wanted such complete secrecy that even our own family would be unable to detect anything unusual. Second, infiltration: joining the Red Guards. This was possible now that the Central Committee had repudiated the Revolutionary dogma that "the son of a hero is a hero; the son of an anti-Revolutionary is an anti-Revolutionary." The third phase was counterattack: wearing a red armband, the symbol of the Red Guard's authority, we would storm the publishing house and force the "Ox Ghosts" now under arrest to sign confessions of anti-Revolutionary acts— specifically, suppression of our parents. Finally, we would present the enormous body of evidence in writing; by the quality of its preparation, it would demand the redemption of our parents and their reinstatement to their former posts. We would send it to Premier Zhou En-li, since we had heard stories of his just actions toward intellectuals and believed that he was the most humanitarian of all those holding power.

We walked along quiet Kang-ping Road, reviewing the plan until its mechanics were second nature to us. Our major concern was that in our service as Red Guards, we might be obligated to commit a morally repugnant act. We decided that, under those circumstances, we would refuse even if it meant ostracization from the Red Guards and failure of the master plan.

It was dusk, and my sister appeared to glow in the sunset. We were drunk with thoughts of heroism and believed that we could move mountains. We assumed everything would go along without a hitch, but the answers to two simple questions would have revealed the gross flaws in our plan: "Is the purpose of the Cultural Revolution to root out the subversive members of the Communist Party and exonerate falsely accused persons?" and "Can the Communist Party ever exist without conflict?"

Kang-ping Road had well-kept trees and gardens, but its beauty and serenity were superficial: The Party headquarters for Eastern China and Shanghai were located here. A chill wind blew through the bare trees. The last rays of the sun disappeared and darkness grew around us. Armed soldiers in People's Liberation Army uniforms patrolled the street, in stark contrast to the workers rushing home to dinner. Rei-qing would return to the farm the next day, and I already felt the acute pain of separation. I wished that we could walk and plan together every evening, but I tried to repress dreams and concentrate on reality. "We need a code name," I whispered.

The streetlights were turned on, revealing my sister's clear, black eyes. She looked young and beautiful. "Because we're sending our document to Premier Zhou En-li, let's call our plan 'En-ligh-tenment'!"

△△△ Later in December, not long after our first visit with Mother at the Basket Bridge, I began the investigation. Wei-chun Ho, one of Father's friends at the publishing house, and another man, Shi-wen Yang, had been close friends of Father's since they were all in their twenties. When Wei-chun Ho graduated from the university in 1936, specializing in biostatistics, he put aside his chosen field in order to help Father train other students to join him in his travels to remote areas to teach basic economics. Although Shi-wen Yang was slightly older, he had been my father's pupil. Separated after the war, the three met by chance in Shanghai years later in the 1950s. Shi-wen Yang had risen to the position of Administrator of Economic Policy for the six Eastern China provinces and Shanghai. Father and Wei-chun were colleagues in the publishing house. As Wei-chun grew older, he lost his idealism and became an overcautious yes-man. When Father was branded a Rightist, Wei-chun broke off their friendship, but I still hoped that he might help.

Two minutes after I hung up the telephone, Wei-chun Ho appeared at the corner of Triangle Park, a few blocks from the publishing house. The hazy winter sun shone dully on the wall posters flapping in the chill breeze. Triangle Park, now Revolutionary Plaza, was, like almost all the parks now, primarily a location for viewing wall posters. The last time I had seen "Uncle Ho," I was a chubby little girl who rolled on the grass in a colorful sweater. This time, it took him a while to recognize me. "You have your father's forehead and your mother's chin," he exclaimed. We turned down a quiet street, and he pulled twenty yuan from his pocket. "Your life must be very difficult. I didn't bring much money with me today, but take this for some emergency."

I flushed, shaking my head. "No, that's not why I came here." Seeing that I was hurt, he put the money back into his pocket and gently asked me what he could do for me.

Gradually regaining my composure, I began by asking him to swear that he would tell no one, not even Father, that I had come to see him. Then I asked him to inform me periodically on the course of the current criticisms of those in power.

"That isn't a problem," he said without hesitation. "The wall posters of the publishing house report all the details."

"I know," I replied, "but I can't go to the publishing house every day, and besides, it might look suspicious. The way things are now, if

I skip even one day of reading wall posters, I could miss the denunciation of someone very important to me."

When Uncle Ho nodded, I asked him if he would agree to help me.

"Yes," he said firmly, then changed the subject abruptly. "Do you remember my son, Xiao Ru? He's your age."

"I couldn't forget him," I laughed. "He once wanted me to taste honeysuckles with him. I didn't like them. They made my mouth tingle."

"He's a lot like me. He likes science. When he was little, he was fascinated with plants and animals. Later he came to love math." Uncle Ho sighed. "Now all of you have lost your school and stay home all the time. You weren't born at the right time."

By six that evening, I was waiting by an overpass near Jiao Tong University to meet Kung-lan Guo. Just as the streetlights went on, we saw each other and stepped through the red iron gate of Jiao Tong University.

Kung-lan Guo had returned from Japan just as the anti-Japanese war began in 1937. Handsome and charming, he had caught the eye of an heiress six years older than he. They eventually married and had children. After the Liberation in 1949 and ten years of marriage, he discovered that his wife had been working underground for the Communist Party. In 1957, he was called a borderline Rightist but was virtually immune to persecution because of his wife's powerful connections. She retired shortly before the Cultural Revolution, and, since they no longer held positions of power, they were not denounced.

Father had spent many of his weekends with "Uncle Guo," patiently correcting his Japanese translations. Although Uncle Guo was the deputy editor-in-chief of a large publishing house and had spent many years in Japan, his knowledge of Japanese literature and language was poor. One of his books was so poorly translated that Father had to rework three-fourths of it. Guo proposed that both their names appear on the final translation, but Father refused. Guo had not visited him during the last year, but only because Father turned away all visitors following his trial.

After Kung-lan Guo had inquired about the family, I got to the point. Although Uncle Guo had passed through the greatest crises of the nation unscathed, he was not unsympathetic to the problems of others. Politically shrewd, he clung to no particular ideals, simply bending with the breeze.

"Xi-ou, do you know at whom this movement is directed?" he asked.

"The Four Obsolete Vestiges and the Ox Ghosts!" I answered automatically.

"You're just parroting! If you're going to recite Revolutionary slogans, you'd better know what they mean," he said, smiling.

I considered the question anew. Finally I replied, "At this stage, I gather from the newspaper editorials and the wall posters that the bourgeois elements of the Party, from local governments all the way up to the Central Committee, are under fire."

"Who would be the biggest of all of these?" Guo asked.

"S. K. Yang? R. Q. Luo? D. Y. Lu? Z. Peng?" I guessed, recalling the prominent names on the wall posters. I had no idea how to tell who had been the most powerful.

"Just the biggest."

"I honestly don't know, Uncle Guo. Please, just tell me straight out who it is," I pleaded.

"Who is the innermost of Chairman Mao's inner circle?"

"I don't know. Who?" I asked.

"Liu Shao-qi."

"Liu Shao-qi," I stammered, shocked, "the president of the People's Republic of China? How could it be he? Only two years ago we voted him into office! The whole country celebrated his victory!"

There were a number of large, makeshift walls for wall posters along the street near the main campus of Jiao Tong University. Three Red Guards were using brooms to apply paste from a huge barrel to one of the walls while two other guards hung the wall posters on it. I watched, interested, but Kung-lan Guo paid no attention.

We passed the library. All of the books had been either burned or locked away, and the building was now dark and silent. Kung-lan Guo suddenly embraced me tightly, kissing me squarely on the mouth.

I struggled free and fled. I felt dizzy, and my face burned as I still felt his rough kiss on my lips. I wanted to wash my face. Angry with myself for trusting him, I did not dare to go home directly, since Father would ask what had upset me so. I wandered through the streets for two hours, wishing the worst for "Uncle Guo." "I hope that disgusting pervert's lips fall off!" I fumed. I also remembered Chairman Mao's words: "Whenever there is a fight, there is a sacrifice." I tried to see this as the first sacrifice I had to make to carry out my plan, and I was prepared to continue fighting. The first phase of the plan would take time, but it was now underway.

△△△ The second phase, infiltration of the Red Guards, took a turn I had not expected. After the 1967 "January storm" when Shanghai workers went to Beijing to force the city government to relinquish the power to the working class, the Red Guards began to lose popularity. The now-organized Shanghai Working Class divided into two rival organizations: the General Association of the Shanghai Working Class and the Shanghai Diesel Assembly Working Class. A woman in my neighborhood belonged to the first group and her husband to the other. Because they were both active members of their respective organizations during the day, they spent the nights fighting. Eventually the wife was sent on a mission to burn down the Diesel headquarters, and her husband died in the fire.

Rei-qing had been sent to the countryside the previous September as part of the "disposable youth," but they returned four turbulent months later, proudly carrying large flags and proclaiming themselves the "Shanghai Farm Workers." Rather than subject themselves to the battles of the two rival factions, they formed their own. Although they had been working in the fields, they had been paid eighteen yuan per month by the government, unlike the unsalaried peasants. Still, no one could deny that a person who worked with his own hands in the fields every day was a member of the working class. Realizing that they were "artificial" and not "natural" members of the working class, and that their popularity would be short-lived, the Shanghai Farm Workers cautiously set up a headquarters in Shanghai. Those with better family backgrounds held meetings to chastise the Neighborhood Committee for forcing them to go to the countryside. Those from bourgeois families stayed in the background but suggested ideas and slogans to those in control.

Everyone classified as a member of the working class could now wear the red armband previously restricted to the Red Guards. Two brothers who had worked with Rei-qing came from a bourgeois family but could now use their titles as Shanghai Farm Workers to expel the Neighborhood Committee members occupying their family's estate. Then they allowed the Shanghai Farm Workers to use their house as a headquarters. A constant parade of farm workers bowed respectfully to the boys' parents, addressing them as "Uncle" and "Aunt." Without knowing it, these farm workers became the family's protectors. Although it was simple for Rei-qing to join this organization, I experienced considerably more red tape in joining the Red Guards.

My classmates had been scattered two months earlier, taking advantage of the opportunity to tour China. It took both raw courage and physical prowess to plunge into a train filled to 400 percent capacity, and it was not uncommon to be thrown from the train while sleeping. When the train passed a station, passengers shut the windows and doors against the Red Guards, who had waited for days to board a train and often threw garbage into the windows or hosed down the passengers in their frustration. Lack of spending money was no problem for some Red Guards. If one found himself running low, he would burst in on a local family to search the home for signs of the Four Obsolete Vestiges. During the search, he would pick up money or items for barter. Lodging was also of little concern. All the primary, middle, and high schools, as well as the colleges, were turned into hotels for the Red Guards. If a Red Guard desired better accommodations, he could always temporarily evict a Black family and use the home for the night.

These Red Guard escapades disrupted ordinary routine throughout China. The Ox Ghosts, pleased that their tormentors were still on the road, acted like mice in a house with its cat run over by a bus. Reports of train crashes and derailments were greeted with secret joy. At the end of 1966, the State Department posted orders in every railway station and shipping port demanding that the Red Guards return home and continue the Revolution there. The orders promised that there would be another Cultural Revolutionary exchange in the spring, but this promise was not kept.

The winter was a cold one; many Red Guards did not own proper clothing and, like Ah-di, would not steal it either. Quite a few had visited areas that were infested by plague, while others returned home crawling with fleas and lice. Many of the women became pregnant. Seeing new things gave the Red Guards the sophistication and maturity they had lacked. Instead of having identical experiences and goals, each wanted to gain something different from his or her association with the Red Guards—most of it having more to do with self-interest than with the Revolution. The unity began to dissolve and splinter groups formed.

I applied to join the "Red Guards of Self-Determination," whose motto was "Not through birth but through self-determination can you be Red." Mostly comprised of students from working-class families, it was diametrically opposed to Xiao-yi Wu's group, the "Revolutionary Army." Ah-di was a member of my group's Executive Committee. By accepting me into their ranks, they were contaminated.

I was excited suddenly to have comrades I could call my own, but I knew that they only wished to exploit my debating skills. Because any public statement by me could easily be interpreted as that of an anti-Revolutionary infiltrator attempting to tear down the work of the Revolution, I was hesitant to speak out. I could not explain this to my comrades, and I was unsure whether Ah-di really understood my reluctance or just acquiesced to protect me. I sincerely wished to contribute, and Ah-di and I worked out the following solution: We would sit together at the debates, and Ah-di would speak while I pretended to take notes. In reality, I fed lines to her.

On the day of the first debate, the classroom at our old school was packed with more than a hundred students, just as there had been several months earlier when Xiao-yi Wu forced Teacher Peng to his knees. Red Guards of each faction, along with the student spectators, faced each other from the two sides of the classroom. The Revolutionary Army, Xiao-yi Wu's group, was larger than ours.

The topic of the debate was a Rolex watch. Six members of the Red Guards of Self-Determination had once searched a bourgeois home with Xiao-yi Wu and another of my old enemies, "Lard Bucket Lin Chu" (also known as "Chubby Chu"), the secretary of the Youth League. Everyone had seen Lard Bucket pocket an expensive Rolex watch, which she did not turn in to the Central Office. Lard Bucket was on the Executive Committee of the Revolutionary Army, and the Red Guards of Self-Determination saw her as an easy target. By discrediting her, the entire Revolutionary Army would be branded as anti-Revolutionary, common thieves.

The debate began with six witnesses describing the incident. As they gave their evidence, Lard Bucket sat with Xiao-yi Wu on her left and Canton Kiss Up on her right. With her arms folded, her legs spread wide, she wore a look of practiced indifference.

"Lin Chu, let me ask you," began Ah-di. "Do you have anything to say against the evidence these comrades have given?"

"Even if it's true, who cares?" Lard Bucket answered. "I only *borrowed* these things for the overall good of the organization. After all, Ah-di Chen, didn't you use the blanket I *borrowed* later that night while you were on duty?"

Ah-di responded, "Our great leader, Chairman Mao, has always told us that we should observe his Three Disciplines and Eight Regulations. One of them is, when you borrow something, return it. Am I telling you something new?"

Lard Bucket replied sharply: "These things belonged to the anti-Revolutionary bourgeoisie! Do we have to obey these rules even when dealing with *them*?"

Ah-di paused. After a glance downward at my notes, she continued. "Everything that the anti-Revolutionary bourgeoisie possesses has been stolen from the working class. These things don't belong to you or me, they belong to the People!"

Xiao-yi Wu had been squirming during the entire interrogation, and now he lost his patience altogether. Jumping up, he said, "You're out of your petty little mind! Our beloved Chubby Chu kept this watch because she wanted to keep track of time so she could see Chairman Mao, the Reddest Sun, as soon as possible! Her motivation was purely Revolutionary."

Da Lu, the chief of my group, spoke: "All right, now that we've seen Chairman Mao and she's realized her Revolutionary goal, why does she still have the watch?"

"Who has it? The day I saw Chairman Mao, I lost it in Tiananmen Square," Lard Bucket said, her voice rising three octaves.

"You can't prove you lost it and you know it!" Da Lu shouted.

"Somebody picked my pocket! Do you think he left an address?" she sniped.

Two members of the Red Guards of Self-Determination, who had defected from the Revolutionary Army only a week earlier, stood up. One of them spit out, "We've traveled with Lin Chu for several weeks. Both of us have seen that watch on her wrist within the last two weeks!"

Lard Bucket began to stutter: "Well . . . my watch, I mean that watch was . . . stolen . . . in Shanghai last week."

Ah-di pounced. "Lin Chu, as a member of the leadership of the Revolutionary Army, in the name of the Revolution, you have embezzled the property of the Revolutionary Mass! Now it is time for justice. If you have it, hand it over now; if you lost it, you must pay the cost of a new watch to the Confiscated Materials Committee."

Canton Kiss Up cleared his throat. The room fell silent in anticipation of a characteristically eloquent speech. "You members of the Red Guards of Self-Determination, don't try to shift the main goal of our fight. Now, all over the country, everyone is focusing on destroying Liu Shao-qi's anti-Revolutionary stronghold. What Chubby Chu did is unimportant. She was only following Liu's orders. Chubby Chu is a victim, not an enemy. You would like us to forget that our real enemy is Liu Shao-qi!"

Xiao-yi Wu smiled with delight, giving his top adviser as approving a look as any master ever gave his pet dog. Lard Bucket, also pleased, crossed her legs, sat up in her chair, and began to tap her fingers on the table. She resembled a poker player who had laid down four aces and was getting ready to claim the pot.

Ah-di—again after a glance at my notes—turned on Canton Kiss Up. "Zheng-gou Wang, according to what you have said, we should go directly to Liu Shao-qi and ask him to return this watch."

The laughter from both sides dispelled the impact of Canton Kiss Up's speech. Da Lu read a formal edict representing the position of the Red Guards of Self-Determination. It demanded that all members of the Revolutionary Army who had stolen property in the line of duty return it.

Seeing that his side was losing, Xiao-yi Wu started to walk out of the room, followed by Canton Kiss Up, Lard Bucket, and his other lackeys. At that exact moment, Ah-di proposed that the group recite some of Chairman Mao's quotations, giving her opponents no choice but to return to their seats and pull out their "Little Red Books." After the readings, Xiao-yi Wu went to the school lobby, where he swore and pounded his fist against the wall.

Such were my new experiences as a Red Guard, something I had never thought I would be.

△△△ By the time Rei-qing and I completed our second phase, it was March 1967. I obtained a letter of introduction from the Red Guards of Self-Determination to the Red Guards who controlled the publishing houses in Shanghai. This served as a passport, allowing me to come and go freely. Since Rei-qing was a member of the Shanghai Farm Workers, she was equivalent to a Red Guard.

First, Rei-qing and I visited the Chinese Encyclopedia Publishing House to interrogate Jiang. The Red Guards were made up of young people, but the older ones had their own groups, and Jiang was being held by "Fish Five Oceans for Abalone." (Like so many other groups, they had taken their name from Chairman Mao's poems.) The leader, a gentle, middle-aged man, showed us to the conference room. He had been a clerk in the Army until retiring a month before the onset of the Grand Cultural Revolution. He then took a job at the publishing house but had never met Father. Although he was a career soldier, he struck me as wise and kind, unlike most members of groups like Fish Five Oceans for Abalone. He summoned Jiang to the conference room and left us alone with him.

When I had been a messenger for my sick father after his return from Qin-hai in 1961, I visited Jiang every month. Even though he had not seen me in seven years, I knew that he would recognize me, so I put on a false air of authority. I started with a standard speech, which included slogans such as, "Speak the truth and we will treat you well; lie, and you will get worse than what you deserve." We also requested him to repeat several carefully selected quotations of Chairman Mao. Then I began the questioning in earnest. Rei-qing took scrupulous notes, since we wished Jiang to sign them at the end of the meeting.

When I asked him if the name Jin-ren Tan meant anything to him, he turned his beady eyes away from my gaze, as if trying to recall something. He looked back with a sneer on his face that seemed to say, "Little girl, do you actually think I don't know who you are?"

"If you don't answer my questions, perhaps the Fish Five Oceans for Abalone will be more persuasive," I said sternly.

"Of course I know Jin-ren Tan," Jiang answered quickly.

It would not have been easy for Jiang to forget him. In 1935, both he and my father took an exam at the Wu Wei Japanese Research Institute in Beijing. The institute needed two bilingual editors, but they had almost a thousand applicants, many of whom were Chinese who had attended Japanese universities as undergraduates. Jiang's Japanese was only fair, so when he saw how many applicants there were, he became discouraged and started to leave, but Father dissuaded him. When they ran into each other several months later, Jiang was envious when he learned that Father had been one of the two accepted.

They met again by chance during the anti-Japanese war. Some of the youth from Zhe Jiang had been turned out of their jobs and schools, and Jiang organized them to go to Yan-an, the center of Red power. He met an elementary-school teacher named S. W. Yang, who desperately wanted to go but was reluctant to do so because of family obligations. His father was handicapped; his mother, illiterate and unskilled; and his older brother, a vagrant. Since he was the second oldest child, he inherited the family responsibilities, including five younger sisters and brothers. Impressed with Yang's ability, Jiang felt that this man could offer much to the Communist Party. Yang told him that in his spare time he studied economics at a local college, and that he had a wonderful young teacher. Jiang was shocked when he learned that Yang's teacher was my father. The three of them met, and Yang openly stated both his desire to go to Yan-an and the reasons for his hesitancy.

"It's not a problem," said Father gallantly. "I don't have any family obligations myself. I make more money than I know what to do with, so I'll set some aside for your family." Yang knelt before him in gratitude. In a jealous rage, Jiang considered denying Yang permission to join the Communists in Yan-an.

Yang rose quickly in the Communist Party. Jiang had left the Party during one of its more difficult periods, and now he served it at a lower level than Yang. An old Chinese proverb states that the road two enemies travel grows ever narrower. Jiang and Father met again in the publishing house. When Father first began there, Jiang was in a relatively weak position, since he was forced to give a written account of his activity during his hiatus from the Communist Party. Writing this confession took most of his time and energy, and Jiang was sorely afraid that the vacant position of editor-in-chief would be given to Father. Fortunately for Jiang, the Anti-Rightist Movement began. Jiang's Party membership protected him, and he was freed from the obligation of compiling his confession. The entire Party devoted itself to weeding out Rightists, and Jiang had Father exiled to Qin-hai.

"Confess how you branded Tan as a Rightist," I demanded.

"I don't remember the exact details, but I do remember that it was Tan's fault. He was always publicly denouncing the New China Bookstore," Jiang said.

"And exactly how did he denounce this bookstore?" I asked.

"Well," Jiang said, after pausing and scratching his head for a few minutes, "he said that the variety of books was limited, that the system was inefficient. He also criticized our party's policy of 'Let a hundred flowers blossom.' "

"Is that all?"

"Yes, that's all."

"Did this satisfy the requirements of being a Rightist?" I asked.

Jiang had been lackadaisical in his previous answers, but he suddenly became animated. He said obsequiously, "No, I don't think so. While he was working with me, he wasn't branded as a Rightist. It wasn't until the end of 1958. The Central Committee made a change in policy. They said that the Anti-Rightist Movement was over, but they knew there were some Rightists who still had not been singled out. To get the last few, they established a quota for every group, and the dictionary division still had to find one more Rightist. Since Jin-ren Tan had just left our group and joined the dictionary division, he was the obvious choice. It happened after he left my group. It was out of my hands."

"That is your story? We heard that you told Jin-ren Tan that he was a Rightist and used this accusation as a means of squeezing him out of your group and having him join the dictionary division. That same afternoon, you also recommended that he be sent to Qin-hai to support the ranchers' construction efforts there."

"Support the construction!" Jiang laughed sarcastically. "Qin-hai was the dumping ground for the country's political garbage."

Wrenched by anger and pain, I slammed my fist on the table and shouted, "How *dare* you call Jin-ren Tan political garbage!" Even as I did so, I knew there was some truth in what he said. Forcing a calm tone, I continued, "Helping the construction was a glorious task. The publishing house asked everyone to apply. All those so honored by being accepted into this admirable venture were presented with beautiful red flowers."

"They asked everyone to apply, right! The inner circle of the publishing house knew long before who would be sent to Qin-hai. I even submitted an application. But there wasn't a snowball's chance in you-know-where that I would be going."

Just as the desire to slap this villain consumed me, Rei-qing put down her pencil and said flatly, "S. Jiang, are you prepared to confess that calling Tan a Rightist and seeing Tan transferred to the dictionary division happened on the same day?"

"How can I remember so long ago?" he asked, throwing up his hands.

"You were planning such a thing for a long time. When the Anti-Rightist Movement began, your old problem had not yet been resolved. You were weak then, and furious that you could not take advantage of this movement to ostracize Tan. But you were lucky. When your turn came, you were not going to waste the opportunity. The dictionary division had wanted Tan to join them for a long time. You chose that time to encourage his transfer. It is you who branded Tan a Rightist. The dictionary division was merely a smokescreen to obscure your true intentions. That way, you could deceive the rank and file and save trouble for yourself." Rei-qing's voice was clear and unemotional; her words were undeniable.

"You must be careful that you do not jump to the wrong conclusion from your reasoning," Jiang said softly.

We ordered him to sign his name to the notes, and he did so, far more meekly than we had expected. Years later, a former friend of his told us that, as soon as Jiang recognized me, he decided to embarrass us by correcting any grammatical mistakes before signing. He had noticed in the notes the statement that Jin-Ren Tan did not fulfill the requirements of being a Rightist. Once he would have denied it, but the metamorphosis brought about by the Cultural Revolution had changed his philosophy. He could not understand why he was constantly having to defend himself politically, nor how someone such as he, who had been given the official title of "Red Expert Party Member and Editor-in-Chief" could have his authority, even his freedom, stripped from him. Previously, he would not have yielded a grain of rice without a fight. Now, he was resigned to his fate and willing to cooperate.

Next we went to the Shanghai Publishing House to see a man named Q. Zhang. Father had taken me there several times when I was a child, and the sounds of the vocalists rehearsing at the adjacent Beijing Opera House had terrified me. Each time I went, I steeled myself to brave the music. Rei-qing saw my discomfort this day and smiled. "Don't worry, Xi-ou. The opera company is so busy touring and giving propaganda performances, they don't have time to practice."

A man in his late twenties greeted us. He was good-looking, despite a long, thin scar from the bridge of his nose to his jawline. His dark, thick eyebrows almost met each other, and I immediately recognized him as "Hardnose" from Uncle Ho's description. Years before he joined the People's Liberation Army, he had earned the scar in a street fight that had also changed his volatile temperament to one of cautious introspection. While Fish Five Oceans for Abalone had a rival group in the Chinese Encyclopedia Publishing House, Hardnose was the undisputed master of the most powerful of the three or four such organizations here.

We showed him our letter of introduction. After reading it through twice, he said, "This letter only introduces Xi-ou Tan. Therefore, I can only admit her."

"I have my ID," said Rei-qing, pulling her card from her pocket.

"Don't bother," Hardnose said, waving his hand. "An ID card doesn't mean anything to me. I must have a letter of introduction."

"Look at us!" I said. "Can't you tell we're sisters? It's our parents' political situation, no one else's, that interests us. This is Revolutionary and good; by understanding their political situation, we will establish our own political identities. We ask that you help us in this."

Hardnose said nothing. After scanning our faces, he walked out, but he returned several minutes later with Q. Zhang behind him. "Zhang," he said, "these two Red Guards would like to investigate the branding of Jin-ren Tan as a Rightist." Hardnose sat down and made himself comfortable.

Zhang wore a long overcoat with countless holes and looked as if he had not shaved in weeks. I remembered a wall poster stating that Zhang had once been a guerrilla fighter before the Liberation. "Jin-ren Tan is a Rightist and an anti-Revolutionary. Down with Jin-ren Tan!" he said coldly and mechanically. He did not notice us arranging our notepads on the long conference table as we prepared our questions.

"Over there," Hardnose told Zhang, indicating one of the chairs at the conference table. Hardnose crossed his legs and waited for the show to begin. The interrogation began with the same protocol and Party propaganda we had used in the Chinese Encyclopedia Publishing House. After some routine background questioning, I attacked:

"At the end of 1958, when the cleanup phase of the Anti-Rightist Movement was in force, how did you and Jiang conspire to brand Jin-ren Tan as a Rightist and send him to Qin-hai?" Although straightforward, the question was loaded and came too swiftly for Zhang to consider a proper defense.

"When they came out with the Rightist quotas, Jiang showed me a report on Jin-ren Tan's actions during the Anti-Rightist Movement. I can't remember the details, but it seems I recall that there wasn't enough evidence to make him a Rightist. He got along well with his coworkers, so it would have been hard to organize a public chastisement meeting. Jiang suggested transferring him to the dictionary division and branding him a Rightist at the same time. When the Anti-Rightist Movement was really underway, Tan was working hard to finish the *New Cultural Dictionary*. Jiang said that Tan had always been a Rightist but was too busy working to follow his Rightist ideals. Jin-ren Tan spoke out any time he didn't like something—how could such a person be anything *but* a Rightist? At the time, I thought that both Tan and Jiang were strong. I could have supported either one, but if I had supported Tan, Jiang would have made things hard for me, so I chose the lesser of two evils."

Zhang was an unrefined man with a primary-school education. Under the philosophy of "The insiders must take orders from the people outside," Zhang rose to an elevated position. To appease the Party cadres, he allowed innocent men to be branded as Rightists. Zhang's confession made sense in the light of the other evidence we had compiled, and I was very excited.

Jumping up, Hardnose shouted at Zhang, "Enough, enough! Just get out of my sight!" Terrified, Zhang leaped from his seat and backed out of the room, bowing and muttering polite phrases as he left. Hardnose remained in the conference room.

"Why did you stop him?" Rei-qing asked.

"You're not trying to establish your own political identity. Aren't you really just trying to have your anti-Revolutionary father exonerated?" Hardnose replied icily.

"We want the facts. As long as there are mistakes, they should be corrected," Rei-qing answered firmly.

"Rebellion is a privilege of the Left Wing. The Right Wing can only submit," he shot back.

"Don't you think we should see if Jin-ren Tan is a Rightist or not before we decide whether he may rebel?" I asked.

"You even dare deny the Anti-Rightist Movement brought about by Chairman Mao?" Hardnose snapped.

"If you agree that Zhang and the other bourgeois elements of the Party have been anti-Revolutionaries and that their actions are consistent, you can't deny that they might have done bad things during the Anti-Rightist Movement," I stated. "Do you dare to say that the publishing-house leadership during that period performed in a true Marxist-Leninist fashion?"

"Overall, the leadership's performance was truly Marxist and Leninist," Hardnose responded, softening slightly.

"You deny the specifics but admit the generality," I said. Forgetting where I was, I continued freely, "Isn't leadership made up of individuals? Let's examine each and every member of this leadership. All of them are now acknowledged anti-Revolutionaries. How can you throw a bunch of anti-Revolutionary scum together and expect to make a Marxist-Leninist organization?" Hardnose was silent.

"All right. Let's consider Zhang. He just confessed to falsely branding Jin-ren Tan as a Rightist. Unless you're still unsure about Zhang's anti-Revolutionary roots, you must regard with suspicion everything he did from 1957 to 1958. Chairman Mao taught us, 'Those whom our enemies support, we should oppose; those whom our enemies oppose, we should support.' Our purpose is to uncover the facts. Exoneration may be a fruit of this, but it is not our goal."

Rei-qing nodded and said, "I think our business is finished, but we still need Zhang's signature on the confession." Handing the notes to Hardnose, she continued, "I don't think it's necessary to ask him to come out again. Could you please take this to him and have him sign it?" When he did not respond, Rei-qing said, "Chairman Mao teaches us, 'It is our duty to be responsible to the people for our words and deeds.' Asking Zhang to sign will fulfill your responsibility to us; Zhang's signing will fulfill his responsibility to his own words. I assume you can do this for us."

Hardnose scrutinized us. The veins in his temple throbbed and his face twitched nervously, making his scar dance. Finally, through gritted teeth, he agreed.

⚊⚊ So far, En-ligh-tenment was proceeding well, and no one, including Father, suspected us of anything unusual. Luckily, the Shanghai Farm Workers were demonstrating at the Municipal Agricultural Administration building located near our home, so Rei-qing could come home for dinner every night. This was the most relaxing time of day for the whole family, but we were careful to speak in low voices, because neighbors routinely listened through the walls. Occasionally Father would pace about the room to keep his leg muscles from atrophying. Although 9:30 was our customary bedtime, Rei-qing often asked permission to stay up later, presumably to write something for her organization. She wrote rapidly until after midnight, when she finally would go to bed. A few hours later, I would rise, read what she had written, and continue the work. Father never guessed it was our document for Zhou En-li.

    △△△ One day, I picked up a pamphlet that read, "Our beloved comrade Jian-qing, the standard-bearer of the Grand Cultural Revolution, once declared at a public meeting that the entire police and judicial system was hopelessly diseased and should be destroyed for its own protection." The judicial and police divisions had been exempt from the Cultural Revolution, as had the armed forces, under the proviso of the Sixteen Principles. Now we would have access to the courts, since it was recognized that those who convicted my parents may have been corrupt. Ming-yuan Ge, the prosecutor, was our first target. On a chilly spring morning, we went to his office.

Ge had very short hair and thick glasses. "I have received your letter," he said openly. "I understand that you have some doubts concerning this trial. I am therefore taking time out of my busy schedule to answer your questions." As he spoke, his hands, covered with chilblains, riffled through our parents' file. Under a ragged sweater with frayed cuffs, he wore a new uniform of the judicial and police system.

"Please, could you explain what 'betraying their country and going over to the enemy' means in the context of this case?" Rei-qing asked.

"Your uncle, Ji-wang Bai, tried to defect secretly to Hong Kong. Your parents not only failed to report this to the proper authorities, they encouraged his treasonous act," Ge replied.

"According to our information, Ji-wang Bai could not find a job after the Revolution, due to his former Guomindang affiliation. It seems that he tried to emigrate to Hong Kong only to start a new life where he could stop being a parasite and support himself," I pointed out.

"*Your* uncle did not attempt to *emigrate,* he attempted to *defect.* Defection is equivalent to treason. This was a very simple case," Ge said, taunting us by emphasizing certain words.

"Then what is the meaning of 'going over to the enemy'?" I inquired.

"Enemy? That is simple: Guomindang, Reactionary, anti-Revolutionary. More specifically, your uncle planned to go over to your grandfather in Taiwan."

"If Z. R. Li, the former president of the Guomindang, could return to the People's Republic of China and be received as an honored guest by Chairman Mao and Premier Zhou En-li, how can you still call my grandfather, a Navy judge, an enemy? But this is beside the point. Bai was headed for Hong Kong, not Taiwan. How can you assume that he was going to Taiwan to join his father?" I asked sharply.

"Don't be ridiculous. Getting from Hong Kong to Taiwan is as easy as dropping your chopsticks."

I responded, "Even if they did see each other, there is nothing necessarily treasonous about a son wishing to see his father after sixteen years of separation."

Ge gave me a quick glance and then was silent for several seconds. After graduating from law school in the mid-1950s, Ge was one of the few intellectuals in the post-Revolutionary Chinese judicial system. At first, it pained Ge to see that jurists, whose job was to uphold the law, broke it constantly, but he slowly became inured. After several years, he decided merely to accept the situation, finding it profitable and rather pleasant to do as others did. After joining the Party, he married a woman who was a People's Liberation Army veteran. Life was dull but safe, and keeping his job became his only ambition.

The trial transcript was filled with contradictions, and even the short verdict contained many inaccuracies. Ge and his group were presented the following facts at the trial:

> Huang, a Cantonese man, was branded a Rightist in
> 1957. His wife immediately divorced him, leaving him to

raise two children. He was eager to be politically reborn.
Chu, one of Huang's coworkers, had been branded a
thief for stealing copper from his factory. His teenage
daughter fought with him constantly, claiming that she
would be forced to leave school because of her Black
family background. In addition, his wife constantly
threatened him with divorce. Chu met Ji-wang Bai at a
dumpling peddler's cart in 1964, several months before
Bai was caught trying to cross the border.

Chu and Huang decided to trap Bai by pretending
to know two guides in Canton who could lead them all
to Hong Kong. At the time, Bai had no hope of finding
employment, and so agreed to go. In actuality, Chu and
Huang went to the police before and after each meeting
with Bai, asking instructions and making reports as
necessary. An undercover agent followed their
movements and took photographs.

Bai told his plan to his only relatives: his sister,
Y-yao Bai, and his brother-in-law, Jin-ren Tan. Since
they discouraged him, he told Chu and Huang that he
did not want to be included. Chu and Huang requested
instruction from the police and were told to threaten to
report the entire affair to the police if Bai refused to go.
Bai submitted to the blackmail. Soon after the train from
Shanghai to Canton left the station that night, the three
were arrested and handcuffed. After spending one night
in the police station, Chu and Huang were released. Two
weeks later, Y-yao Bai and Jin-ren Tan were taken into
custody.

This was all of the evidence on which the trial was based. Ge and
his prosecution team modified these facts as follows:

Bai was from an anti-Revolutionary background
and had joined the Jiang Kai-shek Youth in 1946. He
despised the Communist Party and all that the new
China symbolized. Defecting to Hong Kong was the first
step in his plan to restore the old order. He planned to
meet his Reactionary father, who had served the
Guomindang, and together they would formulate plans

to retake the mainland. Defecting to Hong Kong was therefore tantamount to betraying the motherland.

Y-yao Bai and Jin-ren Tan were both Rightists. Although they took no direct action, they were Reactionary thinkers. Constantly wishing to resume life in their lost paradise, they planned to defect to Hong Kong. With their two henchmen now on the outside planning the counter-Revolution, Y-yao Bai and Jin-ren Tan were ideally placed to serve as spies for the Guomindang. If they were not punished for this attempted espionage and subversion, the Revolutionary Mass would be outraged.

Chu and Huang performed these actions to clear their names. It is only right that they should be restored as members of the Revolutionary Mass in good standing. Ji-wang Bai, his sister, and his brother-in-law were described as "the gang of three betrayers and defectors" and prosecuted. Ji-wang Bai was sentenced to ten years in jail, the other two, seven.

Ge knew that the police had entrapped Bai by blackmailing him into attempting to defect, but he did nothing to stop the proceedings. For the mid-1960s, Ge's interpretation of this case was fashionable. Decades as a prosecutor had taught him two important skills: hiding one's zeal and holding one's tongue. Unsure how to deal with people who had not perfected these skills themselves, he was at a loss when I protested that a son's wish to see his father was not a crime.

He said, "Our government has a policy so that if Bai truly wished to visit his father, he could have applied to do so through proper channels. Defection was not necessary."

"Please be reasonable," I answered. "Do you believe his request would have been granted? He couldn't even get a job for thirteen years! With no job, and therefore no future, all he could do was hope to start over in Hong Kong."

"You're too young and you were cheated by our class enemies. That's really not how things were."

"Oh? Can you deny that my uncle gave up the opportunity to go with his father to Taiwan? He was only eighteen at the time. He was on board the ship, which had already left the dock. He jumped over-board and swam back to be with my parents so they could welcome the Liberation together. Had he not clung to his love for the Revolution, he would be studying in the United States like my other uncles, instead of sitting in jail," I flashed back.

Ge apparently decided that we were two naive girls who were spouting nonsense and needed a lecture. Pulling out his copy of the Little Red Book, he led us in responsorial reading. " '. . . After the armed enemies have been wiped out, the enemies without guns remain, and desperately want to fight against us. We must always stand ready.' " Ge cleared his throat and continued, "Rei-qing and Xi-ou Tan, these events all happened when you were little or before you were born. You've only heard one side of the story. Let me explain. Your parents and uncle really are the enemies without guns. You were born into a Reactionary family and were deeply influenced by it. It's under-standable that you can't always see the problem logically. However, you must be alert so you don't get pulled over to the side of the anti-Revolutionaries. If that happened, you'd regret it."

Detecting the thinly veiled threat, I said petulantly, "If our parents and uncle are the enemies without guns and we were cheated by them, we should doubtless try to correct such mistakes. We've learned much, but today, when we read this verdict, we have many questions. First, the verdict says that a map and compass—incontrovertible evidence against the anti-Revolutionary gang of three—were found in our home. That map was from my ninth-grade geography class. The red ink on it wasn't what you called the anti-Revolutionary Underground Railroad; it showed the distribution of rare metals. It's in every geography textbook. The compass was my brother's, the kind found in any toy store. How could these things be used to overthrow the new China? The verdict also said that my mother's status was 'presently under arrest.' My mother went to the courthouse with my father of her own free will." As I recited these facts, everything that happened on the awful day of the trial, including the debate over my composition, passed through my mind. The lump in my throat caused by remembering Mother suffering in jail stopped me from going further.

Ge picked up the files and the Little Red Book, saying coldly, "I listen to you and hear only the anti-Revolutionary diatribes of your father. You are your Reactionary father's mouth."

Rei-qing and I walked home silently, each wrapped in our own thoughts. I had always thought it odd that the verdict stated that Chu and Huang were not to be included in this case, they were to be tried separately. When we had asked Father about it, he said he knew nothing of Chu and Huang and did not understand their role in his case. In court, Father told Ge directly that he was not convinced by the evidence, arguing that if anyone should be designated the chief conspirator, it should be he, and that his wife and brother-in-law could do nothing but follow his instructions. Ge called Father a fool for this. When Father asked permission to serve Mother's sentence, he did not understand that the Chinese Encyclopedia Publishing House wanted cheap labor from him and would therefore keep him out of prison. The court told him, "Through manual labor you may be politically reborn. For you, this will be writing books." They even arranged for him to have a library card. Within a month, the Grand Cultural Revolution began. If the Revolution had been postponed for a month, Father might have realized that Chu and Huang were being treated differently, and inquired about it, but whenever we asked him about the case, he only replied with clichés, such as, "It's fate" or "That's the way it goes."

△△△ Rei-qing and I worked to prepare the document for Zhou En-li for several months and finally sent it off. A full year passed after this, with no response. While we waited, we made several more visits to the publishing houses and the courthouse and submitted a formal request to the Shanghai Supreme Court for an appeal. Rei-qing resumed her work in the fields, and I visited the Supreme Court at least twice a month, sitting alone on the uncomfortable, crowded benches in the lobby. At the end of each day of waiting, I heard the same words: "This case will not come up until a later stage of the Movement." That could have meant anything.

Our experiences and our ultimate decision to abandon the Enlightenment plan showed that we had gradually become more practical and flexible than our parents. After all, if we cannot learn anything from the sufferings of our parents' generation, then all their pain was for nothing. Man progresses by learning from the past, bettering himself, and shaking off the chains that imprisoned those who preceded him.

The poet Tu Fu once wrote, "When I think about my old friends, I find that half have reached their ends." I am almost certain that Tu Fu is describing a middle-aged man, for the same poem also contains the following:

> When I said good-bye, you had yet to marry.
> Today your children are lined up to greet me.
> "Where did you come from?" they ask so politely.

Many of my peers, however, died at an early age or lost their health due to this Revolution. Two or three died when thrown from trains during the Red Guard excursions, others died in street fights. Numerous others sustained permanent injuries during various Revolutionary activities; several people were even crushed to death during one of the receptions of the Red Guards in Tiananmen Square.

Others developed mental or emotional problems, and some went on to a life of crime. For instance, Xiao-yi Wu joined the Army three years after I joined the Red Guards, and he became a journalist after the "Gang of Four" was deposed. In 1985, he was convicted of raping many women and was sentenced to death to serve as an example. When I read this in an American newspaper, I could hardly believe it. I even wrote a letter home to check, because I refused to accept it until it was proved. Although I damned Xiao-yi Wu, I never wished such a death on him.

I hope that these memories are not tiresome to you, Professor Hu. I very much look forward to reading about some of yours. Please take care of yourself.

Sincerely,
Xi-ou Tan

Spring recess was nearly over, so I went to my office at Cal Tech to make sure that everything was in order. I found two letters in my mailbox, both from Professor Hu. I had sent him my home address, but he had directed his letters to Cal Tech instead.

 Dear Xi-ou Tan,

Your brother returned my notebook to me yesterday. Thank you very much. I was careless and lost it without realizing it. I had gone to the museum yesterday evening to see if there was a model of a Chinese ship. Since few people go there, I would not have expected anyone to find the notebook so quickly. I appreciate your getting it back to me.

Your brother said you had something important to tell me, and that I should wait for a letter. I asked him about you, but it seems that we have never met. I cannot guess what it is you wish to tell me. Regardless, I thank you again for the return of my book.

Sincerely yours,
Yong-hua Hu

 Dear Xi-ou Tan,

Today I received the letter you wrote to me upon your return to California. I was very moved by it and did not know what to say. My suicide note was written two weeks ago after I received a great shock. I am already over forty, so I would not write such a serious letter just for amusement. I did not carry out my plan, because I thought about my poor old mother. She has already suffered more than enough for me. If I died, I would be relieved, but my mother, a devout Christian, could never commit such an act. My death would ruin her remaining years, and I could not do such a thing.

However, if a doctor told me that I had cancer, I would be glad, not grieved. There is an old saying that the most tragic thing in this world is the death of one's spirit. A person with a dead spirit is like an empty shell. You said that perhaps within a month, I will feel differently. I am grateful for your kind thoughts but cannot agree with you.

I liked your story about a cat having four legs, and I was impressed by your courage and intelligence. Although that classroom argument was more than twenty years ago, I could still feel your vigor through your letter. This vitality is exactly what I lack.

Thank you again for all your kindness.

> Sincerely yours,
> Yong-hua Hu

8

Dear Professor Hu,

I was delighted to receive your letters but sorry to find that you are still unhappy. As we Chinese say, sadness can also kill people. I think that since you do not want to hurt your mother, it is not enough for you to live a passive life. I was glad to learn that you agree with me in that your life does not belong only to you. This letter will tell you about how I came to educate myself, since regular subjects would not be taught in the schools for quite some time.

It was 1967, the second autumn of the Grand Cultural Revolution. At ten in the morning, I walked through a street littered with fallen leaves that were slippery from the heavy rains of the previous night. Idly poking them with a fallen branch reminded me of a quote by Maxim Gorky: "If you are a rotten piece of wood, people will throw you in the mud and use you so they won't dirty their feet."

I had just left Chun-pu Chu's house. I customarily visited him at about eight in the morning, since his daughter, Si-qi, would already have left for work, and the Red Guards would be too busy with breakfast to disturb us. Chun-pu Chu had changed his schedule to accommodate this, awaking at four to write or draw until nine, when he went back to bed. At five in the afternoon, he would wake for his second shift. He had a disadvantage that Father did not: He had to hide his work from his own children. Most of them had already married and left home, but Si-qi was still single and lived with him. Extremely frightened after the Red Guards had searched their home, Si-qi had gathered up all her father's art supplies and made a special trip to the Red Guards' headquarters to turn them in. Expressing her Revolutionary contempt for her father, she openly proclaimed that she would see that he never again poisoned the people with his art.

The Red Guards had put all of his "bourgeois" furniture—such as his piano, sofa, and lamps—into his garden shed, locking and sealing it with stern words of warning. Chun-pu Chu extracted a set of watercolors from the shed by crawling into it at midnight while his wife held a flashlight. After rummaging through the dusty paintings, books, and musical instruments, he finally emerged in triumph with the watercolors held over his head. He whispered to his wife, "Of all the things I ever thought I'd be, I never thought I'd be a thief, stealing from myself!"

"Quiet, you old fool!" his wife hissed. "Do you want to wake Si-qi?"

From August through December 1966, Chun-pu Chu had to squeeze into buses filled with hundreds of Red Guards to go to the Art Institute, where he was denounced each day. In 1967, the Red Guards began taking him through the surrounding countryside to receive public chastisements. He wondered why he was taken to places where no one had even heard of his work, since denunciations in such places would not be "antidotes" for his "poison"; he would instead be "poisoning" a new group of people.

While Chun-pu Chu could give up smoking for extended periods of time, he missed drinking. Sympathetic doctors touring with him prescribed a glass of wine daily "for medicinal purposes." One day, while stopped in Chuan Sha county, he went to the outhouse, a hole surrounded by a straw curtain. There he overheard two people talking outside: "We're so lucky to be touring with Chun-pu Chu. Not only do we get a free trip, we can do our New Year's shopping out here in the countryside, where everything's really cheap! Pretty soon, we'll have everything we need."

Then he understood why the Red Guards were parading him around the Shanghai countryside. They also toured several other old, famous painters in the Art Institute. Although the tour dates scheduled for after the New Year were canceled, the artists were instructed to stand ready to resume the trip at the discretion of the Red Guards. Two of them could not endure the cold and died on tour. During this break, Chun-pu Chu began his work regimen and decided to follow Father's example of feigning illness.

People of Asia, especially the Japanese, called Chun-pu Chu a modern-day version of the Soong dynasty poet Tao Zi. Tao Zi had given up his high post in the emperor's service to go back to his home and live a simple peasant's life, and the people loved him for it. His talent had been recognized while he was yet young, and most of his life had been marked by people's respect and admiration, but he remained unchanged by fame. If Chun-pu Chu had not had the spirit of Tao Zi, the insults heaped on him in his old age would have killed him.

On this particular morning, I had found Grandfather Pu (our name for Chun-pu Chu) alone, drinking a little wine and eating preserved turnips. Sitting at his side, I rattled off the rumors I had heard and read. He listened as he drank, smacking his lips and caressing the beginnings of his beard. He was in a good mood that morning and repeatedly interrupted my stories with his own comments. "Confucious hated people who napped during the day above all others. He called them good-for-nothing pieces of rotten wood. In my youth, I didn't dare sleep during the day, no matter how tired I was. But now the Red Guards have inspired me to rebel against the archaic doctrine of Confucius, and I boldly and proudly sleep all day. Now I am the Red Guards' model Revolutionary!"

There was pain behind his jocular exterior, but I was warmed by his humor. Rising, he pulled a large envelope from under a pillow and carefully extricated a piece of tissue paper. "I painted this for your brothers and sister this morning. Why don't you take it home?"

The deceptively simple painting depicted two teenagers, a boy and a girl, riding beautiful horses, the action captured with vivid colors. In the upper right corner, the title, "A Bright Future," was written in graceful, flamboyant characters. I slipped the painting into the large secret pocket Rei-qing had sewn inside my jacket so I could deliver Father's manuscripts to a friend's house to be hidden. It may have seemed overcautious, but I never knew when a Red Guard or a

Neighborhood Committee member would demand to know what I was carrying. Still, I wasn't completely safe, since they could always frisk me.

When I heard the door open, I assumed it was Chun-pu Chu's wife returning from the market. Expecting to see Grandmother Pu, I turned with a smile that froze instantly on my face. A senior PLA officer, dressed in the mustard-colored uniform with red trim, stood in the doorway. He was five and a half feet tall and very muscular, with large eyes and dark, thick eyebrows. His clothes were dusty as if he had been on a long journey, and he carried a suitcase. Although the Central Committee of Defense had in 1964 outlawed external markings denoting the rank of officers and enlisted men, I could tell that he was at least a colonel. The Army was then the only institution not subject to the Cultural Revolution. Chun-pu Chu sat rigidly in his chair, curiously eyeing his unexpected guest. The three of us remained quiet for several seconds.

"Are you Mr. Chu?" the officer asked politely. I breathed a sigh of relief at his courteous manner. "Mr.," "Comrade," or "Red Guard" was an unequivocal sign of the speaker's Revolutionary attitude. "Mr." was a general term with many meanings, most of them respectful.

Grandfather Pu was silent. If he were to tell the truth, his secret connection with Father might be uncovered and I could be accused of being a bridge between two anti-Revolutionaries. He also could not risk being caught in a lie. Without waiting for an offer, the officer pulled up a chair and sat down. He looked at Chun-pu Chu with an expression of warmth and sincerity.

"Grandfather, shall I go make some tea?" I asked timidly.

The visitor started as if he had just realized that there was a third person in the room. "Don't bother," he said, waving his hands. "I'll only be here for a couple of minutes. I have a train to catch." He turned to Chun-pu Chu and asked, "Is this your granddaughter?"

Chun-pu Chu grunted something incomprehensible. The guest looked at me thoughtfully, and I blushed as I smiled shyly, looking down. The guest smiled in return but then saw my armband signifying my membership in the Red Guards of Self-Determination. "Are you a

Red Guard?" he asked, seriously. "The Red Guards have carried the movement very far. Today you should sit down and carefully read Chairman Mao's works to truly understand the spirit of what he was saying. I'm sure you already know all the slogans and can recite quotations at will, but you should fix these thoughts firmly in your heart." He paused and continued, "For example, it is not enough for you to say of your grandfather, 'Down with Chun-pu Chu!' There are two sides to every argument. In one way, he is our enemy, but on the other hand, he is a national treasure who has brought our country great honor. Chairman Mao teaches us not to kill a diseased man but to cure him, and also to exercise mercy in the cause of the Revolution. In my opinion, the Red Guards overemphasize some things."

Finding it impossible to respond, I again blushed and smiled, but I understood his implicit order to be kind to Chun-pu Chu. The visitor opened his suitcase and removed a large parcel wrapped in newspaper. "Master Chu, here is some *tu chong*. It's hard to get these days. From one of your essays, I learned that you have kidney trouble. I came to Shanghai from Fu Jian on business, but I'm taking this detour to give you these herbs. We hope that you will have good health and a long life. Later, perhaps, you will bless us with more beautiful paintings." He stood up, patting me on the back as he said, "Be a good girl and take care of your grandfather."

He departed as quietly as he had arrived. When I left Grandfather Pu's house, I surreptitiously removed my armband. At one time the Red Guards had represented the Revolution—progress, power, and violence—but now people saw them only as hooligans. I never considered myself a Red Guard; the armband's sole purpose was to shield me and my family.

The armband had been useful in the first stages of the En-lightenment plan a year earlier, helping us to unlock the doors that hid the firsthand evidence we needed. Rei-qing and I had had countless heated battles with people to get their testimonies and innumerable sleepless nights trying to make sense out of the documents. We economized on the family's meals to raise money for postage and made our own envelopes from cheap paper, using leftover rice as glue. Within three months, we had a 400-page document that analyzed in detail our parents' case. We broke it into smaller documents and mailed them to Premier Zhou En-li. We usually sent them by airmail but occasionally paid extra for registered delivery.

As we sent out each installment, I thought about our work, written in the dim light of our apartment, traveling across China to Zhou En-li, who would diligently read every word. I imagined him outraged, stamping his feet in anger at the injustice reaped upon two of China's most patriotic citizens. I imagined that Rei-qing and I would receive a mysterious phone call inviting us to a secret rendezvous in a strange part of town. Only when we arrived at the meeting place and learned that the mysterious stranger was from Beijing would we realize that this was a special emissary from Zhou En-li. I would see the opportunity to liberate not only my parents but everyone I knew. I would describe the eight unjustly accused "Rightists" in my school and then detail the progress of the movement in Jiao Tong University and Nan Yang Model Middle School, as well as the publishing houses. Listening keenly, the stranger would take copious notes as he nodded in agreement. He would shake our hands before he left, saying reservedly, "Justice will be done." Two months later, Mother would appear at the door flushed with pride, a small parcel under her arm. Everyone would rush and hug her and see that the cloth wrapping the parcel had a beautiful pattern of lily lanterns.

Reality was much more harsh. Rei-qing and I had done a great deal of work on the En-ligh-tenment plan, so it was we who felt the bitter disappointment of failure. It was difficult to discard a plan that occupied so much time and energy, but Rei-qing readily agreed that continuing with it would be unwise.

During the previous year, the Red Guards had conducted eleven "death searches" of our home. Requiring no more than five or ten minutes, a death search was conducted by a special group called the "Committee Acting and Associating as Red Guards Together." All were sons and daughters of high-level Revolutionary cadres who had been condemned by Chairman Mao for exploiting the Revolution. Wearing surgical masks and foot-long armbands, they waited until midnight to strike. After breaking down the door, they dragged us from our beds to the floor, beating us soundly. By the time we understood what was happening, they were gone. Everything made of glass was shattered, even medicine and ink bottles. Any book or paper in sight, with the exception of Chairman Mao's works, was torn to shreds. The Red Guards pocketed all ration coupons for rice and oil, and all money hidden in drawers.

When they finished with our house, the floor was covered with broken glass and ceramics. Hot water from our broken Thermos bottle made a hissing sound as it trickled onto the cold floor. Our rice pot had a hole punched through the bottom. After each of the eleven death searches, Rei-qing and I attended to any injuries that Father had received and comforted our younger brothers. The whole procedure became routine after a while, and we were all asleep ten minutes after the Red Guards left. Fortunately, the long letters prepared for Premier Zhou and Father's manuscripts, both well hidden, went undiscovered. Returning to my warm blankets with the still-fresh sting of the Red Guards' slaps on my cheeks, I would find myself trembling—whether from fear or cold, I did not know. Shame and terror were replaced with warmth and hope as I repeated encouraging slogans to myself until I fell asleep.

Through our contacts with our parents' former colleagues, we learned about them and about the whole intellectual world of post-1957 China. Our parents' downfall was due to their idealism and complete inability to play politics. We had inherited these qualities, but to rise above our situation, we would have to discard our ingenuousness.

The schools had stopped teaching; the factories had slowed production. Agriculture kept the country alive, only because most of the peasants were so far from the center of the Cultural Revolution that the Red Guards had never gone out to convince them to rebel against the land. Hundreds of millions of peasants kept their faces toward the dirt and their backs to the sun, heedless of the political winds. Their contribution to the nation's well-being was sufficient to bring the country back from the brink of economic ruin to which the Cultural Revolution had brought it.

Neither Father nor Chun-pu Chu was willing to put his life on hold. Although their manuscripts and paintings could have been seized at any time, with accompanying beatings and humiliations, both had resolved to swim against the Revolution's current by continuing to work. Father and Chun-pu Chu had their careers destroyed, but the people I considered good remembered their contributions and gave them as much praise and comfort as they could.

△△△ Every rower knows the saying, "If you are not advancing, you are falling backward." Maintaining my educational level was impossible, since each day away from school made me fall farther behind. How many formulas could I recite now? Could I remember any geometric proofs? When I helped Ah-di with basic physics, I made her sort through incorrect statements to find the facts. Could I myself now tell correct answers from nonsense? Questions like these terrified me. Why had I suddenly remembered Gorky's reference to rotten wood? Was my lot so difficult because my family was truly rotten wood and good only for absorbing puddles?

No country held science and culture in lower esteem than the People's Republic of China, and, subsequently, no country came to need them more desperately. If the Cultural Revolution continued much longer, all Chinese youth, regardless of political classification, would be illiterate. China was a closed system, and the only points of reference were other students—who were, of course, at the same level. The looming crisis went unnoticed.

Following Father on his parade of humiliation through the neighborhood had been my bravest act. Now I felt that I was about to do my wisest one: Just because the schools were no longer teaching, there was no reason that I could not keep learning. "Independent study" was a magical term holding more beauty and hope than anything else in the world. So excited that I could barely breathe, I threw away my leaf-poking branch and raced home. The autumn breeze whipped my hair about my face, the dead leaves in the street crunching under my running feet. Chun-pu Chu's picture, *A Bright Future,* was safe in my jacket pocket. My mind was clear, my soul in bliss.

The date was November 25, 1967.

△△△ Sitting beside Father's bed, Rei-qing and I enthusiastically told him of our plan for independent study. He encouraged us
happily: "I can draw up a general plan for you to master the human-
ities, but I am afraid I won't be much use when it comes to the natural
sciences."

"We've already thought about that," replied Rei-qing. "I have a
friend, Gui-feng Wang. Her father teaches electrical engineering at the
university. He might be willing to teach us math, physics, and engineering. Her younger sister, Mei-feng, is only a year older than Xi-ou.
The four of us can study together." Gui-feng, one of Rei-qing's former
classmates in middle school, was a year older than she and worked in
a factory. She and her brothers and sisters had similarly been branded
as "anti-Revolutionary spawn."

"I want to learn, too!" Jian-nan begged, running from across the
room.

"Actually, they have younger brothers who are a year older than
you and Chi-kai. You four can form another group, and Mei-feng and
I can teach you what we learn. How's that?" I offered, smiling.

Rei-qing and I rushed to Gui-feng's home. Their mother, unlike
ours, was an old-fashioned, semiliterate woman whom not even the
most fanatical Red Guard could classify as an intellectual. The father,
like other professors at the time, was condemned as a "Reactionary
Academic Authoritarian." No classes were held now, but Professor
Wang was forced to go to the university each day to be criticized
publicly. He received only the "Revolutionary mercy" relief payments
of fifteen yuan per month per family member, the balance of his former
218-yuan salary frozen by the Red Guards.

Gui-feng became a worker after graduating from middle school.
Mei-feng, still middle-school age, stayed home as I did. The idea of
independent study appealed to them, and we lowered our voices as
we excitedly made plans. After finding college-level mathematics
textbooks, we would master calculus first, gradually entering
Professor Wang's field of expertise. Mei-feng and I still had to finish

our middle- and high-school courses before moving on to such advanced studies.

We four girls pleaded with Professor Wang that night in the dim attic where they lived. The exhausted man struggled to keep his eyes open as he listened to us. His seemingly endless confessions were a result of evidence presented against him by several of his former students. While explaining the Maxwell equations of electromagnetism, he used the term *universal axioms*. Such a description, it was argued, put these equations on a par with Chairman Mao's doctrine—a heretical act, since Mao's doctrine was the only universal truth.

"Why do you want to study? The Grand Cultural Revolution teaches us that it's pointless. Haven't you learned?" I had not expected a professor from a university to raise this question, but Mei-feng was quick to respond, "What are we supposed to do all day? Studying is better than doing nothing!"

Gui-feng adopted her role as big sister and said, "Since the schools are closed, all of my sisters stay at home, chattering and quarreling like chickens. And if we can't find something for the boys to do, they'll end up running around the street like hoodlums."

Feeling that they had missed the true point, I wanted to tell Professor Wang that teaching us today was preparation for the motherland's call tomorrow. Before I could open my mouth, he nodded to Gui-feng and said, "Yes, you're right. It may be pointless to study these days, but it's harmless as well. The least it can do is tie you to your mother's apron so that you don't do anything bad out on the street."

We all laughed at this, but he did not. Cupping his chin in his hand, he said, "All right, I'll teach you. When do you want to start?"

"How about next week?" Gei-feng asked tentatively.

"Don't you need to make up some high-school courses?" he asked Mei-feng and me.

Rei-qing answered for us: "Mei-feng only needs analytical geometry, but Xi-ou needs algebra as well. I can take care of those courses. And since Gei-feng's books are still here, we don't have to worry about high-school texts."

The attic was perfect for conspiracy. Yellowed newspaper covered the wooden walls upon which our exaggerated shadows were cast. The one window, accessible only by ladder, rattled noisily with the wind as the walls allowed drafts to swirl around us. The thought that I would be educated under these clandestine conditions seemed romantic to me, and I thought of an old couplet by Tien-xiang Wen:

> We study and learn as the storm outside rages,
> Led in spirit by fallen heroes and sages.

Father's reaction to our plan was much warmer. Calling us again to his bedside, he informed us, "If Professor Wang is teaching you math and physics, you're learning under the best conditions possible in China. Not many people get tutors these days. Professor Wang and I aren't doing this for pay but for love. You aren't being ordered to learn; you've made the conscious decision to learn of your own free will."

Rumors and wall posters soon lost their attraction, and even strange events we witnessed did not distract us as they used to. Through the broken windows at home, I once saw the bobbing heads of more than a thousand Red Guards in the playground of the nearby Nan Yang Model Middle School. The East Is Red Red Guards and the Squad 0827 branch of the Committee Acting and Associating as Red Guards Together were in open conflict, and the original battlelines disappeared as everyone engaged in hand-to-hand combat. As each Red Guard attempted to beat the other senseless, he tried to rip off the armband and stars that signified his opponent's affiliation. Although disorganized, the East Is Red group advanced toward its opposition's banner. Then someone threw a torch at the East Is Red banner. As it burst into flames, the standard-bearers threw down their poles and ran, in total chaos. I had an excellent view of the battle, but pity for my peers stirred inside me. I suddenly felt like the only sane person in a kingdom of madmen. I could not run out to the playground to say, "Stop fighting, it's not worth it. Come inside and study math and science with us" so I turned from the degrading spectacle back to my reading.

I began my study regimen by rising at six in the morning, but I soon changed this to 4:30, although it took all of my determination to leave the warm blankets for the chilly room. Had I been a good Red Guard,

I would have contemplated some of Chairman Mao's quotations about overcoming difficulties, but instead I considered the exhortation of Confucian philosophy to overcome laziness.

Within two months, I managed to master the equivalent of two years' worth of high-school-level math, physics, and chemistry and was about to begin college-level calculus. This text was much larger than the high-school ones, and as I weighed it in my hands, I felt that my education was entering a new phase. We four girls shared the single book, published in the 1940s. It was old, but we were lucky to have it at all.

The night before Chinese New Year in February 1968, Gui-feng Wang came to our house, telling us through her tears that her father had been arrested. Two Red Guards had come to their house, taking his sheets, blankets, and toiletries. A new movement, Clarify the Class Rank, was sweeping the nation. Since Professor Wang had studied in the United States in the 1940s, he was considered a spy.

Father comforted her and told Rei-qing to visit Gui-feng's mother to discuss ways of dealing with the Red Guards. The six Wang children stayed at our house that New Year's Eve. There was little food but much companionship. The sound of fireworks did nothing to lift our spirits as we looked with dread to the New Year. We were determined to continue our course of independent study at all costs, so Father told us encouraging stories of famous self-taught statesmen, scholars, and inventors. Warning us that what happened to Professor Wang today could well happen to him tomorrow, he urged us not to take things for granted.

Opening the calculus book on New Year's Day, I began my college-level work. The pedagogical style of the book made it difficult, and I found the concept of infinity particularly confusing. I persevered, and within three months, I had completed five thousand problems in differential and integral calculus. Unwilling to put down the book even to eat or sleep, I worked day and night. Rei-qing and I had a definite partiality for integration, and we dubbed the integral symbol the "bean sprout" because of its shape.

Gui-feng's full day in the factory left her little energy for lessons in the evening; Mei-feng's attention span was minimal. Despite our encouragement, they essentially had abandoned their study. Unaware that each must learn at his own pace, Rei-qing and I were frustrated by their lack of progress. They were, however, devoted to literature. A friend lent them a book of ancient prose, insisting that it be returned the next day, but the two were so fascinated that they spent the entire night copying a hundred pages by hand. Proudly presenting their work to Father the next day, they were taken aback when he frowned and told them that the book was not very important since it was only an interpretation of the works of Confucius.

Father decided to write a textbook specifically for us, beginning with the *Zuo Zhuan,* a book of ancient Chinese history that school-children traditionally memorized. Assigning a composition each week, he gave us the choice to write in traditional or vernacular style. Since it was practiced only before 1919, few young people had the chance to learn the traditional style. We four girls took advantage of this opportunity, writing most of our essays in the older manner. I had never been taught how to write on an abstract theme, and when I first began, I found myself writing in a descriptive style that did not discuss the ideas involved. Ten unsatisfactory opening paragraphs had me almost in tears of frustration before Father came to my rescue: "Anything worth learning takes time. Don't expect to pick up a book and master it in a day. If you can, it's probably trivial."

Gui-feng and Mei-feng enjoyed coming to our home, infected by the nontraditional, democratic atmosphere. With his wit and charm, Father made even the analysis of haiku rhythm interesting and entertaining, but we stifled our laughter, since any noise might alert the neighbors. Jian-nan and Juing-hai, Professor Wang's eldest son, learned classical literature with us girls. Chi-kai and Professor Wang's younger son, Mao-to, acted as lookouts. Sitting in the doorway, they pretended to be playing Chinese chess as they watched for Red Guards or the Neighborhood Committee who might arrive for spot inspections. Father sat in bed as we students crowded around him. Scissors, rulers, thread, old clothes, and a book, *Sew Your Own Revolutionary Uniform,* were laid out on the table. An unexpected guest would find only a semi-invalid with a half-dozen harmless young people sewing earnestly.

⚞⚟ A year and a half of the Cultural Revolution had taught me that smaller movements follow larger ones, just as aftershocks follow an earthquake. Then another large movement would begin, so I could never relax. I attended the sporadic lectures required for the Blacks of Father's age group and turned in his confessions at the Public Security Office. The Neighborhood Committee supervised the Shanghai Patriotic Cleaning Movement, which required me to do my father's job of unclogging sewer pipes barehanded every Thursday. Diagnosing a bad back was difficult, so the committee could do nothing to Father, even though they disbelieved him. They seemed to find it more amusing to humiliate a young girl than an older man, but as long as they did not trouble Father, I did not care.

Reporting to the Office of Housing Administration one April day in 1968, I learned that my family would be moved to a garage with no kitchen or bathroom. Later that day, I went to a small house on An Fu Street, knocked at the door, and entered. A man sat eating at a table, served by his wife. Their surname was Fong. Both had been construction workers for the Office of Housing Administration, but the woman had been retired for the previous year. Respected for his integrity, Fong had been elected to the Revolutionary Committee Overseeing Housing Administration. Neither of the two had more than a second-grade education. They had worked renovating my neighborhood when I was a child. The man was a carpenter, his wife was a painter. In a matter of months, the construction group became acquainted with most of the families in the neighborhood.

The construction workers loved to gossip, and Aunt Fong told us that they especially liked to visit us because we always gave them a cup of green tea and a clean towel to wipe their faces. Since most of the workers were illiterate, my parents would offer to write letters for them to their families back in the countryside. My parents often did this for the Fongs, and soon the four became good friends.

"Xi-ou, come and have something to eat," Aunt Fong called out.

"No, thank you," I refused politely, drawing the two large packages out of my jacket. "This big one is part of Father's manuscript. Will you please put it in the usual place? The smaller one is notebooks, so it should be put in a more accessible place. When things quiet down in a couple of days, I'll come back for it."

Aunt Fong escorted me to the ladder leading to their attic bedroom. The hand-carved wooden chest beside her bed contained everything she valued in life. As Catholics, they had put away a few religious items, such as a figurine of the Virgin Mary and a crucifix. A lock of hair from the son who had died many years earlier had been saved, along with a bracelet he had owned. The trunk, once nearly empty, was rapidly filling up with Father's manuscript.

Uncle Fong, a quiet man, had finished his lunch downstairs. Aunt Fong once said that the only words he spoke to her were "breakfast, lunch, and dinner." Even so, they were compatible, and their marriage was happy. Downstairs, I heard Uncle Fong clearing his throat. "He wants to say something to you today," Aunt Fong said, shooing me down the ladder. "Quick, go down before he changes his mind!"

When I reached him, he said calmly, "I heard you have to move. I was relieved when I found out which garage they assigned you. It's on a small lane where several bourgeois families live. They used to have the whole house for themselves, but now they are packed into just a few rooms. It's good that people with situations like yours will be your neighbors. They'll leave you alone."

It was still misting that afternoon as Chi-kai and I took our mops and brushes to the garage to clean it before moving in. The black garage door was already open, and two workers were knocking a hole in the south wall to make a window. Through it, I glimpsed a garden as the younger of the workers stood to greet me.

"Hi! Are you the Reactionaries who are moving in tomorrow?" he asked cheerfully. The bizarre greeting irritated me, but as I looked at him a second time, my anger melted. This same young worker had been assigned to fix the smashed window in our house two months earlier. He told his fellow workers, "They'll freeze without a windowpane, just as if they were sleeping in the street." His friends had agreed: "If we put acrylic in the windows, they won't have to worry about anything like this again." Standing at the windowsill, the young glazier had fished a cigarette from his pocket and thrown it to Father. "Go ahead, old man, take it! No one will care. We're comrades!" Turning to a colleague, he had said, "I'll never get anywhere if I keep making friends with stupid Reactionaries!"

I was amazed to meet up again with the worker who wanted to make friends with "stupid Reactionaries." I was about to ask something when he winked, jerking his head toward his companion to indicate that the man would not be sympathetic to me. The new window was a godsend. Imagine actually having sunlight in our new home! Realizing that it made no sense to clean the place while work was being done, we assisted the workers.

When his companion went to use a bathroom, the young worker said confidentially, "Trademaster Fong sent *me,* but that tattletale was sent by the director of Housing Administration. Trademaster Fong really had to pull strings to get the window put in. But that's not all. Look over there." Pointing to a pile of iron bars on the floor, he continued, "The director wants me to put those in the window. Fong says to use wood. I'll try to get rid of that fool so I can follow Trademaster Fong's instructions. I want to fix them so you can remove them easily enough to hop into the garden at night for some fresh air."

Fighting back tears, I asked shyly, "Why are you being so nice to us?"

"Quiet," he hissed, waving his hands. Then he bellowed, "You filthy swamp devils! Get out of my way and let me work. What do you want to clean up for, anyway? It's a pigsty, and it'll stay that way. Why don't you clean yourselves instead? You both reek of Reactionism so bad I can smell you a mile away!"

I understood and took Chi-kai home. Rei-qing had been sent back to the countryside in early 1968 with the rest of the Shanghai Farm Workers. Now that it was April, Rei-qing soon would be back for a visit, and I had a great deal of planning to do. Foremost on my mind was deciding how to move Father safely to the new place.

At two that morning, Gui-feng, Mei-feng, Juing-hai, and Li-na, one of Gui-feng's friends, removed their shoes to tiptoe to the third floor, where my family lived. First we had to move Father's bed, to permit him to hide as soon as he entered the garage. Next came Father himself, in a wheelbarrow borrowed from Li-na's factory. We had lined it with newspaper, and Juing-hai pulled from the front as Jian-nan pushed from behind. Mei-feng, Li-na, and I acted as escorts. Gui-feng and Chi-kai guarded the possessions in the old place as Rei-qing waited for us in the new one. Afraid that Father would catch cold in the damp night air, I was constantly pulling the clothes tighter around him.

The air in the deserted street smelled fresh and clean. The rain had stopped hours earlier, and the sky was clear and full of stars. The only sound was the grinding of the wheelbarrow and an occasional thud when we hit a bump in the road. Father was able to see the sky for the first time in two years. There was no midday sun, but the light of the moon and stars and the cool, fresh air on his face were enough. He remarked that he could not imagine any anti-Revolutionary as well cared for as he was.

By dawn, we had moved the larger pieces of furniture. To conceal Father's bed, we made a wall of furniture, books, and clothing. Too small to lift the heavier items, Chi-kai made breakfast for everyone and busily ran around the room, waiting on us. Although Li-na and Gui-feng had had no sleep that night and still had to go to work, they appeared satisfied, if a bit tired.

Rei-qing and I returned to the old room that had guarded our childhood memories, although the eleven death searches of the previous year were clearest in our minds. The picture of a princess and a goose that I had scratched on the wall with a hairpin when I was only six or seven caught my eye. For doing that, Mother had made me kneel on the floor all afternoon. Spattered next to the picture was blood from a beating that Father had received from the Red Guards. I was consumed with an irresistible urge to clean both the bloodstains and the pictures from the wall. They were memories of my family's painful past, and I hated to hand them over to anyone else.

We all retired early that night, but I was overtired and could not fall asleep. Hearing a faint whistle, I jumped out of bed. It was Rei-qing, also wakeful. I followed her away from the side of the room where the beds were. We each pulled up a stool and sat in the light of the moon pouring in through the new window. Remembering the words of the young worker, I pulled on the wooden bars in the window. The three central ones moved with little effort, and we slipped outside.

We talked about day-to-day household matters until it grew light; then we climbed back through the window. In addition to the main garage door to the north and the window to the south, a small door with a large glass pane in the upper half faced west. Rei-qing began to cut into a piece of red paper. Naturally artistic, she was talented in calligraphy, drawing, and painting. Looking closely, I saw that she was cutting characters in the paper mimicking Chairman Mao's style of lettering. She had selected one of his poems, entitled, "A Poem to Accompany Comrade Li Jin's Photographs of the Angel Cave of Mount Lu."

> *The shadows lengthen with the incoming night,*
> *The pine tree an image of ascendant might.*
> *Chaotic clouds dance to a rhythmless song,*
> *But the hardy tree stands, still steadfast and strong.*
> *An angel cave, Nature's perfect creation,*
> *Dangerous peaks hold beauty's vast variation.*

Chairman Mao wrote with a beautiful, ornate hand likened to "a dragon in flight." Greatly impressed by Rei-qing's work, I exclaimed, "And you did this from memory! Even if I had the characters in front of me, I couldn't do anything like that!"

Rei-qing responded, chuckling, "Silly goose. Look over there. There's a tube of Chairman Mao's 'Hardy Pine' brand toothpaste. Can't you see his writing on it? Do you think I'd memorize it?"

Our laughter woke Father. As he adjusted his glasses, I handed him the paper with its cutout characters. After he had admired it for several minutes, he smiled and said, "This gives me a name for our new home. We'll call it the 'Angel Cave.' " Old, dull walls and cold cement floor could not squelch Father's optimism. If the previous grim years had not made him a fatalist, nothing would.

△△△ You see, Professor Hu, I was so happy to receive your letter that I ended up writing you a twenty-five-page one without feeling the least bit tired. Since tomorrow is Sunday, I can write the whole day. I start working again on Monday, but I will still write to you each day.

I will keep my promise, if in exchange you will promise to be my patient reader.

> Sincerely,
> Xi-ou Tan

The Clarification Movement during which Professor Wang was arrested started in the spring of 1968. The Red Terror peaked a second time, although it is hard to say whether it was worse then or at the beginning of the Cultural Revolution. A neighborhood physician used an old newspaper to wrap his galoshes, but when it was found that it contained a picture of Chairman Mao and his wife inspecting the Navy, he was imprisoned for misusing such a "holy" object. Rumor had it that he committed suicide the same night. A famous actor suffered greatly during the Cultural Revolution for his early association with Mrs. Mao. At a special chastisement meeting, he beat himself, repeatedly saying, "I have committed a great sin against Chairman Mao." When the Revolutionary Mass pressed him, he called upon his considerable theatrical skills, feigning nervousness about speaking in front of an audience but finally pretending to confess, "Comrade Jian-qing and I were more than friends!" The news rapidly spread over the city. A fourteen-year-old girl overheard this snippet of gossip as her mother and best friend spoke and broadcast it throughout her school. She, her mother, and her mother's friend were labeled "malicious attackers of our Red Sun" and sent to a forced labor camp.

The Clarification Movement also worked to deify Chairman Mao, telling us that his thoughts could make the blind see, the dumb speak, the lame sprint, and the dead rise. Mountains were said to crumble at the majesty of his words, and rivers and oceans to part to make way for his overpowering rhetoric. People who did not understand his words or actions were told by Vice Chairman Lin Biao, "Whether you understand or not, follow what Chairman Mao says."

.A new neighbor of ours, a cadre and a Party member, developed appendicitis but was terrified of having the necessary operation. He knew that instead of being anesthetized, he would be given a copy of the Little Red Book to wave as he shouted, "Long live Chairman Mao," supposedly working himself up into such a Revolutionary frenzy that he would feel no pain. His wife later told people that visiting Albanians were much impressed that the doctors' and patient's recitation, "Be determined, not afraid of sacrifice, remove all difficulties to fight for the final victory!" seemed to dull all pain. My American friends have trouble believing these stories, but Professor Hu would know them to be true.

Chairman Mao's works became even more popular. People would receive many sets as wedding gifts but of course could not sell them to a used-book store, since they were considered priceless. The typical wedding picture showed the bride and groom posing with red bags at their waists, Chairman Mao's picture pinned to their chests, Little Red Books held in one hand over their shoulders, and stacks of Chairman Mao's works in the other. A sunflower in the background represented their loyalty to the Red Sun.

For the average worker, the Clarification Movement changed the daily routine. After arriving at work at 7:30, everyone lined up before a large portrait of Chairman Mao and waved Little Red Books for ten minutes in the "morning consultation with Chairman Mao." The first step was the "wish" that he and Lin Biao would have a long life and eternal health. The "sing" followed: "East Is Red, Rises the Sun. . . ." "Recite" was the final step, during which people recited vintage articles of Chairman Mao as well as his newest and highest instructions. Instead of a morning break at 10:30, a "ballet of loyalty" was performed, an improvisational dance in which the workers used all parts of their bodies to demonstrate their loyalty to Chairman Mao. In some factories workers gave thanks to the Chairman before eating. When the shift was over, a political study lasted for at least an hour, but before leaving, the people again lined up in front of the picture to perform the "late progress report to Chairman Mao." The workers were expected to examine their thoughts and confess any selfishness or doubts, either to themselves or out loud.

If a new two-hour "Revolutionary sample movie" was shown after work, the workers paraded through the streets in celebration of another victory of Mao Zedong's thought in "art." Even though only eight such movies were made during the ten years of the Cultural Revolution, they were shown every day. They were considered not entertainment but a Revolutionary task that the faithful Maoist fulfilled happily. After the movie, the workers returned to the workplace to discuss why they loved the Chairman even more after seeing it. If the nationwide broadcast at eight o'clock announced some new pearls of Chairman Mao's wisdom, all workers were expected to participate afterward in "spontaneous" parades to rejoice over the new gifts to the nation.

The approach of May Day of 1968 was ominous. While shopping, Rei-qing and I saw posters of fifty-one people who were to be executed on May first (fifty-one because the date was 5/1). Condemned to die as a salute to the holiday for the Proletariat, most were innocent of any crime except for offending some person in power, or walking down the road at the wrong time. Seeing the pictures of the men and women who were going to die on the "happiest day for the people," I felt both grief and shame. I had been taught that Chairman Mao had removed the three mountains crushing the Chinese people—feudalism, imperialism, and the capitalist bureaucrats—but I felt that the deaths of these people smacked of both fascism and moldy feudalism. It was less of a shock for me that fall when for National Day, October 1 (or 10/1), 101 people were sentenced to death to express the wish that the People's Republic of China would have a long life.

During this evil time of death and fanaticism, people still married, had children, and carried on with their lives. I thought that reminding Professor Hu of this period might make him realize how much better his life really was now, and that he should allow himself to enjoy it.

9

Dear Professor Hu,

In my mind, the spring of 1968 went by without a smile as the class struggle tightened like a noose with the Clarification Movement. Now that the Red Guards were out of style, the two groups in charge of the schools and universities were the Army Propaganda of Mao Zedong Thought and the Workers Propaganda of Mao Zedong Thought. Because our Angel Cave was very close to our old home, I still attended the same school. No classes were being held, but we had to study Chairman Mao's works and criticize our class enemies, the teachers, six days a week. The previously chastised nine classes of Blacks had been given a brief respite from the fury of the Revolution but were now being reexamined. "Student Rightist," "bourgeois beetle," "Reactionary roach," and "loyal Royalist" were some of the new labels. Those who had been branded earlier as Rightists or anti-Revolutionaries again came under scrutiny.

There was a new rash of suicides among the teachers from my school who were being investigated. The first was a twelfth-grade-level Chinese-literature teacher whom the Red Guards had accused of being a Guomindang spy. Shortly after they confined her to a classroom, she jumped out of the window of the women's bathroom on the fourth floor. Upon removing her clothes, the Red Guards found that she had torn up her sheets and wrapped them tightly around her body in the widely held belief that this ensured death after jumping out of a building. I often heard classmates say, in matter-of-fact voices, "Well, another teacher committed suicide last night." I never asked who it was, fearing that it might be one who had befriended me. If the teacher jumped to his or her death, the Red Guards would write slogans on the pavement where he or she had fallen: "Good riddance, traitor! Even death cannot pay for your sin!" Some of the Revolutionary music played by the Thought Squads was sad, and I secretly thought of it as dirges for my dead teachers.

Entering the school gate one morning, I saw dozens of people running in the same direction, and I knew that there had been another suicide. I hesitated to follow, but I soon heard people shouting, "Old Man Xue!" He had jumped from the fifth-floor men's room. Not daring to approach the body, I stood apart from the crowd and trembled. The old Rightist of the biology division had survived the years when he was the only one being chastised, so why could he not manage now that he had the principal and the Party secretary of the school for company?

"Thearch hith pocketh," a female Red Guard nicknamed "Slab-Tongue" shouted. "Thee if there are any exthplothiveth inthide!" The crowd murmured reasons for his suicide. Two students who lived on the same block told people that his daughter-in-law had left with his grandchildren when the Clarification Movement started, and that his son had poisoned himself a few days later.

Such stories were common. The bonds between brothers, husband and wife, father and son, mother-in-law and daughter-in-law were severely tested. Old Man Xue's daughter-in-law had endured much during her marriage, but perhaps this new movement had made her think more of her children's future. The suicide of his son may have been Xue's final straw. After enduring ten years of insults, he may have felt defeated and seen death as the only option. I wondered whether the chain reaction would continue, leaving Mrs. Xue as the final victim.

Relishing the situation, Slab-Tongue ordered people to fetch the wheelbarrow that Old Man Xue had used to transport flowers and saplings for more than ten years. Now it carried the body of the gardener as the mock funeral procession passed through the crowd. I summoned all my courage to take a final look at his body and silently wish him farewell. The body was so mangled in the fall, it did not even look human.

Ah-di appeared next to me, and we returned quietly to the classroom. She never exploited a tragic situation to attract attention to herself, due both to her gentle nature and her fear of the Buddha. I, however, was angry and wanted to punish Slab-Tongue. After I convinced Ah-di to help play a trick on her, we found two other friends and went to Slab-Tongue's classroom. She was telling her classmates of her brave deeds beside Old Man Xue's body. Ah-di motioned to her.

"I have a secret to tell you," said Ah-di bluntly. "Let me see your hand!" Although it was early spring, Slab-Tongue was sweating profusely, and the beads of sweat collected on the thick down of her lips as she extended her left hand.

"Other paw!" Ah-di snapped. "Left for a man, right for a woman!"

Confused, Slab-Tongue meekly obeyed and extended both hands. All four of us crowded our heads together, staring at her palms. "Whath the matter? Ith thomething wrong? Tell me!" she said nervously.

"Look at this line on your right palm! It goes all the way across! You have a crossover hand! Don't you know that this means that if you beat people, they'll die? No wonder Old Man Xue died!"

"You lie! I didn't beat Old Man Thue today! Bethideth, I don't have a crothover hand. I ought to know."

None of us had expected her to know anything about palm reading. Ah-di shouted, "Who told you that you don't have a crossover hand? Look, all three of you! Isn't this a crossover hand?"

"Oh, yes, it's definitely a crossover hand if I ever saw one!" we all agreed.

"All right," said Ah-di, "do you want me to ask everyone in the classroom to classify your hand?"

Slab-Tongue trembled. "Why can't I thee it? No, no, pleathe don't athk the clath. Even if I do have a crothover hand, I didn't beat him today. You all thaw that he killed himthelf!"

Ah-di laughed derisively. "You don't understand anything, you bumpkin! You said you didn't beat him *today*! But it's not like you'd never beaten him before!"

Slab-Tongue confessed: "Ith true. I beat him latht week with my belt!"

"There you have it! You didn't beat him today, but you did last week. It was a delayed reaction. It took a while for your beating to take effect. Everything about you is different. Look in the mirror! You're a woman, but you look, act, and smell like a maaaaan!" Ah-di said, lowering her voice.

Self-conscious about her masculine appearance, Slab-Tongue was particularly ashamed of her mustache. She floundered helplessly: "But what ith tho different about a woman who lookth like a man? Why thould it affect everything elthe?"

Ah-di opened her eyes wide in an innocent fashion. "Oh, there are many things. Just now, all four of us girls can see that you have a crossover hand, but you missed it! That means you're losing your visual acuity. And," she continued gravely, "you will lose other abilities if you do not atone for your sin."

"How can I atone for my thin?" asked Slab-Tongue desperately.

"Well, I'm not an expert in these matters, but my grandmother says that you have to chant a mantra one hundred times, twice a day, for a thousand days. But in a more practical sense, I personally think that you should keep house for Old Lady Xue and take care of her." Ah-di cleared her throat. "People who die like Old Man Xue did can become restless demons walking the earth, seeking revenge on those who did them harm. If you can get the old lady to pray and appease the demon, you might be safe. But I don't know. . . ."

Slab-Tongue was sweating even more, filled with awe at Ah-di's understanding. When we all parted, she apparently considered us four her new friends. "And when you thee your grandmother, athk her what elthe I thould do to pay for my thin," she called to Ah-di over her shoulder.

△△△ Ju-jin Xiong, my father's best friend, was also caught in the net of the Clarification Movement. Because Uncle Xiong had spent six years in Western Europe, studying forestry, he was placed under arrest in the Railway Administration Office where he worked.

He was cut off from his family. The Red Guards interrogated him in three shifts for many days, and the cumulative fatigue caused virtual physical and mental collapse. "Why, in 1939, after receiving your Ph.D., did you refuse a lucrative offer from an American university and return to the mainland? It's obvious you must have been on a special mission if you turned down such a high-paying job in the United States to work for low pay in a Chinese university during the war. Who would believe it was mere stupidity?" Xiong always answered that he had returned to China to fight in the anti-Japanese War. Had it not been for his ailing father-in-law, a Chinese citizen who had moved to Germany, he would have returned at the outbreak of the war instead of waiting until 1939. When his father-in-law died, Ju-jin and his wife went home to China.

"You're a spy for the whole world! You have four eyes in your head: One sees for the Americans, one for the Guomindang, one for the Japanese, and the last for the Germans!" his tormentors stated.

Outraged by such a ridiculous accusation, Ju-jin finally lost his temper and screamed his defenses until his mouth was dry. The interrogation continued, each of his arguments going unheeded and his punishment increased. When the Red Guards threatened to rip out his tongue, he realized that all defense was useless.

"So then, are you a spy working for these four countries?"

He took a deep breath and rocked back on his low stool. Looking up at his captors, he replied, "Yes, I am."

The Red Guards exchanged glances. At last they were getting somewhere. "What is your code number?"

"Five-six-seven-eight."

"Where is your rendezvous point?"

"The third tree to the left of the gate to the Railroad Middle School. There is a hole in the tree for messages."

"And when are your meeting times?" The questioner was becoming visibly more excited.

"Sundays from three in the afternoon until eleven at night, every two weeks."

The Red Guards were euphoric. In just a short time, they had broken the largest international spy ring that had ever threatened

Chairman Mao. "What an incredibly complex network!" they thought. "It's too bad old man Xiong didn't work for the Soviets, too! Then we could kill five birds with one stone! Then again . . ."

The investigation was reopened. "When you returned from Europe, did you happen to spend any time with those Revisionists?" one of the Red Guards asked, pointing roughly north.

Ju-jin caught on immediately. "Oh, yes," he replied, "but the Soviets were not yet Revisionists."

"What difference does that make? Our time is valuable and you are wasting it with whining excuses! How many days did you spend there?"

"At least ten days, maybe even two weeks." Ju-jin shrugged, unconcernedly.

"Did you receive any espionage or terrorist training while you were there?"

"Of course! I said I was there for at least ten days. Did you think I was sightseeing?" Ju-jin laughed out loud.

The leader handed him the notes of the meeting. "Sign it," he demanded.

Without hesitation, Ju-jin signed the paper, which read: "All of the above confession is true. I will never retract this confession, nor will I ever attempt to have my name cleared."

He returned calmly to his cell. The sunlight coming through his west-facing window cast a shadow of the bars onto the east wall of the cell. He estimated time according to the sun, since his watch had been confiscated as "evidence" when he was apprehended. Watching the sun set each day, he felt a deep guilt about the way his life was being wasted. When the Red Guards had threatened to hang his tongue on the wall, he had even considered suicide. Years later, he told me that it was the thought of my father and his own son Tao-ran that kept him from leaving the world.

Hoping to trap Ju-jin's fellow agents, the Red Guards went to the gate of the Railroad Middle School the following Sunday and waited from three until eleven. Of course, there was no contact. "He said, 'Every other Sunday,' " one of the Red Guards pointed out. "This must be the odd Sunday." Disappointed, they left, but they returned the next

Sunday to wait for another eight fruitless hours. Furious, they summoned Ju-jin from his cell and interrogated him further.

"Yes, it's true," he sobbed piteously. "I did lie to you. I was afraid that you would beat me if I told the truth, so what else could I do? I'll tell you what you want to know, but please don't beat me!" His new saga was embellished with bits and pieces from detective movies he had seen. They were old tricks, but the young Red Guards had never seen any Humphrey Bogart movies. The farce continued for months while Ju-jin patiently waited for his captors to become bored. He hoped that when they realized that they had not uncovered an international spy ring after all, they would cut their losses and release him. When Tao-ran visited every month to bring fresh clothes and sundries, Xiong told him, "On payday, every month, please don't forget to send some money to Tan's family." Were it not for this man, my family doubtless would have starved to death. Uncle Xiong was finally released in 1971.

△△△ Professor Wang was not released until the end of 1970. Still not recovered mentally from his detention in the university, he thought of little besides the personal and political accusations made by his Red Guard captors. Rather than ask his own family for advice, he asked his daughter Gui-feng to send for Rei-qing, for whom he had a great deal of respect. While waiting excitedly for her return from seeing him, I arranged all of the calculus and physics problems I had been working on since his imprisonment. Now that Professor Wang was back, my days without a teacher were finally over.

Rei-qing returned at midnight, and, to my delight, she was carrying two copies of a classic textbook on microwaves. I was chatting with Father, but when I saw that she was upset, I asked her what was wrong.

Shrugging nervously, she answered evasively, "Well, I don't think we should go over to Gui-feng's anymore." She went on to explain that she was so late returning home because she had spent six hours helping Professor Wang write his confession. Apparently he had told her everything he had done since he was eighteen, even describing his marital problems. Rei-qing was so disgusted that she refused to study with him further.

"How can you judge him like that? He may have personal problems, but that doesn't mean he isn't a brilliant electrical engineer," Father said quietly. "I hope you understand that you must learn to hide evil and spread only goodness." The idol of the "teacher" was again broken in my mind, but I reluctantly agreed to ask Professor Wang my questions. Father told me, "When you admire somebody, you make a god out of him. When you find that your god has feet of clay, you decide he's worthless. That's too extreme, Xi-ou, and you'll only be unhappy if you keep thinking this way. No one is all good or all bad. We all show different facets of our characters in different situations." Shaking his head with a little smile, he said, "When I was young, I was pretty extreme in my views, too. Apparently you've inherited this from me."

The "City of Heroes" in my mind was filled with scientists, engineers, philosophers, writers, and artists—all pure and good-hearted. When I read the book *Madame Curie,* I found it easy to relate to the poor Polish girl. Our backgrounds and lives were similar: an older father living alone with four children in a poor home where patriotism and education were held in high regard. Even the finer details were similar: Marie Curie's father was a naive intellectual who suffered because of one of his wife's relatives. Identifying each member of my family with one of the Sklodowskas, I saw myself as the next Madame Curie.

Professor Wang, on the other hand, was the first scientist I had met in person, and I was cruelly disappointed. Although I had lost respect for him, I tried to be kind to his children and invited them to our home for the New Year's Day dinner. In our part of China, the traditional Chinese New Year's celebration lasts for thirty days. The dinner seven days before the New Year's Eve is called the "minor feast," while the one on New Year's Eve is called the "major feast." My family was on such a tight budget that we had only gruel for the minor feast, but Father taught us an old folk song:

> *Today is the day of the small New Year feast!*
> *You'd think we'd have salt on our turnips, at least!*
> *In the mountains up north is hidden our meat,*
> *A thousand miles south is our rice and our wheat!*

But on this New Year's Day, we were not thinking about the meager dinner we had had a few nights earlier. Instead, we were dutifully playing host to our best friends by piling food on their plates while they protested that we had used our entire month's allotment of some of the rationed ingredients. When the Cultural Revolution began, Father was forced to report all of his visitors and so refused to receive any. The tremendous burden on such a naturally hospitable man was alleviated a little by visits from his children's friends.

Gui-feng came to our house several days later, clearly distraught. Her father objected to her fiancé, even as a boyfriend. How could she tell him that they were planning to marry within a month? "Why does your father object to Xiao Zhang?" Father asked softly.

"He thinks I should marry someone with a college education. Xiao Zhang and I have only finished high school," she sobbed.

Father asked how they met and decided to marry, and what Xiao Zhang was like. After glowing answers from Gui-feng, Father said, "It takes proper family and class origins to get into college these days, not just good grades. So it's only marginally important that your future husband have a college education." Gui-feng could see no farther than her love for Xiao Zhang, but since her father was strongly opposed and her mother's views were not respected in her home, she wanted a second opinion from a wise man. Out of politeness, I went to the other side of the room and pretended to do problems in my notebook, even though the conversation interested me far more. I was touched that Gui-feng had such faith in Father, a man who had long ago been politically damned.

After Gui-feng and Xiao Zhang's ceremony in February 1968, Mei-feng and I accompanied her on the bus to her new home. The bus was packed, and, since I was bigger than Gui-feng, I did my best to protect the bride from being jostled. It was not as crowded as it had been when the Red Guards toured the country, but it was still far from comfortable. Gui-feng's new leather shoes were scuffed from the dirty feet of other passengers, so before she entered her new home, where the groom was waiting, I cleaned them with my handkerchief. Then I helped fix her hair, insisting that she remove her brown overcoat to show the red jacket underneath. I examined her from head to toe several times, making sure that she was ready to begin married life.

Their new apartment building consisted of dozens of rooms with a common cooking area. Their own room was only eight square meters, but the walls and the old furniture had been newly painted by friends. Rei-qing and Li-na prepared the marriage feast with Xiao Zhang's sister, his only relative in the city. A large board was placed over the table to extend it, and the couple, Li-na, Me-feng, Xiao Zhang's sister, and their best man, Rei-qing, and I all crowded around it in the tiny room and began the traditional wedding feast.

Xiao Zhang's eyes were red and watery—not from crying, but from having stayed up several nights to make the room habitable. Their wedding was not the kind that was fashionable for the Clarification Movement, and the only symbol of Revolutionary conjugal bliss was the requisite life-size portrait of Chairman Mao over their door. I was disappointed by the complete absence of books in the room. In preparing for the wedding, Gui-feng had not attended Father's lessons for weeks. "From now on, will she simply eat, sleep, work in the factory, come home from work, and eat and sleep all over again—have babies, cook, clean, and never study?" I asked myself sadly. "But if this is what she wants and what makes her happy, what's wrong with it?"

Xiao Zhang's sister proudly praised her new sister-in-law to the curious neighbors, who wanted a peek at the newly married couple. "My brother got the daughter of a professor!" she repeated over and over. The impressed neighbors made admiring comments: "No!" "Really?" "Is that what a professor's daughter looks like?" "That's really something!"

Gui-feng had drunk some wine at the meal and was truly the "blushing, shy bride" as she hid her face from the eyes of the envious, respectful neighbors. I was puzzled; the Cultural Revolution had been going on for three years, so how could a professor make such an impact in a working-class ghetto? I found it ironic that the man who had most violently opposed this marriage had given Gui-feng the best wedding present she could ask for—the title of "professor's daughter."

Xiao Zhang was grateful that such a highborn woman would marry a man like him. After the neighbors left, he closed the door and made a hearty speech: "We're just a couple of workers. We don't make much, not even eight yuan together. We have no parents to sponge off. This isn't a rich folks' wedding dinner, but we practically had to go into hock for it. The minimum price for a wife these days is three chickens and seventy-two legs. Can't afford those chickens now, so I owe her. But I'll work hard all my life and save my pennies and one day I'm sure I'll be able to pay for Gui-feng."

After speaking, he stood with a stupid, innocent grin. Li-na shouted, "Come on, Xiao Zhang, you're not that bad off. In this room you already have two chickens and twenty-four legs!"

Rei-qing and I looked at each other in total confusion. Finally, Rei-qing embarrassedly asked, "What are 'chickens' and 'legs'?"

Li-na explained: "A chicken is just a machine that can move or talk. The three 'traditional' chickens are a radio, a sewing machine, and a bicycle. The legs are furniture legs. The more legs, the more furniture you have." Looking around the room, I saw two bicycle "chickens" propped against the wall.

Seeing that Xiao Zhang's shame and promise were sincere, Rei-qing held Gui-feng's hand and said, "Gui-feng certainly didn't marry you for your money. She loves you for yourself. Don't be too concerned about these things. We hope that you'll be happy together until your hair is snow-white."

Xiao Zhang's sister left the room and then returned, accompanied by a woman who lived down the hall and her son, a plump three-year-old whom Xiao Zhang's sister introduced as "the number-one son." Then, from under the bed she pulled a new chamber pot, the traditional wedding gift. It was filled with candies, peanuts, colored eggs, and dates. She asked the little boy to reach in the commode and pull out something. He pulled out a date, and the entire wedding party applauded and shouted: "He pulled out a date! Look, he pulled out a date! You know what that means! Gui-feng will have a son soon!"

△△△ So you see, Professor Hu, even through the Red Terror, people still married and had feasts with their friends and loved each other. Some people gave up and committed suicide, but others sought the sweet parts of life. The human spirit can rise above any amount of misery and find joy. Life is so much more secure for both of us now. Please allow yourself to enjoy it.

Sincerely,
Xi-ou Tan

 That morning, I received an Express Mail letter from Professor Hu. It seemed thicker than his last two letters, and I tore it open quickly.

 Dear Xi-ou Tan,
I have received all your letters. Your story is full of blood and tears, and no one could remain unmoved after reading it. I have become afraid to read them, for your courage makes me feel ashamed. On the other hand, I look forward to them because your stories are gripping. You may be younger than I, but your experiences were far more difficult than mine.

I told you in one of my letters that I had recently received a great shock. Three weeks ago, one of my best friends during my adolescence passed away while visiting an American university on the West Coast. He was only forty-six, but he was the best contemporary Chinese mathematician. At nine years old, his mental arithmetic was faster than his father's calculations with an abacus. Because his father once worked as an accountant for a bank owned by the British before the Liberation, he was not permitted to go to the Soviet Union for graduate school as other promising students did in the 1950s. After graduating from college, he was assigned as a middle-school teacher in a mining area. In 1980, he was transferred back to the Academy of Science in Beijing. He had been pushed into the background for years, but now that he was in the limelight, he was so grateful that he worked sixteen hours a day, producing more than thirty important mathematical papers in six years. No woman wanted him during the twenty years he taught in a mining community, but after he returned to Beijing and became famous, thousands of women mailed him their pictures, proposing marriage. Still, it took him five years to find the right one. He called me the week before he died to tell me that he was going to be a father. He did not once mention any of the awards he had won; he only told me of his excitement about having a child. One of the Soong dynasty lyrics says:

> *The sea is boundless, so is the sky,*
> *The east wind our ally, but then, why*
> *Do they not help our heroes on the courses they try?*

If I were a filmmaker I would make a film featuring a thin ox plodding along a narrow, tortuous road with a tight, heavy yoke cutting into his neck so that his blood dripped down onto the grassless, waterless road. The hungry, dry-lipped animal would drop on the road and die. I feel that my friend did not die of an illness, but rather from overexertion due to his effort to make up for his wasted years. I want to cry, but I have no tears. I want to say something, but I cannot. The poet Xin Ji-qi wrote:

> *When I was young, I did not know the taste of grief.*
> *I wanted to climb the highest tower,*
> *Imagined sorrow gave my writing power.*

> *Now I am growing old, and I know the taste of grief.*
> *It bites keenly, but I hold it back as mine,*
> *Saying empty words: Isn't the weather fine?*

The reason I hold back is twofold: First, who would listen to me, and second, how much would any listener understand? Another famous poet, Ye Fei, our national hero in the Soong dynasty, wrote the following:

I confide to my lute all my feelings,
For appreciative listeners are rare.
If I played so long that I broke the strings,
Still no one would understand, or care.

I sent this letter Express Mail to tell you not to spend so much time and energy writing to me. I look forward to your letters, but I should not be so selfish. I can imagine the pressure you are under in the "publish or perish" American academic world. Although you have not finished your month of stories, I want to assure you that I will try to develop a better outlook on life.

Thank you for all your kindness.

Sincerely yours,
Yong-hua Hu

Dear Professor Hu,

Thank you for your Express Mail letter. I
know you paid extra so I would receive it before
the spring recess ended. I started working again
today, but instead of concentrating on my project, I find
myself still thinking about what to write you. The story of your
friend, the outstanding mathematician, reminds me of another
scientist I knew when I was a teenager, and his sister.

 In 1968, while working on the farm, Rei-qing made a
friend called Lao Mo. This woman, at twenty-six years old, constantly
lamented, "I'm so poor, and besides, I'm almost thirty. That's too old
to get married." So her coworkers nicknamed her "Grandma" Mo.
She had a twenty-nine-year-old brother who did classified military
research.

One night in late spring, Rei-qing went to borrow a pair of scissors
from Lao Mo and found her sitting on the bed, tearfully thinking of her
home and family. Lao Mo motioned for her to sit down next to her.
"Being away from home is killing me. My father is seventy-five, and I
don't know how much longer he's going to live. He began as a factory
apprentice when he was fourteen, and his first boss treated him very
badly. He vowed that he would someday be a boss and never have to
call anyone 'master' again. He put in fourteen-hour days, scrimping
and saving for twenty years until he was able to buy a rundown paper

factory. He married my mother when he was forty-two, so they call us the children of his twilight.

"My brother studied hard even when he was a little boy. He did well in all of his subjects, and the school recommended that he enter every mathematics and physics contest, even the national ones. He dressed like a ragamuffin in college so no one would suspect that he was the son of a wealthy capitalist. He graduated from college in 1962 with a degree in physics and was assigned his present position in a military research institute. Since it was considered part of the Army, he and his project were not affected by the Cultural Revolution. He knows that to be successful in science he needs to join the Party, but that will be nearly impossible. He's very modest. Even if something is his idea and he did all the work, he doesn't care if someone else gets the credit. All his colleagues like him.

"I'm completely different from him. I've never worked hard at anything. I used to get Fs in all my classes except physical education. I never would have been promoted if I hadn't passed the makeup exams they offered in the summer. I'm not only lazy, but I also like to snack all day." She stopped talking and reached into the tall, thin jar of salted meat and preserved turnips that she kept by her bed. Instead of eating the handful of food right away, she tilted her head back and lowered it slowly into her mouth, savoring every morsel. When the afterglow of the snack faded, she handed the jar to Rei-qing and encouraged her to eat.

"This is your dinner. I can't take the food out of your mouth," Rei-qing said.

"Hasn't this movement had any effect on you, bourgeois madam? We don't have fine divisions of 'dinner' and 'snack' anymore. We just eat when we're hungry. It doesn't matter how much food I bring back when I go home for vacation; it's gone in a week. After all, Lao Mo is almost thirty and has to take care of herself." Rei-qing smiled, recognizing the beginning of Lao Mo's usual speech.

She left the room, contemplating the story of Lao Mo's brother. Because sixteen-year-old Jian-nan showed a fine flair for physics in our independent study program, Rei-qing thought that he might like to visit Xiao Mo. Lao Mo agreed to arrange a meeting during an upcoming vacation. On a stifling summer evening a month later, she, Rei-qing, and Jian-nan went to visit Xiao Mo. The physicist appreciated Jian-nan's inquisitiveness, and he offered him some reference books and old journals. Overjoyed, Rei-qing and Jian-nan thanked him profusely.

Two days later, our dinner was interrupted by an urgent pounding on the door. Fearing it was the Red Guards or the Neighborhood Committee, Father dove into bed. Father's seat was nearest to the bed, so Rei-qing slipped into it to divert suspicion. When everything was secure, I opened the door. Lao Mo burst into the room, crying hysterically: "He's gone! He's gone! How could he leave us like this?"

I stood in the doorway with my mouth half-open. Rei-qing came over and put her arm around Lao Mo, trying to find out what happened. Lao Mo told us that Xiao Mo had awakened with a tight feeling in his chest that made breathing difficult, but he attributed it to his asthma. He had insisted on bicycling to work to complete an experiment. Then he went to the paper factory on his lunch hour to pick up the monthly pay for living expenses for his parents. The Revolutionary Committee of the paper factory claimed that Xiao Mo lost consciousness while unlocking his bicycle in front of the factory, and he was rushed to the emergency room. He was pronounced dead from a heart attack less than thirty minutes later. The hospital notified the administrators of the institute, who in turn called the public telephone station for his parents' neighborhood. His mother fainted in the telephone booth, and Lao Mo went to the hospital with her. When she could leave her mother, Lao Mo did not yet have the strength or composure to tell her old, weak father the news, so she ran to our house instead.

With a suspicion born from seeing too many "accidental" deaths, Rei-qing asked, "Have you seen your brother's body? Are there any unexplained marks or bruises on it?"

Lao Mo shook her head, crying: "The hospital didn't let me see it. They said it was already in the morgue. The cadre from the Personnel Division of the paper factory wanted me to sign the identification papers right away."

"Did you sign them?" Rei-qing interrupted.

At Lao Mo's weak nod, Rei-qing said angrily, "You shouldn't have done that. Now no one will really know how your brother died.

Don't you know that thousands of people are beaten to death and thrown out of windows and then branded as suicides? Then the Revolutionaries say that the victims killed themselves because they were afraid of being punished for their crimes. How could you so easily believe that he died just unlocking a bicycle?"

Lao Mo bowed her head and the tears ran silently down her face. Rei-qing stamped her foot, saying, "Now that you have already signed and the body has been taken to the morgue, the die is cast. You have no recourse."

Father calmed Rei-qing, who offered to go with Lao Mo to help her. Father agreed: "When you're telling Uncle Mo the news, remember that how you say it is as important as what you say. Outliving a son, especially in one's old age, is a father's greatest pain. That the boy was so outstanding only makes it more difficult."

Rei-qing left with Lao Mo and the rest of us returned to the table, although no one felt like eating. Father did not turn on the light to write his manuscript that night. Instead, he sat in the dark under the small, southern window, with my brothers and me in a tight circle around him. The night was windless, and Angel Cave was full of hot, sticky, mosquito-laden air. As if we had an unspoken agreement not to disturb the air with noisy paper fans, Jian-nan lit the mosquito-repelling incense. In the bright moonlight, I watched the incense smoke rising in graceful plumes up through the bars, and I wished with all my heart that Xiao Mo had indeed died of a sudden heart attack. He was a good man and deserved better death than one at the hands of the Revolutionaries.

Xiao Mo was his parents' only son, and they were devastated. Later, I once saw the mother sitting on the exact spot where her son had fallen to the sidewalk, but I barely recognized the filthy woman with matted hair and no dentures who cried uncontrollably, oblivious to the staring crowd. Old Uncle Mo was a self-made millionaire, but he watched the Red Guards steal his fortune in a single night. The next morning, he awoke back where he had been fifty years earlier, a member of the Proletariat. He accepted these things because he still had a phenomenal son, beyond price, who could not be confiscated in a raid. With the loss of this last treasure, Uncle Mo lost his will to live.

After two months of halfhearted existence, he fell asleep on a drizzly autumn night and did not wake again.

Lao Mo, deadened to the outside world, decided to stay in Shanghai without a job. She had grown accustomed to a life free from worry over money, but now she found herself in unexpected financial trouble. She took her brother's books, journals, and notes to the recycling plant to receive a tiny sum before Rei-qing could find out about it and stop her.

On a cold December day, Rei-qing was home on a vacation, and Lao Mo came to visit. They were talking about Xiao Mo, and I heard my sister say, "Jian-nan is very interested in the concept of entropy, but he can't fully grasp it. It's so unfortunate that your brother died; he could have asked him."

"That's easy enough," Lao Mo answered with some of her former exuberance. "My brother had a good friend named Wu. He's a wizard at math and physics. He's teaching at Wu Han University now. When he came to Shanghai last year to get married, he made a point of visiting us. I'll send him a letter with Jian-nan's questions."

When Lao Mo came back with Wu's reply two months later, she handed the letter to me. She seemed depressed as she said, "Here. Read it." Unaccustomed to reading other people's mail, I played with the letter for a few minutes before finally opening it.

> My dear Su,
>
> I received your letter. When I learned of your brother's death three months ago, I figured that your parents wouldn't live much longer. So I wasn't surprised when I read that your father had passed away. I feel that your mother isn't long for this world either. I know you don't want to hear this, but I'm determined to be honest with you. Truth is often the most difficult thing for people to accept. I decided to tell you these things directly, because there are too few people in this world to do this for you.
>
> I often feel that you shouldn't grieve for your brother. It's better to die than to continue living as he did, although you might think it is cruel for me to say

so. I really believe that I knew your brother better than anyone, so I know that his pain was beyond your comprehension.

When I went back to Shanghai last year, I knew that you were deliberately avoiding me, but I still wanted to visit you no matter how hard it was. I knew that our relationship had to end, and I had to tell you face to face.

Actually, four or five years ago, when I learned that I was assigned to Wu Han, I realized that there could be no future for us. For one thing, your mother wouldn't allow you, her only daughter, to leave Shanghai. Besides, my salary of fifty-six yuan a month isn't enough to support you in the style to which you are accustomed. Maybe you didn't know that your mother took me aside several times to ask me to use my achievements in mathematics as leverage to stay in Shanghai. I didn't try, because I was very loyal to the Party at the time. If the Party told me to go somewhere, it wasn't for me to disagree or question their reasoning. I suppressed my feelings for you and left without saying good-bye. I convinced myself that I couldn't get along with that "snobbish capitalist old despot" mother of yours and used it as an excuse to sever all relations with you, a capitalist daughter. Your brother wrote me several letters later, but I never wrote him back.

I didn't realize how the storm of the Grand Cultural Revolution had changed me. I used to be at the pinnacle of my field because of my prowess in mathematics, but I was cast down and made a model of Revisionism. In 1964, it was revealed that my father, along with many of his coworkers, had joined the Guomindang before the Liberation. I was accused of the more severe charge of concealing my background. There was only one way left to keep the ten-square-meter room in Shanghai that my parents lived in: If I got married to a Shanghai girl, we could claim the room as our legal right. . . .

I did not want to continue reading. I had never dreamed that Lao Mo had hidden such a sad love story behind her cheerful exterior, and now I understood her obsession with the notion that she was too old to marry. I could not understand why she would want to show me such a personal letter. "I really don't think I should read any more of this. It's really too personal," I said nervously.

"It doesn't matter. I think of you as a little sister. I don't care if you know these things about me. Keep reading. You'll see that he does finally get around to Jian-nan's questions."

> . . . You know that my wife and I were introduced by some mutual friends and were married a week later. I didn't really know her. At that time, her only attractive quality was that she was in Shanghai, teaching elementary school. When I look back, I can't understand why I felt as I felt or did as I did. Why did that ten-square-meter room become more important than anything else in the world? Needless to say, the room is owned by the Office of Housing Administration. Even if it belonged to us, it could have been taken away in one night. Isn't that what the Red Guards have been ramming down our throats for years?
>
> In the eleventh grade, your brother told me in confidence, "My IQ isn't much above average. The only reason I did well in these courses is that I worked far harder than anyone else. Even you—I made a statistical study of it and found that I spent five times as much time on my math and physics as you." At first I didn't believe it, but when I looked, I found it was true. At graduation, he had the highest composite score of the 400 people in our graduating class. When your mother saw his achievements, could she appreciate that he worked so much harder than anyone else?
>
> Such an academically ambitious person, in addition to everything else, carried an insupportable political burden on his shoulders. How could anyone survive? Although his mind still wanted to fight more than ever, his body finally said, "Enough!" and he was released by death. In spite of my deep grief over losing him, I rejoice over his well-earned rest in the next world.
>
> It's a pity that I don't have the courage to die.

Every day I live like a beast. I work like a peasant in the fields, where the university sent me. I till the earth from sunrise to sunset in the most primitive way possible. There aren't any books or newspapers or studying. What was the point in learning mathematics if I was going to end up here?

That friend of yours, I think that he's either too young to understand or he's very lucky and lives in another world. Even now he boldly and unrealistically studies science. One thing I can predict: In the very near future, he will surrender to our society.

The letter was unsigned, but two crossed swords were drawn at the bottom. Lao Mo explained, "Wu, my brother, and a third student were so close that they were known as 'The Three Musketeers.' When they wrote each other, they signed their letters with a sketch of three crossed swords. With my brother gone, there are only two."

Seeing that her eyes were red, I quickly tried to change the subject: "Wu doesn't seem like a bad person, only a depressed one. I think you should keep writing him. It might make him happy."

Lao Mo fished a small photograph album from her knapsack and paged through it. "I found this when I went through my brother's belongings. This picture was taken when the Musketeers won the top three prizes in the national high-school math competition." In the photograph, three teenage boys were standing in front of a statue of Pushkin in a Shanghai park. All three had awards in their hands and carefree smiles on their faces. "This is Wu; he won first prize. When he visited our home last year, my brother told me that he was bald and looked about ten years older than he was," Lao Mo said.

He must look even worse now, I thought. He didn't even say a word about entropy in that whole long letter. How could I explain this to Jian-nan?

△△△ When Rei-qing came home for a visit in February 1969, we discussed the matter and decided to tell Jian-nan the truth. We first asked him why he thought we were studying.

"To understand the mysteries of nature, of course!"

Rei-qing licked her lips: "If someone told you that studying is hopeless and that you should simply surrender to the wishes of society, what would you say?"

"Why would it be hopeless? Why should we surrender to our society?" he asked indignantly.

I felt a sudden wave of sorrow for my brother. I did not want to play games with him, so I told him the whole story. Rei-qing said little, only toning down portions of the story so his feelings would not be hurt. Jian-nan had been looking forward to Wu's response, but the unexpected result did not make him lose hope. After a period of deep thought, he asked, "Can I write a letter to Big Brother Wu? I want to quote him something from Evariste Galois: 'Wherever there is sunshine, the violets blossom!' "

△△△ Not everyone was as discouraging as Big Brother Wu regarding our independent study. Rei-qing developed a fever during her vacation and I took her to the hospital, since there was a rule that anyone with a fever over 100 degrees was entitled to two days of sick leave. While I certainly did not want my sister to be ill, I wished in a way that she could have a fever for the rest of her life.

"It's not like I'm afraid of working in the fields," she said. "Planting, harvesting, feeding the pigs—as long as other people can do it, so can I. What bothers me is what happens after work. The men and women know that they're never going to be able to get married and have families, so they do what seems to them like the next best thing. They have a different partner every night. We live like animals in the countryside. We eat, we sleep, we work; we don't think. Our brains become smaller while our muscles get bigger," Rei-qing lamented.

Rei-qing was fully recovered within a week. Determined to do whatever it took to get her out of the countryside, we decided to try our luck first with the countryside hospitals, where the doctors were said to be more lenient with sick leave than those in the city. It was a four-hour bus ride to the country hospital nearest to Rei-qing's farm. She was exhausted by the trip and looked so pale that I was afraid she might have a relapse. A tall doctor called both of us into an examination room. After looking over Rei-qing, he scribbled something on a form. I could not decipher his entries, but I could see from the form what information he was to supply. He wrote out a prescription and left.

Our effort appeared to be a waste of time. Stepping out of the examination room, we realized how much of our hope had been wrapped up in this visit. I left Rei-qing on a bench in the lobby while I went to the hospital pharmacy. The line was long and the pharmacist was new. When my turn finally came, he claimed that he could not read the prescription and I would have to go back for a legible copy.

I returned grimly to the examination room and said, "Dr. Wei, what's this supposed to mean? Your handwriting is so bad the pharmacist wouldn't even look at it!"

"Well," he said, laughing, "if my handwriting is so bad, how did you figure out that my name is Wei? All right, give it to me and let's see what you can't read."

"Wait a minute, I think I can figure this out. Your name is Jun Wei, the same as the minister of records to the second emperor of the Tang dynasty," I said, and continued decoding. Examining the characters carefully, I discerned a familiar beauty. Dr. Wei's handwriting was almost an exact copy of Me Fe's continuous script, Father's favorite style. He used to post Me Fe's characters next to his desk. "I'm sorry, Dr. Wei. Your handwriting is of the same style as Me Fe. It's very easy to read and I should have recognized it immediately. Please forgive me."

The doctor looked surprised. "You knew that there was a minister of records named Jun Wei? You could even pick out Me Fe's style? That's impressive. My nephew is fourteen and he's much taller than you. When he wrote to his mother, who works in another province, he even forgot how to write 'Mama!' He got the characters confused and wrote 'Horse-horse' instead!"

"You can't really blame him. When the Grand Cultural Revolution started, he was still in elementary school. After two or three years of not reading and writing, anyone could forget that," I said. Despite my cheerful words, I felt depressed. If the Basket Bridge would not allow me to communicate with Mother, I myself might forget how to write "Mama."

Dr. Wei stared at the prescription. Frowning, he shrugged his shoulders and made some changes. Bringing out Rei-qing's record form to modify it as well, he saw our address. "You live in downtown Shanghai? And you came all this way today? That's a long trip," he said.

"Yes, we are going to return home now," I replied.

"Well, I think I should authorize some sick leave for your sister."

My heart began beating rapidly. Dr. Wei pulled out the forms and said very seriously, "I'm writing that the patient is still very weak, and without a good rest, she may develop pneumonia. I have authorized a month of sick leave. Let her have a good rest at home." He stamped the form with the red seal of the country hospital, tore it from the pad, and handed it to me.

He was such a large man that when he stood up, I came only to his chest. "At your age, you should develop both your mind and your body. Continue enriching yourself. Someday you will be glad you did," he said, offering me his massive hand. I was so nervous that I gave him my left hand. It was the first time anyone had treated me as an adult.

△△△ Professor Hu, I had meant at first only to tell you about Xiao Mo and his sister, but it did not seem right to send you a letter full of discouraging stories. Even though most of the people felt the same way as Big Brother Wu about our independent study, there were a few who encouraged and helped us, like Dr. Wei. The visit with Dr. Wei also made us realize that there were legal ways to get around being sent to the countryside. Since Chairman Mao had declared in December 1968 that all students should go to the countryside, such considerations were extremely important to me. I will tell you about this in the next letter. Meanwhile, take care of yourself, and write soon.

Sincerely,
Xi-ou Tan

Under the policy of "the working class rules all," instituted in 1968, the squad of the Workers Propaganda
Team of Mao Zedong Thought occupied my middle
school. They ordered the warring factions of Red Guards to stop fighting and join together in the "Revolutionary Union," and they expelled
the Red Guards from the Ox Ghost Reeducation Ranch, where many
teachers had been confined to perform slave labor. Some teachers were
liberated in the process. The working-class representatives led students
to the countryside and factories to help with the harvest and production. In the summer of 1968, it was announced that the classes of 1966
and 1967 would leave the school to begin work. The working class was
now in control; the era of the Red Guards' dominion was over.

Most of us welcomed the change. We were growing older but
acquiring neither skills nor knowledge. Out of sheer boredom, students
had been starting street fights or vandalizing local stores. Those willing
to get out of bed only to eat were considered good children, because
they stayed out of trouble. Even Xiao-yi Wu was bored with the routine
duties of a leader of the Red Guards and looked for a new form of
stimulation.

The working-class squad assigned our jobs. Factory jobs were the
most desirable; we all wanted to stay in Shanghai. Most of the upper-
grade students received them. The younger students, such as I, waited
patiently, hoping that there would be some factory jobs left.

Routinely patrolling the school grounds, the working-class squad
wore no uniforms, although all were dressed in overalls with armbands
reading, "Working Class—Mao Zedong—Thought—Propaganda,"
and pouches designed to hold a copy of Chairman Mao's Little Red
Book. Claiming to be totally unpolluted by education, they frequently
boasted of the virtues of ignorance by repeating a fashionable slogan,
"The more you learn, the more anti-Revolutionary you are." They felt
that their vulgar speech demonstrated their Revolutionary honesty.
Although they did not request it, people called them "master"; the rest
of us were regarded as their apprentices. The title "comrade" was no
longer popular.

My class, that of 1969, had not yet been assigned, but we were led to the countryside for two weeks to help bring in the harvest. We worked in the fields with the peasants during the day and attended indoctrination sessions at night. The philosophy of these evening sessions was, "By contemplating the bitterness of the past, we can relish the sweetness of the present all the more." In a ceremony that resembled a Passover seder, we ate a paste made from bitter herbs and rice husks. Then a working-class master would recount tales of the harshness he suffered in the old, pre–Mao Zedong society.

On one of these autumn evenings, a red-nosed master approached the platform to begin his oratory. When the enthusiastic applause died down, he began: "My father died when I was three years old, and my mother when I was about eight. Never had shoes. Never. Even in the winter. Walked in the snow with feet bloody from the cold. My overcoat was full of holes. I had to wrap a belt made of straw around me tightly to keep warm. I worked years day and night for a despot landlord, and then, when the weather was so bad that nothing grew, my landlord told me to go beg in Shanghai. In Shanghai I met a foreign priest and I cooked for him. That was fun. He taught me to speak French. I learned a lot, like 'shi vous prate' and 'cafe au rate' and 'flomage.' "

A burst of laughter from the others prompted by the poor pronunciation was followed by requests that he teach them some more French phrases. Even during this moment of amusement, some instinctively shouted, "Don't forget the class bitterness! Always remember the bloody score we have to settle with our hated foes!"

Fearing that the working-class master would be branded as anti-Revolutionary for his affectionate reminiscences of the foreign priest, I did not laugh. Looking around, I saw everyone, even the leaders of the working-class squad, laughing and trying to imitate his French words. For the first time, I realized that the working class was far more simple and open than were the intellectuals.

Seeing so many in the classes of 1966 and 1967 becoming members of the working class made me jealous. When friends who had been assigned to the factory returned to visit our school, they flaunted fancy dresses copied from North Korean movies instead of the drab, con-

ventional student clothing. They owned brand-new bicycles and fancy watches.

I wanted a salary so that I could ask people to stop helping my family. I saw a job as the answer to all of our problems, but I failed to realize that I would be a low-paid apprentice for years and that my friends had simple luxuries because they did not need to support families.

Chairman Mao's "Newest Instructions," on December 21, 1968, shattered the hopes of my class of staying in Shanghai. "The young intellectuals," he announced, "must go to the countryside to be reeducated by the poor and lower-middle peasants. We must persuade the children of the cadres and all those in the city who have completed middle school, high school, or college to go to the countryside. We must mobilize the country to bring this movement to fruition. All comrades in the countryside should welcome these young intellectuals."

When the instructions trickled down to my school's level, the working-class leaders halted all urban assignments. Shanghai middle-school students now had two official paths open to them: They could join the Construction Corps or relocate individually to the countryside. The sudden change in policy was unexpected, and those who had factory assignments rubbed it in our faces. Students in the younger classes schemed to get the best possible assignments. They decided that the Construction Corps was more glamorous than moving to the countryside, since that at least provided salary and a handsome uniform. Members of the Construction Corps would have a status similar to People's Liberation Army soldiers, and their foremen would automatically become PLA officers. Consequently, the Corps found itself besieged by thousands of applicants.

Those who thought both choices unattractive found a third option: joining relatives already living in the countryside. The provinces close to Shanghai, such as Zhe Jiang or Jiang Su, became popular, and the cadres in charge of the People's communes suddenly received warm invitations to visit Shanghai with all expenses paid by parents who wished to choose where their children would go. Some bold girls married local peasants to avoid being moved too far from home. Never had there been such an enthusiastic exchange between city and country.

11

Dear Professor Hu,

Within two months of Chairman Mao's announcement in December 1968 that all students should go to the countryside, more than half of my class was gone. Xiao-yi Wu used his father's name to obtain a desirable position in the PLA. Lard Bucket Lin had been admitted to the Northeast Construction Corps. Before leaving, she breezed through the school, sporting her brand-new uniform and well-tailored heavy overcoat. Her new Omega watch was eyed admiringly by the former Red Guards, who had learned a considerable amount about timepieces from their death-search duties. Canton Kiss Up had been away for months, and it was rumored that he had been excused from the working-class squad. He carried his family's identification papers and planned either to seek or to create a relative in one of the nearby provinces. He managed to find a "grandmother" in Su Zhou, less than a hundred miles from Shanghai. When Slab-Tongue heard of the new instructions, she joined a group of girls who lived together in one of the working-class slums. Rising at dawn to dress in their newest finery, they paraded through the market to turn the heads of the young peasant boys who were there to sell produce. Several couples were joined for life in one morning, and Slab-Tongue was proud to be one of the brides. Her new husband was a peasant whose education was limited to recognizing his name, but he was hardworking and good with money. She never again needed to be self-conscious about her mustache, her lisp, or her masculine looks and smell. The next time Slab-Tongue saw Ah-di, she gave her a lecture on "how to catch, keep, and thatithfy a man."

Ah-di's congenital heart problem allowed her to remain in the city, but she seemed reluctant to do so. When I heard that she had not eaten well for several days, I went to visit her and bumped into a handsome young man in a People's Police uniform when I entered her home. Sitting on her bed with a sweater draped over her shoulders, Ah-di said, "This is Xu. He resigned from the Army and is now in charge of criminal investigations with the Public Security Office." Realizing that this was Ah-di's boyfriend, I smiled at him as he walked out. A strange look in his eyes disturbed me.

Ah-di's grandmother handed me a hot-water bottle to warm my hands, saying, "Fool girl wants to go and join the Construction Corps today. Talk her out of it! With her heart, she can't go. And even if her heart were perfect, I'd keep her here forever."

"Have you really decided to join the Construction Corps?" I asked. Ah-di had encouraged me to remain in Shanghai with her when we first heard the new instructions for young intellectuals. I also had never known her to act impulsively.

"Yes," Ah-di said, blushing. "As soon as Xu resigned from the Army, he was assigned this job with the Public Security Office. He's very well respected and is in charge of many important investigations. I don't want people saying that a Revolutionary Army man's girlfriend is holding him back."

"Who would say that?" her grandmother shouted with garbled speech and a heavy accent. "Xu just said that five minutes ago. You are just repeating it to protect him."

Ah-di blushed again and nudged her grandmother, saying, "Yes, he said it, but I feel that way, too." She turned to me, continuing, "Xi-ou, please forgive me, but I can't fight to stay in Shanghai like you do. I still think you shouldn't leave—I'm very silly, right? When you get a boyfriend, you'll be just as silly. Can you understand?"

I grabbed her hands and held them tightly. She began sobbing softly on my shoulder, and soon our tears mingled.

△△△ I had no chance of getting into the Construction Corps, because its members usually were assigned to border areas, and the working class would never risk the defection of a person with my background. People working in the countryside made so little money that they were supported by family remaining in the city, so I was unwilling to relocate voluntarily. I also refused to enter a loveless marriage. The only remaining option was to be assigned to a rural area far from Shanghai. Quotas had been established for some extremely poor, backward regions. When I heard that there were openings for young intellectuals to work in the timber forests in the Northeast, I immediately discussed the matter with Rei-qing, who was still home on sick leave.

She shook her head, saying, "Absolutely not."

"Rei-qing, be practical. This is as high-paying a job as exists. They'll give me sixty yuan a month. That's a fortune!"

"It wouldn't matter if it were six hundred! No matter how bad it gets here, we have to stay together," she insisted.

Rei-qing was correct; I had no right to leave home. If I were gone, there would be no one to deal with the Red Guards, the Neighborhood Committee, and the bureaucracy. My independent study was still very important to me, and I had not yet completed the equivalent of a university's general-education requirements. If I left Shanghai, progress would end.

Because sick or handicapped people could remain in the city to await further assignments, we decided that I would have to "contract" a disease. After poring over all the medical textbooks we could find, we identified rheumatoid arthritis as the ideal malady. The two important diagnostic features of this disease were an increased density of red blood cells and an elevated immune system, both determined from blood tests. An increased heart rate and an irritated throat also were associated with the disease. Red swellings on the scalp and deformed joints signaled the advanced stages.

The blood test cost a half-yuan. On the report, I changed the red blood cell (RBC) sedimentation rate from "4" to "14," a value higher than normal. Doctoring the immune-system report was much more difficult, because only certain values were listed: 333, 500, 833, 1250, and greater than 2500. Normal was "333"; "500" and "833" indi-

cated two degrees of some disease, and the other two were patholog-
ically high. I took four blood tests, hoping for a "500," which could be
changed to ">2500." Unfortunately, the test results invariably came
back as "333." I changed the first "3" to an "8" to make the immune
response value "833."

I gave these results to the working-class squad. The head of the
graduation unit was Lao Li, a white-haired man of about fifty. He told
me to take them to Lao Zhuang, the former principal. Zhuang had
recently been liberated from the Ox Ghost Reeducation Ranch and was
now a clerk at the school.

I went to his corner of the administration office. He put on his
bifocals and looked at my test results. Opening one of his desk drawers,
he pulled out a chart listing a variety of diseases and their accompanying diagnostic features. He stared at the results and the charts for
several minutes before looking up to say, "You can't have rheumatoid
arthritis. Your RBC sedimentation would have to be at least 20. Yours
is only 14. And your immune response report is just slightly over
normal. It should be greater than 2500."

While not surprised at his reaction, I remembered that the book
had clearly stated that a sedimentation value of 10 or more was
abnormal. I stood my ground. "The doctor said that over 10 means
you're sick," I replied.

"That is an obsolete standard. The new movement," he said,
petulantly waving the chart in my face, "has set new standards. It
would have been better for you to have applied for a countryside
assignment sooner." Reaching into another drawer, he pulled out a
report. He paged through it, explaining, "This is a report about two
counties in An Hui. These figures represent the number of young
intellectuals who have already applied for relocation. You'd better
hurry, or all the good slots will be taken. For the rest of your life you'll
regret missing these fine opportunities."

Realizing that he was trying to sell the Party line, I responded,
"Lao Zhuang, thank you for the insights, but I think you've missed the
point, as I can understand, since you've just been let out of the Ox Ghost
Ranch. You're encouraging me to act in an anti-Revolutionary manner
by fighting for the best slots. Our Party teaches us to take the most dif-

ficult paths or, in any event, to go where Chairman Mao points. I don't deserve these soft slots, and I want to make a sacrifice for the Party to leave these more desirable openings for those who truly deserve them."

When I returned to Lao Li the next day, he had already been briefed by Lao Zhuang. I fought hard, saying, "Everybody's born with a different physical condition. Everybody reacts differently to a stimulus. My RBC sedimentation used to be less than 3. When it reached 14, I knew I was sick, but for some people, that's normal. It's just the way they are. Anyway, look at my immune response. That's unambiguous."

I hammered away with my arguments without giving Lao Li a chance to interrupt. He listened carefully to every point I made. Taking a breath, I realized how quiet the office had become. Lao Li smiled at me, his serious, bureaucratic countenance changed to one of amusement.

"Are you finished?" he asked softly.

"Yes," I answered sheepishly.

"You know Teacher Peng, don't you?"

"Yes, of course. He used to be our class adviser."

"He's just been liberated. Our secretary has nominated him sub-chief of the graduation unit. Go find him and tell him that Lao Li has ruled that your name should be removed from the list of those who are to be relocated. There was never any question in my mind about your staying in Shanghai," Lao Li said, kindly but firmly.

I was paralyzed.

He smiled again, saying, "You're quite a debater! And so well prepared! You educated people are different from us. I think it is good to be educated."

I giggled, thanked him, and left to find Teacher Peng. Teacher Peng's liberation did not surprise me. As the Cultural Revolution went on, the Party regained power as that of the Red Guards waned. Although I had not approved of my fellow classmates' treatment of Teacher Peng, his stand on my composition still gnawed at me. When I presented myself to him, it was with a forced, unnatural tone.

"Lao Li asked me to tell you to cross my name off the list of those to be mobilized. I am to remain in Shanghai on account of my rheumatoid arthritis," I said, handing him the test results.

"All right," Teacher Peng said. He pulled out a large notebook and crossed off my name.

Everything now was taken care of, so I turned to leave.

"Wait a minute," he said. "You must take care of your arthritis. Have you heard that one of the Army hospitals uses acupuncture to relieve it?" Looking Teacher Peng in the eye, I saw that he was truly concerned for me. "You need a certificate to visit this hospital. I'll write one up for you. You'll feel much better, I'm sure." Without waiting for an answer, he took a sheet of paper with a letterhead and wrote a note:

> To the Revolutionary Committee of the Shanghai PLA Hospital:
> This is to certify that our student, Xi-ou Tan, is suffering from advanced rheumatoid arthritis. Any help that you can provide for her will be greatly appreciated.
>
> Revolutionary yours.

He stamped the letter with the red seal of the Revolutionary Committee of the middle school. I noticed that he weighed the words carefully as he wrote them, and that he paused particularly long before writing the word "advanced." I reflected on Teacher Peng's actions on the way home, but I could not understand why his attitude toward me had changed so much.

Rei-qing was as surprised by the letter as I had been. Her eyes shining, she said, "This letter is your talisman! No one can touch you as long as you have this! And did you notice that he said your arthritis was 'advanced'? I can't think of anything better!"

"But why should he treat me so well? He never struck me as someone who could be so kind," I said, still confused by his actions.

"People change all the time," Rei-qing said. "Maybe he lost his fascination for power when he was on the ranch."

Teacher Peng told us many years later that the entire time he was being humiliated, he was plotting his revenge. He had searched for my name on the wall posters condemning him, since my composition had been the fuse of the bomb that destroyed him. The thirty-eight signatures included some of his favorite students, but my name was missing.

He knew that he had damaged me by not taking my side, but now he had a chance to do me a good turn.

Within several months, all those deemed capable of leaving Shanghai, either of their own volition or by force, were gone. Those of us who were left had long since committed ourselves to fighting relocation. About 15 percent of my class remained, and the Mobilization Office for our school was unable to get us out. Frustrated by these last holdouts, and knowing that they would soon have to deal with another class of students, they put us under the jurisdiction of the Neighborhood Committee, who had plenty of time and energy to devote to us. Having the added advantage of possessing detailed information about all the families involved, the Neighborhood Committee was far more efficient than the school.

Some of the strongest, most athletic people in my class began to complain of debilitating weaknesses. Some of these people were far safer than I was, for if a doctor told them that they were healthy, they could always find a friendly "uncle" or "aunt" with medical training who would give them a contrary opinion. The school Mobilization Office, also aware of this, insisted that those who claimed to be sick provide them with convincing evidence before they were handed over to the Neighborhood Committee. Rei-qing and I had to find a better way to alter laboratory results. Noticing that the hospital made test results accessible to the public, we deduced that the testing lab itself must have copies. To protect ourselves, we devised a plan to change all of the existing records.

We went back to the laboratory. I had taken several tests over the previous few days, and the latest results were "6" and "500." Although it was simple for us to change these to "26" and ">2500" on my own copy, we needed to change any other copies to agree with them. At the information desk, Rei-qing said, "One of my colleagues asked me to pick up her test results, but I couldn't find them in the information room."

"What is her name and when was she tested?"

"Her name is Y. F. Lu. She was here about a week ago to have her RBC sedimentation rate and immune response measured."

The technician went into the lab, returning several minutes later with a large, black notebook. "You try to find it. I didn't see anyone named Y. F. Lu who came in a week ago."

After pretending to examine the notebook page by page, we finally returned it to the technician, saying, "This is very strange. We can't find it either. She must have given me the wrong date. Thank you for your time."

We had seen my name, but since we were unable to alter the results while people were watching, we returned that night. In the brightly lighted lab, only two people were on duty, so there was no one manning the information window. We asked the man in charge of the night shift about the results for Y. F. Lu. He brought out two large notebooks and checked name by name for Y. F. Lu. He did not seem to mind spending a great deal of time with us.

"It's usually so boring here at night. We never have pretty ladies coming in. What was your friend's name again? Y. F. Lu. . .Y. F. Lu. . . . Let me see. . .I. F. Lu. . .M. Lu. . .Y. Q. Lu. . .M. F. Lu. Is this maybe Y. F. Lu's sister?" he asked as he ran down the names with a plastic ruler.

Just then, a wailing ambulance drove up to the emergency entrance. Dropping his ruler, he ran to the emergency room with the other technician, leaving us alone. While they gathered information about a young girl who had committed suicide, we completed our mission. Now I felt sure that I would not be sent away.

Ah-di was among the last accepted into the Northeast Construction Corps. Her parents invited me to the going-away party, seating me between Ah-di and her grandmother and across from Inspector Xu. There was plenty of the excellent Yang Zhou–style food. Her father, a brickmaker, made a speech: "Since Ah-di is so physically weak, we wish she could wait here for an assignment. But you know Ah-di when she has made up her mind! She insists on joining the Construction Corps. We, her parents, can only wish her happiness."

Ah-di's grandmother buried her head in her hands. She had arranged the entire feast herself, getting up early each morning for a week to stand in line at the markets and spending another three days preparing the dishes. Today she did not even taste the food; she only sat and cried. Ah-di's mother, also a brickmaker, did not say anything or smile even once throughout the feast. Ah-di's sister, Ah-mang, and her brother-in-law were the only ones playing host. Ah-di and Ah-mang were very close; Ah-mang burst into tears every time she offered Ah-di more food or wine.

I was the only real guest at the party. Inspector Xu, already accepted in the family circle, declared his plans to ask for a transfer to the Northeast after Ah-di had settled down. Neighbors passing the open door stood watching the festivities. Ah-di's family was well loved, and the neighbors let Ah-di know that she would be missed. A few people brought wrapped packages for Ah-di, and Inspector Xu took them, thanking them for her.

Everyone spoke so quickly in the Yang Zhou dialect that I comprehended nothing, but I laughed when everybody else did. Whenever I laughed, Ah-di smiled, too, as if her mind were not on the conversation. She looked nervous and sad.

Halfway through the party, a girl named Jin-mei arrived, seeming to know everyone. Ah-di insisted that she join the farewell feast, and Ah-mang left to find another pair of chopsticks and a bowl.

"Xi-ou, this is my fourth cousin, Jin-mei," Ah-di said. When I had met her about a year earlier, she had been shy and frail, but now she was plump and exuberant, with a wild light in her big, bright eyes. Her beautiful laugh made her even more charming.

Ah-di took me into another room of the house after dinner to speak with me privately: "I'm leaving. I hope you can visit Grandmother and my parents regularly. Father has an ulcer, so if you see him drinking, take it away from him. On July 15, the Day of the Dead, Grandmother cooks a feast for our dead ancestors. My parents will help her if it's on a weekend, but otherwise, I have been the only person who could. If you can, would you give her a hand when I'm gone?"

I lowered my head sadly and agreed.

Ah-di continued, "Don't forget to write to me every month. I'll be so lonely out there. The very thought of it terrifies me! I might die of loneliness."

Putting my hands on Ah-di's shoulders, I said, "Don't think that way. You'll be able to set your watch by my letters. Besides, Inspector Xu will be joining you soon, right?"

Ah-di turned slowly toward the window and stared out at the

darkness. Finally she said, "My intuition tells me that it's not going to result in anything. All I can do is let it go."

Alarmed, I asked, "Have you two fought? Doesn't he want to go to the Northeast anymore? What's the point in your going, then?"

Facing me again, she said, "No, we haven't quarreled. It's just my intuition, but it's never been wrong before."

Talk of unpleasant intuitions always frightened me, and I said no more. Tomorrow at this time, my best friend and I would be separated by hundreds of mountains and rivers. We were both rushing blindly into an uncertain future, but one thing was clear: We were adults now. Our lives as students were over, and we had to face life directly.

Professor Hu, it is already three in the morning. I must get some sleep now. Later I will tell you more about Ah-di and her boyfriend. Although we were adults, we were not prepared for all of the cruelties life still had in store. We persevered, and I am glad that you have decided to do so, too. Please write back soon.

Sincerely,
Xi-ou Tan

 The morning after I wrote Professor Hu about Ah-di, I read an article in a Chinese newspaper about a diplomat famous after the Revolution of 1911. Although I did not know him personally, I knew his niece, an extraordinary woman named Kang-li, who was very important to me.

Kang-li Soong was born in Moscow into a family of diplomats. Her father and uncles worked in foreign embassies under the Guomindang. She had an older brother and three younger ones, but no sisters. She lived extravagantly until she graduated from high school, when her father suddenly fell ill and died. Kang-li's immediate family returned to China to live with the rest of their relatives.

It was not until her return that she realized her immediate family had been fervent Christians for generations. In Moscow, there was nothing unusual about this. Her mother was a Catholic, and Kang-li's father had converted to Catholicism to marry her. The five children had been raised Catholic as well, so they and the new widow suddenly found themselves outsiders in a family that was anti-Catholic. However, Kang-li's mother was a determined, independent woman who would not modify her beliefs just to be like others. She became a tutor of English and Russian for wealthy families and established a bookstore specializing in imported books. During her years as a medical student, Kang-li also managed the store. The business did well enough to send two of the brothers to Canada to study medicine.

After the Liberation, Kang-li's mother was jailed for her anti-Revolutionary religious activities, and the bookstore was closed. One night, Kang-li went to a political meeting at her university where the students were celebrating Chairman Mao's rise to power. Fueled by outrage at her mother's treatment, Kang-li jumped onto the stage and shouted, "It's the Communist Party that stole my family's business and threw my innocent mother into jail!" She was immediately seized and stifled. Only twenty at the time, she did not understand the newborn power of the Proletariat and the serious consequences her words could bring. However, she was clever, energetic, and charming, and everybody liked her.

When Kang-li was in detention, her brother sent her a few oranges. She ate the inside but carefully left the rind intact. With a hairpin, she turned the orange peel into a small lantern. When a young PLA guard demanded the lantern, Kang-li graciously handed over her one luxury. She was forced to work as an orderly in a hospital, but menial jobs did not bother her. She stripped the beds each day to wash the filthy sheets by hand, and then she remade them. When the police realized several months later that she was not part of a conspiracy, that she had simply been bitter over her family's treatment under the Revolutionary Government, she was released and allowed to take her final medical exams.

Her wisest decision was to marry Fong Qin. This reserved young engineering major wore thick glasses and came from a poor family. He was less interesting than the other four or five men seeking Kang-li's hand, but she eventually put aside her vanity for his integrity and dependability. Kang-li was much more sophisticated than most women her age, yet she practiced the traditional Chinese feminine qualities of self-sacrifice and loyalty. In her sixteen years of marriage, she always rose first to make herself "presentable" to her husband. She cooked and served his breakfast and attended to his needs until he left for work. No matter what shift she worked at the hospital, she adjusted her sleeping schedule to her husband's convenience. They could recall only two severe disagreements in their whole marriage, and these consisted only of stamping their feet and not speaking to each other for a day. Fong Qin in turn was a good husband, never interfering with his wife's management of the household.

A dedicated wife and mother at home, she was just as dedicated a doctor in the service of others. She devoted tremendous energy to virtual strangers, because she believed that she never could tell when she would need them as friends. As a result, people from the top hospital secretary down to the orderly's assistant were always willing to help her in any way possible. Whenever she entered any store in the neighborhood, she was greeted by one of her acquaintances with a respectful bow and a courteous but warm hello. Such popularity had great advantages in everyday life. Orange juice, powdered milk, fine soap, and toilet paper were always in short supply, but store clerks always held them aside for her. She even won the affection of the guards at Basket Bridge, which was convenient for her jailed mother, and later for mine.

Kang-li emerged unscathed from the 1957 Anti-Rightist Movement. Even at the peak of home searches in the Grand Cultural Revolution in 1966, Kang-li's home was not violated. A society can sustain itself for brief periods without pure scientists, artists, journalists, poets, philosophers, and critics, but it would immediately deteriorate without physicians and engineers. Kang-li and Fong Qin thus were left in relative peace during the purges of the Cultural Revolution. Doctors and engineers were still put into prison, but because of their invaluable knowledge and skills, they usually were given good jobs in the prison hospitals or factories.

Kang-li and I got to know each other when my family was going through its most difficult period. Her love colored those days so that when I look back, I feel no sadness.

12

Dear Professor Hu,

I know that you love and respect your
mother from your letters. You are lucky to have
her. As I have written, my mother was put in prison,
and I missed her very much. Fortunately, I met a wonderful woman who became a second mother to me and helped
me through some of my hardest times. I would like to tell you
about her.

A visiting day was announced at Basket Bridge in
January 1969. The transit system was shut down because of heavy
fog, so we had to walk the six miles to the prison. Rei-qing, Jian-nan,
and I woke on our own, but we almost had to tip over Chi-kai's bed
to get him up. After drinking several cups of hot saltwater to warm us
for the journey, we plunged into the thick fog.

By the time the fog burned off and traffic returned to normal, we
had lined up outside the Basket Bridge with dozens of other shivering
people stamping their feet to keep warm. Most came early so they
would be able to get to work on time without having to tell anyone that
they had been visiting jailed relatives, but we had come early so that
Mother would not have to wait long to see us. Over the years, the other
visitors' faces became familiar.

In our group was an elegant middle-aged woman. She had a broad
forehead; long, curved eyebrows that accentuated large, beautiful eyes;

and a well-formed nose and mouth. She was of average height and slightly plump, and her simple, well-tailored dress was made of fine material. When people spoke to her, she listened with a look of genuine interest and compassion in her penetrating eyes. The self-confident walk that marked her as a career woman drew attention to her.

Like any growing girl, I desperately needed a mother's advice. I deeply loved the other members of my family, but since they only partially satisfied this need, I looked for motherly qualities in this woman, who was about my mother's age and reminded me of her. She fit my ideal perfectly, and I referred to her from afar as "the Queen." Although most of the visitors kept to themselves because they distrusted each other, the Queen approached an old man waiting behind us. "I haven't seen you for a while. Are you feeling well these days?" she asked.

"The weather's been cold lately. As long as the temperature doesn't jump around too much, I feel all right and don't bother going to the hospital. Thanks for asking, Dr. Soong," the old man replied, smiling. I had often tried to guess the Queen's profession. Now I realized that there was no occupation that fit her better.

When the huge iron gate finally opened, two PLA soldiers stood behind me with rifles in their hands and cold expressions on their faces. The warden of the women's section of the Basket Bridge mechanically inspected people's identification papers, and the silent crowd slowly entered the gate. At the Queen's turn, the warden smiled slightly and said, "Dr. Soong, you have time to visit us today?"

"Well, I usually can't fall asleep after the night shift anyway, so I came here," she said, smiling, as she presented her identification.

"Oh, that's not necessary, Dr. Soong. Go on in," the warden said, signaling the soldiers to let her pass.

Between the guards' inspection of the items we had brought Mother, and the visit itself, I lost sight of the Queen. Filing out of the hall when our visit was over, Rei-qing jerked my arm. Following her gaze, I saw the Queen standing outside the hall talking with a female guard whom I recognized from behind and whose laugh made me tremble.

Why is the Queen talking to the Alley Cat? I thought. That's impossible! Besides, I've never seen the Alley Cat in uniform before! The Alley Cat was a prying, troublemaking neighbor who bullied us and others in our complex. Her nickname was the worst thing we could say about a woman. I had never known what she did for a living, and I could not understand why our neighbors played up to her. Among four children, there are eight eyes, so there could be no mistake: The prison guard talking to the Queen was the Alley Cat. When we passed the two women, the Alley Cat turned her back and kept her face from us.

△△△ Chi-kai had to register to attend the Nan Yang Model Middle School that day, so we decided to take the bus back. The Queen was waiting at the bus stop also, and twice we transferred buses together. She smiled at us and asked, "Do you live in Xu Hui district?"

Acting as spokesman, Rei-qing replied, "Yes," while the rest of us only smiled. The Queen asked us about school and told me that the working-class squad at my middle school went to the hospital where she worked under the country's national health-care program. We talked pleasantly until the bus stopped in front of the Central Hospital, where the Queen said good-bye to us with a smile. I thought it strange that I had never run into her during my many visits to the hospital to be tested for rheumatoid arthritis.

The next night, Chi-kai complained of a stomachache. Rei-qing fixed a hot-water bottle for him, but he was so uncomfortable that we took him to the emergency room the next morning. Diagnosing appendicitis, the doctor recommended immediate surgery. Rei-qing hurriedly filled out the forms while I went home for money. We had saved twenty-five yuan to buy fabric so that our brothers could have new clothes for the New Year celebration, but now we only hoped that it would be enough to pay for the operation.

When the doctor emerged from the operating room, he told us that if we had waited any longer to bring in Chi-kai, his appendix would have burst. According to the hospital rules, we could not visit him until three in the afternoon, so there was nothing to do but go home and wait.

While we sat in Angel Cave, a girl yelled through the garage window that there was a telephone call for me. She handed me a note that read, "Call Mrs. Sun" at an unfamiliar number. I ran to the public telephone, trying to think of who "Mrs. Sun" could be. When I called the number, a mellow voice answered: "Is this Xi-ou Tan? This is Kang-li Soong. Do you remember, we rode on the bus together yesterday?"

"Yes, Aunt Soong," I said, realizing that the girl had gotten the name wrong. It was my Queen.

"Is the boy who just had his appendix out your brother?"

"Yes," I said hesitantly.

"Come to the hospital right now. I'll be waiting for you at the entrance in twenty minutes."

I arrived a few minutes early. The sunless day was cold and the wind made it unbearable. I thought of a Chinese expression, "It's the wind that makes the weather cold, it's the debt that makes the worker sold." If the twenty-five yuan was not enough, we would be in debt. As this thought ran through my mind, I saw the Queen coming toward me. Her gentle expression warmed me.

"Would you like to see your brother?" she asked. Looking at her watch, she continued, "At two o'clock I make my rounds, so why don't wc go to my office? That will give us fifteen minutes to talk."

Noticing that my face fell, the Queen laughed, "Oh, I know you wanted to see your brother first, but I've just returned from the ward and he's fine. He's napping right now."

We went to the doctors' lounge and sat together on one of the couches. "Well," said the Queen, "since we've known each other under *those* circumstances, we don't need any further instructions. I was working the midshift this afternoon when I recognized your brother's name on his chart. I noticed that you put your father's name where both your parents' names should have been, but you left the occupation section blank. I take it your father is out of work? So, if I'm not mistaken, you went *there* to see your mother. That means that you have no income. I think I should help you. No matter how great your financial problem is, please tell me about it."

Blushing, I stammered, "I, I, we have n-no difficulties. We have *lots* of money! We have planned well. D-don't worry about us."

The Queen smiled and her eyes widened as she mimicked my tone, "You really have *lots* of money?"

I was too proud to take charity from people, but the kind look in her beautiful eyes comforted me. Standing up, she told me, "Here, let me give you a certificate that will allow you to spend the night in your brother's room. He won't have any problems, but at times like these, children need special attention."

A kettle of water whistled merrily on a stove in the warm, cozy lounge while frost covered the window. My desire for warmth and security was so intense that I wished I could stay in that room the rest of my life.

A variety of juices and nutritious snacks sent by the Queen covered the nightstand next to Chi-kai's bed. As I lay on a cot beside his bed that night, thinking of my Queen, I sensed the door being opened and looked up to see her enter. Her broad forehead and bright eyes shone under the red EXIT sign. She looked around the room, smiled, and closed the door silently. I jumped out of the cot and ran into the lobby to talk to her. The lobby was deserted, but I was unwilling to believe that the vision had been a dream.

The following afternoon I was napping at home, when I received a telephone call from Rei-qing, asking me to go to the hospital immediately. I thought this odd, because Rei-qing had specifically told me to sleep during the afternoon to make up for the previous night.

A heavy snowfall had stopped traffic, so I trudged toward the hospital. I saw children having snowball fights, and their laughter brought to mind pleasant, youthful fantasies. The whole city was blanketed in a peaceful atmosphere.

When she saw me, Rei-qing dragged me through the lobby to the Queen's office. "Look, Aunt Soong, Xi-ou is all right!" Rei-qing said triumphantly.

The Queen smiled: "All right, you win. But I hoped I'd lose the bet when we made it."

I eventually learned that when the Queen saw only Rei-qing, she had concluded that I had hurt myself on the way home. Unconvinced by Rei-qing that I was all right, she demanded evidence. I was deeply touched. At the time when I needed it most, I had been granted the most precious of loves. The whole world was transformed, and my troubled life seemed less ugly.

The Queen's shift ended at eight that night. Visiting hours also ended, and since Rei-qing had already left, I decided to walk the Queen home. It was snowing again, so she opened a beautiful parasol and covered us both as we walked arm in arm. She told me all about her family—her husband, Fong Qin, the engineer, and their three sons. The oldest was twelve, Chi-kai's age, and the youngest was eight.

"I've never liked girls. Mother was put in jail for being a Roman Catholic. She always told me, 'Kang-li, children are a gift from God that cannot be refused. I always hope that the Lord will bless you with a daughter.' I told her, 'Mama, I have never refused anything that God has given me. I only have sons, but I'm very satisfied, because I only wanted boys.' "

"Why don't you like girls?" I asked, puzzled.

She looked at me gently and I held her eyes. A glowing red neon sign behind the Queen read, "Long live Chairman Mao! Long live the Proletariat Grand Cultural Revolution!" The white snow covering some of the ugliness made me feel as if I were lost in some strange fantasy world.

"Girls are always crying, and their minds are weak! They don't have any self-confidence," the Queen said. She continued dramatically, "Of course, I must confess, a lot of my thinking is just sour grapes because I don't have any daughters. Why did we meet in the first place? You've made me change the way I think about girls."

My blush was hidden by the snow and darkness, and I said haltingly, "I . . . you don't know, but I have many feminine shortcomings. I cry, and I look down on myself a lot."

"Really? But you have many fine traits that girls usually don't have," she said. "I like all four of you children very much. From that day on the bus, I liked you. And Chi-kai's operation makes me feel even more drawn to you. It seems like I've just been given four more children. But, you know what? You're my favorite. I don't know why, but maybe it's because we're so much alike."

I was overwhelmed. I started to tell my Queen all the stories of my family. She shook her head as she listened, interrupting only to praise my family's courage. When she said, "But you have arthritis! And you look so healthy!" I wanted to assure her that I was indeed perfectly healthy. I was proud of the adventure in the laboratory, but it was a deep secret between Rei-qing and me; we had not confessed the details of the scheme even to Father. The Queen's genuine concern for me made concealing the truth unbearable, but I had to remain silent.

"I would like to visit your father," she said. Suddenly changing the subject, she asked, "Xi-ou, how old are you?"

"I just turned nineteen."

"When I was about your age, I had a boyfriend whose first name was the same as your father's. Jin-ren is such an unusual name that I was startled when I saw it on your brother's chart!" Firmly grasping my hand, she said, "Are you a headstrong girl? I hope not. I was when I was your age. Once I was invited to Jin-ren's house for dinner. The cook's cousin, who lived in the countryside, had brought a dish of fresh peas, and everyone kept saying how delicious they were. I refused to touch even a single pea! It wasn't that I was allergic to them or anything like that—I just didn't particularly like peas. But my refusing them put a damper on the party. The cook's cousin told me later that my refusal had made him lose face. To this day, I remember his hurt tone and expression. Whenever I don't want to do something, I always remember how badly I hurt that poor boy."

The snowflakes were getting smaller, when we stopped in front of a tall building. She said, "This is my home. I live on the ninth floor. Come up with me and let's have something to eat."

It was hard to leave the Queen, but I was afraid that my family would be concerned about how late it was. "Aunt Soong, I'm afraid that my father and sister will worry. May I come back another time?" I asked.

"Please don't call me Aunt Soong; call me Mother Qin. Just take me as your mother. Can you do that?"

Mother. Although I had a mother who could love and be loved, her imprisonment sometimes made me feel worse than if she were dead. The Queen hugged me tightly. I cried. "Dear child, from now on I'll watch over you just as if you were my own daughter and I were your real mother."

She took money from her pocket for my bus fare home, but I refused. "Unless you show me that you have enough money to get home, I'm not going to let you leave without taking this," the Queen said firmly.

The five feng I had hidden in my glove were not enough even for the first bus. But I said adamantly, "Don't worry about me. I have plenty of money."

△△△ Chi-kai recovered quickly from his operation. After he was released from the hospital, I often visited Kang-li in her home, sometimes accompanied by Rei-qing. Insisting that I needed the exercise, I refused to ride the elevator and ran up eight floors of the spiral staircase. Kang-li would wait on the landing on the ninth floor, calling down to me in her musical voice.

Mother had attended boarding school as a child, and her stepmother had been a career woman with little time for housework, so she learned relatively little about cooking. Before I met the Queen, I only knew how to cook rice, since our family had no money to spend on experimenting with food. "You must learn to take care of other people," said Kang-li. "You need more than a good heart; you also need skill. You should learn how to take care of your father and brothers now, and when you're married, you'll have to take good care of your husband."

I blushed, but Kang-li continued seriously: "Every good thing has to end sometime. I'm so happy whenever you visit, but I know things will change. Sooner or later, you'll leave home and go someplace far away to fight for your future. You'll fall in love, get married, and have children. But I worry about you. You're so giving, you could easily be deceived by some man."

Mercifully, Kang-li changed the subject when she saw my obvious embarrassment. "I've been wondering why we like each other so much. In some important ways, we aren't similar at all. For example, from the time I was a little girl, my mother told me that any success a woman achieves can only serve as a ring on her husband's finger. The more successful or educated a woman is, the more beautiful this decoration is. I'm a doctor and of course well educated, but I've never put my career before my marriage. This will always keep me from becoming a well-established member of my profession. You're different; even though you can't go to college, you fight for your independent study. If education were only to be the ring on your future husband's finger, what would be the point in suffering so much now?"

"Times are different now," I said. "All the girls in my class think as I do. Everybody made fun of one girl named Y-nan, because her name means 'dependent on her husband.' She would go home crying, begging her parents to change her name. They refused, saying that according to the palm readers, it was her fate to depend on her husband for most of her life. But with the Cultural Revolution, she could shake off her parents' feudalistic influences, so she changed her name to Ban Bian Tian."

Kang-li laughed, saying, "Didn't she take that from one of Chairman Mao's quotations, something about women having to hold up half of the sky, or 'Ban Bian Tian,' on their shoulders?"

"Exactly," I said. "But my independent study has nothing to do with my being dependent on a man. I hope I can be a scientist someday, so I'm doing my best to prepare for it. Besides, what else would I do with all the time the Cultural Revolution has left on my hands?"

Kang-li said, "That's exactly the reason I like your brothers and sisters. A lot of children waste their time wandering around doing nothing. But you shouldn't go to the other extreme; you still need a social life. I was very sociable at your age. Mother said, 'If there are fifty people in a room, you should make all of them happy at the same time.' So I learned how to deal with many kinds of people.

"I remember an American-born Chinese woman who came to China to live. She was married and had a son, but she wasn't faithful to her husband. I thought that she was forced into it for economic reasons and decided to help her. Because I managed my mother's bookstore, I had a little extra money, so I had a month's supply of rice and coal sent to her home every four weeks. She didn't change her ways, but I didn't want to give up. My mother finally went to her house and begged her to refuse to let me inside. I had a quarrel with my mother over it."

Although I had suffered more than most people my age, I had remained ignorant of many things. Kang-li taught me a great deal, treating me as a daughter as well as a confidante. Committed to seeing that I understood society better, she taught me certain social graces. When a young man came to visit her one day, I rose respectfully from my chair. Kang-li told me later that even though the man had been a little older than I, young ladies should remain seated when a man enters.

That winter we spent many nights sitting at the window, shoulder to shoulder, talking about life and the future as we watched the snow fall. She taught me Russian and American folk songs, and sometimes I looked for her beautiful eyes in the dim light. She did not seem like a woman of forty-five—she still had all of the energy of youth.

△△△ "Half of your daughter is mine," Kang-li said to my father when she met him for the first time. Making a rare exception, he rose from his bed to greet the honored guest as my brothers stood guard at the door. Father reminded her of her older brother in Canada, so she spoke as if she had known him for a long time. She looked all around Angel Cave, admiring every bit of furnishing we had built for the nest. She checked to make sure that the blankets were warm, the mattresses firm, and the pantry clean. Seeing Chairman Mao's poem on the glass windowpane, she remarked, "A seraph and four cherubs live in this Angel Cave."

"I invited your children to come to my house for New Year's Eve dinner, but they turned me down," she said to Father. "They said they not only wanted to be with their father, they also had a very important task: they couldn't welcome the New Year without finishing the old year's assignments."

Father smiled: "Last year, even Chi-kai was awake until three in the morning making up his work. They're racing each other, and nobody wants to be the snail."

Kang-li said, "If that's the case, I'll bring my children to your place the day after New Year's!"

She sent her three children to us the next evening with packages of food. When Kang-li arrived later that night, she ran into the Alley Cat in the kitchen, the very event we had feared. I overheard the Alley Cat asking her for a prescription and then offering to walk Kang-li to our door. Taking off her scarf and shaking the ice from her coat, Kang-li told us that the Alley Cat suffered from a chronic ailment. She implied that the Alley Cat could be bribed with some expensive medications and thus would see that Mother was treated well at Basket Bridge.

"It's ironic that the only person in the entire world who can see all four of us and Mother every day is the Alley Cat," I said bitterly. The room went silent for a while.

Kang-li broke the ice by proposing a toast to Father. "If we can believe the courts," she said wistfully, "in three New Years from today, your mother will also be able to sit with us. And a year after that, my mother will join us." A few tears came to her expressive eyes. She rose gracefully from her seat and stood in front of Chairman Mao's portrait. She raised her glass and said, "Now, let every one of us wish our great leader, Chairman Mao, a long, long life!" We doubled over with laughter, temporarily forgetting our sorrows.

Fong Qin was in Nanking that holiday season, building a power plant. Kang-li had hand-sewn a package containing more than fifty different food items for him to enjoy. She was at the center of so many lives, and those around her benefited so greatly by her existence. She gave all she had and asked virtually nothing in return. I resolved to follow her example.

◮◮◮ Professor Hu, the first silver rays of dawn are coming up in the East, and I find that I have once again written throughout the night. Although I have written more than twenty pages, Kang-li is even lovelier that I could describe. For a long time, I tried to emulate her, but I could never be her equal. Because I was helped by people such as Kang-li, I want to try to help you. Please take care of yourself.

Sincerely,
Xi-ou Tan

13

Dear Professor Hu,

Yesterday I told you about my second mother, Kang-li. Today I would like to tell you about my best friends. Ah-di, about whom I have already written, is still living, but another, Xiao Ru, is not. While he and I were never romantically involved, we were very close, so I can well understand your pain over your mathematician friend.

Ah-di wrote to me at least once a month after she joined the Construction Corps. She had been assigned to drive a tractor near the Soviet border but was soon transferred to the regimental headquarters to study Russian because of her good political background. After several weeks, she knew enough Russian to shout Maoist propaganda across the border to the Russian workers and guards.

Several young men were attracted to her as soon as she arrived at the corps, and two of them had gone to the headquarters to welcome her. When the two rivals met, they shed their overcoats, rolled up their sleeves, and began fighting in the playground in front of the building. There was no clear winner; both were bloodied and bruised. News of the fight spread throughout the corps, and Ah-di was very disturbed by the scandal. She wrote me that she had already given her heart to Xu, and her first two letters were full of her anticipation of their future happiness. Six months later, she learned that Xu had been assigned to an emergency mission and would be delayed in joining her. She did not mention him for a year after that, but her deep depression was evident in every letter. I did not dare to ask about him, but one day I received an urgent letter from her.

> Dear Xi-ou, my best and most trusted friend in this world:
> You are the only one I trust now. Xu wrote me a letter saying that my whole family was insulting him in public and spreading rumors to separate us. But my father wrote me a letter saying how welcome they made him. Father said that they invited him to dinner at least once a week and treated him as if he were already my husband. Then last month Father wrote me again, saying that my cousin, Jin-mei, was pregnant with Xu's baby! I didn't believe this and wanted to hear it from Jin-mei, so I wrote her a letter. It's been three weeks and I haven't heard anything. . . .

Jin-mei? I thought, puzzled. Then I remembered Ah-di's going-away party and a wild, laughing girl. None of the guests had had any appetite for the delicious food except Xu, who ate so heartily that the sound of his lips smacking seemed deafening. At the time, I had thought nothing of the way Xu and Jin-mei had looked at each other, but now I realized that even then, there had been something between them. The letter continued:

> . . . Xi-ou, I need your help. I don't know if this is true or not, and I must know. Please go see for yourself and tell me the truth. To preserve Xu's reputation as a Revolutionary Army man, I applied to the Construction Corps and came to the Northeast. Now I've developed an ulcer in addition to my heart defect. I'm in almost constant pain. Sometimes it's so bad I can hardly breathe. A person isn't a piece of stone or wood, a person has feelings! I hope that Xu hasn't cheated me, but if he hasn't, then my family has, and this is hard to bear. Xi-ou, please go now. If I keep on feeling like this, I'll go insane.

I went to her family's house the day I received the letter. I knew that only the grandmother and Ah-di's younger sister would be there, since her parents worked in the suburbs and returned only on weekends. Stopping through the door, I saw dozens of long, narrow pieces of red paper glued to the furniture. Most of them were on Ah-di's bookshelf, now dusty from disuse. The grandmother wiped her eyes with her sleeve and said, "A devil in uniform drives Ah-di mad with his lies! These red strips will frighten him and make him release her from his power!"

She continued the lament in her thick Yang Zhou accent, so I could barely understand her when she told me that even before Ah-di had left for the countryside, Xu was sleeping with Jin-mei. After Ah-di had gone, he had affairs with two other women at the same time. Jin-mei had indeed been pregnant, but she attempted to abort the child in the fifth month by striking herself in the stomach with a beer bottle. This brought about the desired miscarriage, but it also caused massive internal injuries, and she nearly died. At that point, her affair with Xu could no longer remain secret.

Ah-di's younger sister left to find Ah-mang, who lived several blocks away. Ah-mang read the letter I brought and cried, saying, "Ah-di's been cheated and she still hasn't realized it."

"Didn't Xu say that he was applying for a transfer to the Northeast to be with Ah-di?" I asked.

Ah-mang snorted. "To the Northeast? Are you joking? He's just been promoted to director of the local Public Security Office! He's not going anywhere!"

I sighed. "He was promoted so quickly. Ah-di was just a stepping-stone for him."

"Exactly! After she left, Xu was invited to give lectures all over the district. He talked about how he used Mao Zedong thought to persuade his fiancée to answer Chairman Mao's call to go to the countryside. He was written up in the local newspaper for that. Every weekend, when my parents came home from the suburbs, they invited him to visit. Our neighbors told us that they had seen him with other girls, but we took it as idle gossip. Jin-mei wasn't showing her pregnancy yet, so we were still in the dark."

I believed Ah-mang, but Ah-di had wanted me to see Jin-mei with my own eyes. I went to her middle school pretending to be her friend so I could get her address. I had no trouble finding her classmates, but when I asked where she lived, some of the girls giggled, while others acted disgusted. "You're looking for that tramp? She plays around more on a Saturday night than ten whores do in their whole lives!" said one.

These fourteen- and fifteen-year-old girls wore low-cut, V-necked shirts under their overcoats, a style copied from a North Korean movie, and had curled their hair with a homemade curling iron. They took turns making insulting remarks, and I was struck that they seemed far more worldly than Ah-di and I had been at that age. As I left, they called after me, "Don't go away yet! Let's negotiate! Do you want a man yourself? Now that Jin-mei's gone, all the boys are lonely! You can take your pick!"

That night, I wrote Ah-di a long letter. At the end, I suggested that she come to Shanghai for a vacation and settle the problem. I imagined my friend reading with anguish each word that I wrote. It was painful to write the whole truth, but I believed it was the best way to help her.

I visited Ah-di's family each weekend for the next month, discussing how they could help her accept the situation. When Ah-di finally returned, she apologized to her family and expressed her hatred of Xu. The emotional strain forced her to bed for two weeks. I went to see her every day until a healthy color returned to her cheeks.

Ah-di was in an unusually happy mood one afternoon, insisting that she and I go shopping. We walked toward the shopping square for a few blocks, but then she made us double back and start in a different direction. "I wanted my grandmother to think that we were going shopping, but actually I want to visit Jin-mei," she said.

I was too shocked to say anything. We eventually stopped in front of a thatched hut with the door ajar and the heavy smell of medicinal herb emanating from it. Ah-di knocked on the door a few times, but without waiting for a response, she pushed it open and entered. I followed reluctantly.

Jin-mei was lying on her side with her back to the door. Assuming that it was the woman hired to take care of her, she began giving orders without even looking up: "Dump out the commode! It's stinking up the place! Then go to the market and get half a chicken to make some soup tonight." Ah-di and I said nothing, so Jin-mei continued, "Go get a basin of hot water and wash me! And don't forget to put the perfume in my shirt!"

Not hearing "Yes, mistress," she started to get up, shouting, "It's just my luck that they'd give me a dumb, lazy girl like you to take care of me in my time of need! All you do is drink my soup and eat my food and sleep all day while I do all the work around here! They told me that you had three children already and knew all about these things, but all you really know how to do is lounge around and get fatter! Tomorrow I'm going to have Xu throw you out! No more free—" She paled when she saw Ah-di.

Ah-di held my hand and took a step toward the bed, asking icily, "So what have you been up to in the last two years?"

Jin-mei lowered her head. The room was silent for several minutes, and I saw Ah-di start to tremble. Finally, Jin-mei whispered, "I'm sorry I hurt you, Ah-di." Both were crying, and although I understood that Ah-di wept out of forgiveness, grief, and sympathy, I was unsure of Jin-mei's emotions. I hated the woman bitterly.

Ah-di and I left when the maid arrived. Jin-mei's remorse had taken away Ah-di's hatred, and now we were ready to shop. When we reached the shopping square, Ah-di said, "Would you wait here a minute, Xi-ou? I want to go into the general store."

Waiting outside the store, I heard Ah-di say, "How much is brown sugar today? Well, can I get some? A close friend of mine just had a miscarriage. In that case, how many ration coupons do I need?" When Ah-di came out, she said, "That preserved bean-curd looked delicious. I bet Grandmother would love some. I'll have to come back later with some money." I pretended not to have heard anything, but I was moved by her mercy and charity.

Xu later visited Ah-di, begging her forgiveness and asking her to marry him and promising to accompany her back to the Northeast. She realized that he was trying to exploit her for his own political gains, but she let the shameless libertine plead for hours, while her grandmother tried to chase him out with a broom. Xu was as immovable as the Great Wall, so Ah-mang was summoned. Ah-mang had better success, and after a few threats, Xu scurried out of the house with his tail between his legs. The two sisters then had a loud argument—Ah-mang accusing Ah-di of being too weak and Ah-di accusing her sister of being too tough and unfeeling.

Ah-di tried to explain to me why she did not hate Xu. She had once loved him with all her heart, and there would always be a remnant of these feelings inside her; she would be unable to forget all the little things she associated with him. Seeing the effect of such a bitter love on Ah-di, I realized that mere friendship paled next to the love between a man and a woman.

△△△ When I visited China in 1984, I saw Ah-di. She had returned to Shanghai permanently because of an accident she had had while driving a tractor in the Construction Corps. The blades ran over her whole body, crushing three ribs. At first she could only get temporary jobs doing physical labor, but finally she got a position as the manager of a hotel. Because of her many years of Party membership, she is obeyed, although she still has little education. Ah-di is now tough and uncompromising. "The cold wind in the Northeast blew away all my warmth," she told me. She studied English and mathematics to pass the examination for the high-school diploma that everyone in China now needs. Her face is wrinkled and her hair is graying at the temples. Her body slants to one side because of her missing ribs, and she told me teasingly, "I'm just like Teacher Peng, but he tilted to the left and I tilt to the right."

She has two children, but since her husband was still in the Construction Corps in the Northeast, she raised them alone. He is an alcoholic but not a bad person. I accompanied her to the Children's Hospital, because she worried that her son had roundworms. It normally took an entire day to see a doctor, but Jin-mei was a nurse there and opened a "back door" for us within fifteen minutes.

Jin-mei still looked young, and she smiled broadly when she saw me. She asked me to buy some 1980s American-style panty hose for her: black, with a pattern. I heard that Xu had an easy life. When the elementary school that Ah-di's son attended asked the Public Security Office to send someone to talk to the children about how detectives solve crimes, they sent Xu. Ah-di does not write to me very often, because she cannot afford the expensive postage. Her life is hard, and my heart sometimes aches for her.

△△△ At the beginning of our En-ligh-tenment plan, when I had asked Wei-chun Ho to keep me informed about the progress of the Revolution and the current situation at Father's publishing house, he had mentioned his son, Xiao Ru, but it was six months before I met the boy. After I visited them several times, Xiao Ru asked if he could call on my father. I agreed but insisted he not reveal that it was I who had initiated the visits between our families. I still did not want Father to know about En-ligh-tenment. To explain how I happened to become friends with the Ho family again, I told him I ran into Xiao Ru at the hospital.

To my surprise, Father was pleased by the prospect of Xiao Ru's visit. "Where is he? Did he give you an address? How are Uncle Ho and the rest of the family?"

I was amazed that Father could so easily forgive Wei-chun Ho. I told him that Ho's family was the same as always, and that their home had never been searched.

"Good! I'm glad to hear it. Uncle Ho's always been cautious. It's not easy for an intellectual to avoid abuse by the Red Guards!" Father continued in a concerned voice, "What kind of disease did Xiao Ru have?"

Drawing my brows together, I said, "Diabetes. It's pretty bad. He has to watch his diet and give himself insulin injections every day."

Xiao Ru had developed diabetes a year before the onset of the Cultural Revolution and had grown very thin. He was a model student who smoothly walked the career path chosen by his parents: He would attend a famous university and fight to be assigned a lucrative research position in Shanghai. He would marry a nice girl, have one son and one daughter, and live comfortably. A responsible father, Ho considered it a duty to have a politically acceptable image. To protect the future of his descendants, he meticulously eliminated every element from his existence that could be interpreted as bourgeois, anti-Revolutionary, or Rightist, for more than ten years, including cutting off relations with his oldest friend, Jin-ren Tan.

Xiao Ru indeed looked forward to a successful career, but two things were out of Wei-chun's hands: the Grand Cultural Revolution and his son's disease. The universities closed and the entrance examinations were ended when the Cultural Revolution began, and no one knew when or if the educational system would ever be restored.

To make matters worse, Xiao Ru's poor health prevented him from joining the Red Guards, although at least it protected him from being politically perverted. With the schools closed, he had unlimited time to read, particularly works of Western literature and philosophy. His battle with the insidious disease strengthened his will and instilled in him sympathy for the sufferings of others.

Xiao Ru's health killed his political career, and the Revolution killed his academic one. These were terrible blows to Wei-chun Ho. Before the Revolution, he had devoted himself to his biostatistical research, but with the onset of the movement, all research was viewed as anti-Revolutionary. Since only Marxism and Mao Zedong thought were worthy of study, it followed that biostatistics was a pseudoscience that had to be chastised. During the day, Wei-chun Ho made wall posters, wrote polemic articles, and attended meetings as would any good follower of the Revolution. At night, however, he returned home to his unemployable children and kept his feelings and tears to himself.

I was different from Xiao Ru in many respects. I had been oppressed from childhood, so I had a passive role in the Grand Cultural Revolution. I had no right to be a spectator as he was, nor could I be on the front lines like Ah-di. Constantly punished, although I did nothing wrong, I actively despised society and what it represented. I had little free time to develop myself, since my main concern was finding the quickest—although not necessarily the best—solutions to everyday crises. My greatest asset was health. While Xiao Ru was strong because of his disease, I knew that if I were to become ill, I would lose hope altogether.

Xiao Ru and I complemented each other. Although there was no romantic attraction, we saw each other frequently and became close. After only a few weeks of visits, I told him of our independent study and urged him to begin one of his own. "If you don't have any textbooks, you can use mine," I told him enthusiastically. "I also did all the problems for advanced calculus and general physics. You can borrow them if you like." I produced several volumes I had hand copied and hand bound, but to my surprise, Xiao Ru opened his book bag and removed a stack of hardbound notebooks, saying playfully, "I have something you might like in return. I copied the Chinese translation of Victor Hugo's *Les Misérables*."

I was speechless. A hand-copied thousand-page novel! While I had enjoyed many of Balzac's works, the only Hugo I had read was *Notre Dame de Paris*, and that was when I was in middle school and too young to understand its deeper meaning. I had regretted not being able to read more of the works of this giant of literature, but now Xiao Ru was giving me the chance.

"If you're interested, I also copied Dumas's *The Count of Monte Cristo*. I also have some essays by Kant, Huxley, Voltaire, and Rousseau, and some Sherlock Holmes stories. Just let me know when you want them," he offered. I rubbed my hands greedily. These books had been illegal for years, but now a buffet of Western literature was laid before me, and I could barely wait to devour it. In fact, I stayed up reading almost until dawn for weeks, using a piece of newspaper to shield the lamplight from my sleeping family.

Xiao Ru came running to my house one summer evening in 1970, panting from the effort. He told me that his father, through one of his old colleagues who worked in secondary education, had procured for him a position as a middle-school substitute teacher. "You need this job more than I, Xi-ou. You're more competent than I am, anyway, so I think you should take it."

I certainly realized what having a job would mean for my family, but I replied, "Thank you, Xiao Ru, but your father went to a lot of trouble to give you this chance. It's precious and you must appreciate it. Take it; don't worry about me."

"Xi-ou, please don't refuse. You need the job more than I. We don't have to tell my father right away. We can wait until you fill out the forms and start work. We'll say that the school didn't want me because of my health and that I recommended you for the job."

Although touched by his generosity, I continued to refuse. I could not help noticing the contrast between Xiao Ru and his father. While

Father had forgiven Wei-chun Ho for his disloyalty, I still resented him. Self-sacrificing Xiao Ru valued friendship above all else. Realizing my own shortcomings, I rebuked myself for being closed-minded and unforgiving. I recounted Xiao Ru's altruism to Father, commenting, "Who said, 'Like father, like son?' Xiao Ru always puts other people first."

      Xiao Ru took the first entrance examinations for the universities in December 1977, when they resumed after a twelve-year hiatus. Although he ranked third in mathematics for the city, his health kept him from being admitted. The part-time universities offered classes mostly at night and did not have such strict health requirements, so Xiao Ru attended one of these after working all day in a factory making small boxes. His diabetes frequently sent him to the emergency room, but when he broke the blood vessels in his eyes, his vision was irreparably damaged. When he took his final examination in the summer of 1982, he had to ask his professor to read the problems to him, but still his score was the highest of the four hundred people in his class.

When I visited him in 1984, he was completely blind. Although he had to stay at home, he did not give up working. I found him surrounded by the dozen mathematically gifted teenage middle-school students he coached in the evenings for the mathematics competitions. He told me, "I don't want to be a burden. There's still some residual value left in me. The progress of a society is like a relay race: Each generation passes the stick to the next. It takes only ten years for a tree to grow, but much longer for a person. Perhaps I won't live to see their success, but that's not important. What I wasn't able to do, they can do for me, and their success is just as meaningful as though it were mine."

I had prepared many words to comfort him, but when I heard this, I knew they were not necessary. A diploma from a part-time university was worthless in some people's eyes, but Xiao Ru was a strong person and a hero. I gave him a transistor radio so he could hear people's voices whenever he wanted. He gave me two poems and a cassette of Beethoven's Symphony no. 5 in c minor ("Fate"). I did not think that it would be a farewell gift, but he died the following autumn as the red leaves fell.

△△ Professor Hu, you said that you wanted to cry but had no tears, that you wanted to say something but could not. I understand, for I have felt this way many times myself. Since Xiao Ru's death two years ago, I search every fall for the blood-red autumn leaves with their mature, sad beauty. Tu Mu wrote a poem:

> *I stop my cart in the woods as the fall sun is setting,*
> *The beauty of autumn's leaves surpasses the flowers of*
> *spring.*

My generation has been called "lost," but the survivors are like the autumn leaves that have turned the cold in the air into flaming brilliance. We mourn the passing of your friend and Xiao Ru, but their spirits still live. There are thousands of people like Ah-di, bravely fighting. They live a difficult life, but they will overcome and hold up the earth, like Atlas. I do not think the generation is lost; although sincere people have a harder life than those who are cynical, their lives are more meaningful. From your letters, I know that you are sincere yourself, and I hope that you are realizing again how meaningful life really is.

Sincerely,
Xi-ou Tan

 While Ah-di was far away in the frozen Northeast in the late 1960s and early 1970s—racked by thoughts of Inspector Xu in Shanghai—the trains, once full of Red Guards visiting Chairman Mao in Beijing, now were filled with many of the same people, without armbands, on their way to China's remote countrysides. The streets were full of banners and wall posters saying, "Go to the countryside, go to the borders, go where you are needed, follow the Party's orders!" and "Bring the movement of relocating to the countryside to a climax!" Red flags fluttered in the breeze, and the

sounds of drums and the shouting of slogans were deafening. Families whose adolescent children had not relocated to the countryside were deep in forced study of Mao Zedong thought, jointly led by the representatives of the parents' work units and the local Neighborhood Committees.

Parents and children were exhausted by the workshops, and since the indoctrinators worked in shifts, there was no time when a family could talk alone. The cadres used public chastisement, the same tool perfected by the Red Guards, to drive home their points. The doorways of these unfortunate families were filled with cadres waving red flags, banging drums, and shouting quotations during the day. At night, the cadres read from Chairman Mao's Little Red Book until the family members dropped from exhaustion.

When some former neighbors decided to keep their youngest daughter at home, the joint indoctrination squads set up floodlights and a stage outside the house. The daughter ran away before the chastisement began, telling no one where she was going. Her father had a heart attack when he learned of this, and his wife took his place on the stage. Their eleven other daughters were part of the Revolutionary Mass witnessing the chastisement. Some of them also were forced to the stage, but others who felt that their parents had not treated them fairly took advantage of the situation to add to their discomfort. The mother lost consciousness before the event was over, and the old couple committed suicide together at dawn. The youngest daughter had fled to a small city in Canton but failed to sneak across the Hong Kong border. Saved by a friend after a suicide attempt, she did not reappear in Shanghai until 1978, by then married with two daughters of her own. The relocation movement, like the beginning of the Cultural Revolution, simply provided a new excuse for a wave of violence and turmoil.

14

Dear Professor Hu,

In one of my earlier letters, I told you about
feigning illness so that I would not have to go to
the countryside. Since the movement to relocate
young intellectuals to the countryside lasted several years,
my "illness" was an ongoing concern.

By the early 1970s, many new and sometimes rare "illnesses"
appeared throughout Shanghai. Drinking copious quantities of chicken
or duck blood, for example, will imitate symptoms of a peptic ulcer. A
healthy woman's urine during menstruation may appear bloody, a
symptom of a urinary tract or bladder infection. Ephedrine, an anti-
asthma drug, increased blood pressure. People could even simulate the
symptoms of lupus. Twelve hundred years ago, Ju-Yi Bai wrote a poem
called "A One-Armed Man," which told of thousands of young men
who severed their arms to avoid the Emperor Tang's military draft.
These stories were no longer ancient folktales but modern reality, and
young people sometimes even caused permanent damage to themselves.

One classmate of mine took an excess of ephedrine and gave
himself hypertension for life. Rei-qing and I resolved not to touch any
drug that could cause physical damage. If circumstances arose that we
could not otherwise handle, we could only trust in God. Two such
situations occurred.

Each week, I went to see a doctor about my "arthritis," for it
would arouse suspicion if a person with a painful disease never saw a

physician. On one visit, I was received by a middle-aged female doctor who carefully scrutinized my chart. When her eyes fixed on the entry Rei-qing and I had changed, she said nothing but dragged me to the lab as if I were a thief. She told the technician to check the master copy of the test results, but of course I feared nothing, knowing that the entry would be verified. It was. Furious, frustrated, and still suspicious, she ordered another test.

The doctor watched every move, from the needle entering my arm to the sealing of the sample tube with my name on it. Satisfied, she left. It would be an hour before I would learn the results of the test that decided my fate. If they were within normal limits, my entire file would be suspect.

I paced nervously in front of the laboratory door. I thought of running away instead of fighting the battle ahead of me, but as an old Chinese saying pointed out, "A monk can retreat, but the temple cannot." My records in the doctor's hands had my name, address, and status. It was my "young intellectual" status that made the doctor suspicious in the first place. By the time the hour was up, I had turned everything over to God and was completely calm. And a miracle occurred.

"Your sedimentation rate is 20," the technician called out.

I returned to the doctor's office and handed her the official test results. The piece of paper had the strength of steel in it. Unable to argue further, the doctor grudgingly prescribed the medicine with the most unpleasant side effects. I had vivid, confused dreams that night. My mind bounced between the day's events and those years ago when the mob chased me through the streets. I screamed and struggled in my sleep, waking my father, who tearfully stood watching me. Only at dawn did I sleep soundly.

After breakfast, I went back to the hospital to wait for Kang-li, who had been working the night shift. (I had confided to her the truth about my "condition.") When I told her what had happened, she said, "That woman's name is Jian. She's always pretending to be a big supporter of the Party. She already sent her seventeen-year-old daughter and fifteen-year-old son to the Northeast. Of course she'll hate a young intellectual who's still in the city."

We walked slowly, enjoying the first warm days of May. Huai Hai

Road was as crowded as if a movie had just let out, even though it was a weekday. Turning down a smaller street, Kang-li took my arm and said gravely, "Xi-ou, promise me that if such a thing ever happens again, you will come to me immediately. In my position, I can do more things than you can. I also think I should examine you a few times myself and give you some important documents."

"I always look for you whenever I'm at the hospital," I responded quickly. "All your colleagues know me. You must be careful. Your handwriting should not appear on my file. My sister and I resolved not to bring you into this. We gave our word to each other, and I can't go back on it. But, actually, I do have one question. How come my test result jumped to 20?"

Kang-li mulled over the question and said, "A test like that is very subjective. Whenever there's a human element, some uncertainty is introduced." I was dissatisfied with such a vague answer, but another adventure in the near future proved Kang-li correct.

△△△ The Central Office of Relocation was not slow to learn that many "strong oaks" feigned sickness to avoid being transported to the countryside and told the Neighborhood Committees that we needed an occasional lightning bolt to reveal us for what we were. They complied, and at eight o'clock one August morning in 1970, Madame Couvre, our family's old nemesis, came pounding on our door. She was as ugly as ever, her face covered with large, hairy moles. She pointed at me: "Get your clothes on! We're going to the Central Hospital to see if you're really sick!"

A different female doctor met me in the examining room. Kang-li had already briefed me on her, so I knew that she despised her husband, a PLA officer who was rarely at home. She pursued other men but became bored quickly and did not keep any lover for long. The jilted men nicknamed her "the Rabbit," because she hopped from bed to bed. She and Kang-li had both graduated from prestigious medical schools—unlike the multitudes of "doctors" who had only completed a first-aid course. She was a Party member with a good political background, trusted by and indispensable to the hospital.

Madame Couvre pulled out a badge with the Relocation Office's red seal and handed it to the Rabbit. She whispered something in the doctor's ear, her mouth almost touching it. The Rabbit edged back, as if repulsed by Madame Couvre's appearance. I felt a nudge at my back and turned to see a worried Kang-li. I remembered her saying, "Every time I hear the Mobilization Squad's drums, my heart beats along with it, and I worry that they're drumming for you."

"Xi-ou Tan, get over here," Madam Couvre shouted in her cracked voice. As I walked toward her and the Rabbit, I motioned with my hands behind my back for Kang-li to leave before being noticed. The Rabbit put on her stethoscope and listened to my heart. She stared at her watch, trying to calculate my pulse rate, but Madame Couvre interrupted before fifteen seconds had passed: "I don't think her pulse means much. Everybody's heart will beat faster when they're threatened."

The Rabbit pretended not to hear. Removing her stethoscope, she wrote on my chart, "Heart rate = 160/minute."

"How do you feel?" she asked me.

"Sometimes I get very nervous. I get sore throats a lot, too. And in the afternoon, I often break into cold sweats."

Madame Couvre was irate: "Of course you feel cold when you sweat! Everybody does! Why do you think you sweat in the first place? And you're nervous? I'd be nervous, too, if I were trying to avoid Chairman Mao's call to go to the countryside! And a sore throat? Who told you a sore throat could let you loaf in the city?"

The Rabbit threw her pen on the table: "Who's the doctor here, you or me?"

Still Madame Couvre did not let up. Pushing in my nose with her index finger, she hissed, "Anti-Revolutionary whelp! You look strong enough to me! You and your anti-Revolutionary scum father both pretend you're sick! You expect to be pampered and think someone will come and save your worthless hide! We'll watch you rot and enjoy the show!"

People were crowding around to see what was happening. The Rabbit stood up furiously and shouted at Madame Couvre, "This is a sick girl here! If she's a worker, she should be on sick leave! I'll give her seven or eight years of sick leave at least. And we'll feed and take care of her! This is the advantage of the Socialist system! Do you understand me?"

Madame Couvre stepped back. Kang-li came forward to help the Rabbit disperse the spectators. Pretending to be an unconcerned witness, she asked, "What is all this about?"

The Rabbit replied angrily, "This girl is very sick. The Neighborhood Committee sent her here for a checkup. Before I could examine her, this loud-mouthed cadre started telling me how to do my job and wanted me to rubber-stamp what she had already decided. She even wanted me to write a statement saying that this poor girl was malingering and was unquestionably fit to go to the countryside. How could I do something so immoral?"

Nodding in agreement, Kang-li took the record and pretended to read it carefully. She exclaimed, "Oh dear! Heart rate 160! Her heart could give out at any time. Don't get her excited or she'll collapse!"

Realizing that she had lost, Madame Couvre solicitously escorted me to the pharmacy. She waited with me the whole thirty minutes required to get the anti-arrhythmic drugs the doctor had urgently recommended. Not until Madame Couvre was once again in her neighborhood, where her word was law, did she breathe easily again.

I asked Kang-li later about the Rabbit. "Actually," Kang-li told me, "I think she multiplied wrong when she was trying to calculate your heart rate. Still, it's unusual that she didn't cooperate with the cadre. The Rabbit isn't known for her kindness, and she's certainly capable of amoral actions in the service of the Party. This time, it was like sulfuric acid being thrown on caustic soda: The reaction was violent. All people have many facets, and life itself is always changing. There's always a random element in the response to any particular stimulus."

Since I had been saved from so many close calls, I had always thought a mysterious power watched over me. Kang-li turned to me and, with a serious expression, told me the mysterious power was God. "God has His plan for you, just as He has His plan for everything in the world."

I listened politely as Kang-li explained some basic Christian theology, but I felt a vague dissatisfaction with the dogma. I could not understand why God would help me so many times but never ease Father's suffering even a little. I suspected that He might exist, and constantly feared His punishment, but the contradictions in life made me shy away from faith in a loving God.

I suppose that there are many things in life that I will never understand. Throughout the ages, people have wondered why God permits evil to exist, and why some of the best men and women have suffered so greatly. I will not pretend to understand these things; all I know is that I felt protected at that time and still do. I do not know what your beliefs are, Professor Hu, but please continue to hope.

> Sincerely,
> Xi-ou Tan

Dear Xi-ou Tan:
I went to Harvard for a seminar this afternoon, and afterward to its Yan Jin Library. I thumbed through *Lyric Tune Patterns*, my favorite book when I was a student. I like classical Chinese literature, especially Tang and Soong Ci poems. I was punished for this hobby during the Grand Cultural Revolution, so I did not pick it up again for a long time.

Have you read the Yuan lyric by Zhang Shang-ming named *Satirical*? It describes an evil man who was favored by the emperor several hundred years ago:

> His face as cold as a fog on a winter's night,
> He rolls up his sleeves, an invitation to fight.
> His words are but noise, and offend our whole
>   nation:
> "I am your savior!" his mouth's declaration.
> Peel off the overcoat, his identity fix!
> A five-eyed chicken boasts that he is a phoenix,
> Dragon's cleverness claimed by a two-headed snake,
> A tiger's power would a three-legged cat take.

I never joined the Red Guards. When they went to see Chairman Mao at Tiananmen Square and then on a tour of the country, I hid myself at school and read Tang and Soong Ci poems to pass the time. I was impressed by this particular one. When I practiced calligraphy in my dorm that night, I copied it and then threw it away, as I always did.

Several years later, Chairman Mao finished his nationwide inspection and published his "Newest Instructions" when he arrived back in Beijing: "I would describe the political situation as 'major good,' not 'minor good.' But in a few months, it will be even better." I was doing physical labor in Hu Pei countryside at the time. Everybody burst out of their dorms when they heard this, beating their drums and gathering together for a parade to "celebrate another victory of Mao Zedong thought."

I mimicked Chairman Mao's quotation in a teasing way to one of my colleagues: "I would describe the meteorological situation as 'major cold' not 'minor cold.' But in a few months, it will be even colder." This colleague was my roommate when we studied at the university, and he was also from Shanghai. He laughed when he heard me say this, but then reported it to the secretary. I was considered an anti-Revolutionary who attacked Chairman Mao. Placed on exhibit was the thrown-away paper on which I had practiced my calligraphy several years before I arrived at the university. I was accused of using the old, dead poem to attack Chairman Mao and the Red Guards.

There were 136 chastisement meetings for me, of various audience sizes. I was supposed to have been sent to jail, but the head of the Army Mao Zedong Thought Propaganda Team saved me, and I was allowed to stay and do manual labor, watched by the Revolutionary Mass Committee. If the Gang of Four had not been deposed, I would not have been able to go back to the classroom to teach or to come and do research in the United States.

I am not very good at expressing myself, and I rarely write letters. I enjoy yours but feel guilty that you spend so much of your time on them.

Sincerely yours,
Yong-hua Hu

15

Dear Professor Hu,

Thank you for your letter. I did not know that you had also suffered because of "anti-Revolutionary" literature. Your story reminded me of a time in 1970 when I took advantage of a Public Security officer's ignorance of classical Chinese works.

"Quick! Open the door! We're from the Public Security Office!"

The shout startled me out of a beautiful dream of a colorful phoenix. It had flown into the Angel Cave through the southern window and circled over my head. The dull walls had burst into brightness as I stood breathlessly watching the wondrous metamorphosis. The voices outside were an evil intrusion. Putting on a coat, I left the garage and passed the kitchen on my way to the main door of the house. With the shining phoenix still in my mind, I tried to force myself awake. I opened the door.

"We're here to check your family's identification book!" the leader of the group said, and walked through the door, followed by three Neighborhood Committee members. The leader was wearing a police uniform, and two who followed him were people I recognized only vaguely. The third was Madame Couvre.

I took the family's identification book from under my mattress. We had stopped keeping important papers, money, or ration coupons in drawers ever since the first searches by the Red Guards. The eyes of the forty-year-old policeman were barely visible beneath his official cap, because he wore it so low. I had often gone to the local Public Security Office to turn in my Father's confessions, but this man was a stranger to me.

The officer examine each page of the book while Madame Couvre and the other two sniffed around the Angel Cave, from the pantry to commode, hoping to find something anti-revolutionary. Father remained in bed. Rei-qing was on "sick leave," so she could only stand helpless with my brothers. Returning the identification book, the officer asked, "Is there anything else under that mattress?"

"Only some ration coupons," I answered, with dread.

"Why did you put this under the mattress?" he asked.

"Because it's important."

"Pick up the mattress and let's see what else you think is important!"

My heart sank, for along with the coupons, I had a single piece of paper containing a poem by Su Shih, "A Rhyme of Chi Bi." I had recited it before falling asleep that night. Father's mattress covered manuscripts we had not yet taken to be hidden. Under my brothers' were the homework, copied books, and notes for our independent study program.

Thinking fast, I said, "There's a work that is a poisonous weed under this mattress. I'd like to turn it in to you." When I lifted the mattress, the officer snatched the piece of paper. "Inside is a conspiracy! Listen to this":

> A boat of lilacs and two lily oars
> Floats through the night, miles from shore.
> The face of the moon on the water gleams
> Which the lily oar scatters to a thousand beams.
> But empty and meaningless is all that I write,
> As is life when my Love is far from my sight.

"Do you know who this 'Love' is?" I asked.

Neither the officer nor Madame Couvre said anything.

"This is the peoples' common enemy, Jiang Kai-shek!" I said angrily.

"Who wrote this?" the officer demanded.

"I don't feel comfortable discussing it now," I replied. "If necessary, I will accompany you to the Neighborhood Committee office or the Public Security Office headquarters right now and tell you everything."

The five of us left the house. A cold wind blew, and I trembled as I wrapped my coat more tightly. My back was soaking wet from nervous sweat. Although I was surrounded by enemies, I had gained control of myself. I looked up at the twinkling stars and thought of the dream of the brilliant phoenix. Perhaps reading the poem before going to sleep had caused the dream, the most beautiful one I could remember. In ancient times, an imperial minister supposedly dreamed every night that he was a valet. When he awoke in the morning, he bullied the people. I mused that if I had a wonderful dream every night, at least half of my life would be beautiful.

We sat in the reception room of the Neighborhood Committee office, the policeman flanked by committee members. "This poem is very anti-Revolutionary," I began, before the policeman could ask. "Lilies and lilacs are fragile! It would be impossible to use them to make oars, let alone a boat. The author accuses our Socialist society of being a fairy tale that could not come true! As far as the 'Love' is concerned, I already told you that it is Jiang Kai-shek. The author is looking over the ocean to Jiang Kai-shek in exile and begging him to come restore the 'paradise' that has been lost." The committee seemed impressed by my theoretical Revolutionary analysis.

The officer suddenly developed an uncontrollable urge to smoke. After finding a cigarette, he frantically searched his pockets for a match. The three Neighborhood Committee members dutifully took part in the search until one was located. He then insisted that someone find a piece of paper so he could clean his cigarette holder. Madame Couvre handed him Father's "Quarterly Report on the Progress of Thought Reform."

"Who wrote that poem?" asked the policeman. "Was it your anti-Revolutionary Father?"

"No," I answered. "It was written by someone named Su Shih."

"Who is 'Sushi'? Where is he? What's his relationship to your family?"

I was not surprised by his ignorance. If he did not recognize the poem, it was unlikely that he had ever heard of the author. "Su Shih was a Northern Soong writer. He was helping the anti-Revolutionary class to oppress the masses. I learned of this poem in my school's literature club."

Realizing that he had been fooled, the officer shouted, "You could have said this hours ago! Why did you want to come down here to say all this?"

"This material is so poisonous that if we had discussed this at home, the rest of my family would have been affected," I responded gravely. "I want the reading of this material to be forbidden, which is why I wanted to talk of this only with you who are immune to such propaganda."

Slapping his forehead, he turned away. Madame Couvre, slower to understand, said excitedly, "This Sushi lives in Northern Soong? Let's bring that anti-Revolutionary scum here and tar and feather him! How far away is Northern Soong? Can we walk?"

In the sweetest tones I could muster, I informed her, "Northern Soong was a dynasty that ended almost a thousand years ago. Chairman Mao teaches us, 'All those who are mistaken, who are poisonous weeds, who are Ox Ghosts, should be chastised. We cannot allow them to spread freely.' Although this anti-Revolutionary Su Shih and his anti-Revolutionary poem have existed for a thousand years, as long as they are mistaken, as long as they are poisonous weeds, they should be chastised incessantly and mercilessly."

The officer could not respond to this sophisticated Revolutionary speech. He stretched and said, "All right. Go home and get some sleep."

My entire family was waiting for me in the dark. Father greeted me, saying, "My child, it's been a rough night, hasn't it?"

I laughed. "It's been a lot rougher for Mr. Sushi living in Northern Soong. If that old man in his grave heard what I said, I hope he forgives me."

It turned out that the Public Security Office had picked that night to check our identification papers because Prince Sihanouk and Princess Monica of Cambodia were to arrive the next day. The two were then the biggest stars in the Chinese film and political communities, and the government wanted no trouble during the visit. After being expelled from Cambodia they organized a Cambodian government-in-exile center in Beijing. Considered honored guests during their stay in China, they toured the country and were treated to the best accommodations, food, and entertainment. Prince Sihanouk was the stereotypical profligate son of a royal family. He would dedicate rhymes to his "generous Chinese hosts." One of his better efforts was:

> *Stronger than a tower, higher than a steeple,*
> *Are Mao Zedong thought and the power of the*
> *people.*

His wife had a partly Western background. When she became the focus of documentary movies, her clothes and hairstyles were secretly imitated in several big cities. It was said that their son knew a few ballet movements. Portraying a political commissar, he was featured as the only male dancer in one of the modern Revolutionary ballets, *The Red Ladies' Army*, as part of a movement led by Madame Mao to reform the old ballet. In a time when China had virtually no diplomatic relations with any country and therefore no honored guests, this family filled an empty role on the Chinese political stage.

△△△ I was relieved that we had averted danger once again, but learning the cause of the peril made my pleasure disappear. However, the episode was not over. The police officer who had interrogated me was the director of the district Public Security Office. Below him in rank was an officer we called "the Runt." After endlessly recounting how he had found an anti-Revolutionary poem at the Tan home, the Runt, humiliated because his superior had uncovered the anti-Revolutionary nest under his nose, personally led surprise searches of our house about twice a week for a full year. Sometimes he dragged Father out of bed, patted him down, and searched the bed. One day, when only Jian-nan was at home boiling water in the kitchen, the Runt appeared. Without speaking, he made a beeline for Father's bed. Jian-nan said, "Hello, Comrade Xiao Liu!" hoping to warn Father, but it was too late.

By the time Father looked up from his manuscript, the Runt had snatched the entire work, all three hundred thousand characters. I had retrieved the original from Uncle Fong's for Father to revise. While it was tragic to lose the whole manuscript, it was good that nothing remained in Uncle Fong's home that could have led to his being named an anti-Revolutionary conspirator. Four years of hard work lay in the Runt's hands, so I went to visit him later that day.

"What can you possibly say in your defense?" he sneered. "This is ironclad proof that you've been protecting your anti-Revolutionary old man. Every time your father submitted a confession, the characters looked like they had been drawn by somebody half-dead. They were so crooked I could barely read them! But look at these!" He pointed to the manuscript. "They are strong and firm! Isn't he acting? Aren't you just lampooning the Proletarian Dictatorship?"

"This is a valuable scholarly work. I sincerely hope you will turn this over to knowledgeable committees who can render a true judgment," I almost begged.

"Scholarly work? What's that? I'll tell you. It stinks of bourgeois liberalization! We don't need this trash. And further, we don't need any anti-Revolutionaries to write 'scholarly works' anyway!" The Runt paused a moment. "Our vice chairman, Lin Biao, recently gave his first directive to the Chinese people. He calls us to prepare for the coming war by emptying the cities and filling up the countrysides. Your family are unsuitable residents of the city. You have two options: You can return to Hunan, your province of origin, or you can go where we assigned you, An Hui."

"We don't have anyone left in Hunan," I said firmly. "If you make us move, we'll go to An Hui." Humility on my part was one thing, but I refused to see Father's pride hurt. For him to return to Hunan under these circumstances would have been a disgrace. An Hui was unfamiliar, but I believed that Father would be under less mental and emotional strain there. Lin Biao's directive had already been carried out in many of the smaller cities surrounding Shanghai, and I had heard that some residents of Wu Xi and Su Zhou had been forced into the poorest communes of Jiang Su province.

My second problem was Madame Couvre. Upon hearing that the

Runt had found incriminating evidence in our home, she jumped on her desk and began to dance, whereupon she lost her balance and fell to the floor, causing a compound fracture of the femur. I learned of Madame Couvre's injuries when I went to hand in Father's next confession. The doctors had decreed three months of bed rest, so her assistant met me. I had expected that there would be a special chastisement meeting for Father, but none was planned. If Madame Couvre had not been injured, such a meeting would have been inevitable.

All this talk of the "Four Obsolete Vestiges" makes me laugh! I thought, contemptuously. These fools are so superstitious, they probably think Madame Couvre's accident was a sign from the gods. Now they're scared to do anything!

"Go home and start making bricks!" the assistant spat at me. "The United States and the Soviet Union are preparing for World War III. We, in turn, have to protect ourselves, and that means every family has to turn in twenty bricks a month. Since your family is anti-Revolutionary, your quota is twenty bricks per family member. Get moving."

Professor Hu, since you spent most of your time in Wu Han, you might not know the details of the Brickmaker's Movement of 1970. A district was told what size bricks to make and the families gathered the mud and then shaped, pressed, and dried it. The half-finished bricks were left in predetermined locations to be picked up by trucks and kiln-dried in local brickmaking factories. This was the response to Chairman Mao's call to the people: "Prepare for World War III, prepare for starvation. Dig deep the hole, gather rice from all quarters." Work units organized squads to build underground bomb shelters, the first step toward the goal of a massive network of tunnels and halls beneath Shanghai. Not only would this system protect those living in the city, it also would be a strategic base for launching guerrilla attacks. The underground construction originated at the Spanish-style house that the three old ladies had lived in only a few years earlier. Floodlights illuminated the half-naked workers shoveling mud while electric pumps removed water from the ground twenty-four hours a day.

Chi-kai built our family's wooden brick mold. Realizing that other families might try to fill their quotas with bricks stolen from us, I asked

Mei-feng if we could dry them in the playground of the nursery school that their home overlooked. Mei-feng and I went with our brothers to the local cemeteries in the early morning hours to steal dirt, since this was not supplied. We mixed it with water at home and kneaded it, then dropped it on the ground until it turned rubbery. When satisfied, we transferred it to the mold. The bricks became brittle if exposed to direct sunlight, so it was necessary to find a shady spot for drying them.

The first hundred bricks were a backbreaking task, but as our skill improved, we were able to fill our quota effortlessly. To avoid having to make bricks every month, we stockpiled a large supply. When my brothers and sister vacated the Angel Cave in 1985, they still found twenty-odd bricks, even though the six-month-long Brickmaker's Movement had died fifteen years earlier.

△△△ We had yet another major problem: Father had to deal with droves of unexpected, unwelcome visitors. At the start of the Grand Cultural Revolution, many people in power were accused of exploiting the Party to pursue their bourgeois goals. A new movement, "Check In and Look Out," demanded reevaluation of those serving time on the Ox Ghost Reeducation Ranches. Two or more trusted cadres studied the confessions of those previously chastised. Armed with letters of introduction from their parent Revolutionary organizations, they went to the Revolutionary Committees to interview the individuals who could corroborate the evidence given in self-criticisms. This was an excellent travel opportunity: Since many of those who could provide information lived in different parts of the country, the investigators could tour China free of charge.

△△△ In the early 1940s, Father had helped support the family of Shi-wen Yang. In 1964, after our uncle, Ji-wang Bai, was arrested, Father had been apprehended and placed in a holding cell for interrogation. Alone with the four young children, Mother remembered how her husband had helped Shi-wen Yang's family. Hoping that he might at least offer some advice, she sent Rei-qing and me to his high-rise apartment with the news of Father's predicament. I was only thirteen, but I have not forgotten the plastic smile on his cold, emotionless face.

"It is undivided loyalty to the Party—turning away from friends, lovers, and family—that makes the Communist Party the strongest force in the world," Yang told us. "Yes, your Father once helped my parents. But those parents of mine were the Guomindang's cadres. Early in 1955 I sent them back to where they came from and told them I wanted no more to do with them. You must follow my example and cut off all relations with your parents."

As we spoke, Yang's maid came in repeatedly to change the hot-water bottle he held to his stomach, to freshen the coals in the fireplace he used to warm his feet, and to bring ginseng soup. He escorted us down to the lobby, his military overcoat draped around his shoulders. Pushing the elevator button, he said, "Go home and think deeply. Contemplate any anti-Revolutionary actions or statements of your parents. Write them down and mail them to me, or give them to one of my assistants. I'll be happy to see that your reports reach the proper committees."

With a mirthless laugh, he patted me on the head and said, "I know you've loved to read ever since you were a little girl. I have lots of Revolutionary books on my bookshelf. When you have time, come back so you can gather strength from these stories of Revolutionary heroism and raise your Revolutionary consciousness."

The elevator bell rang, and the red light came on. As we walked into the elevator, he struck a dramatic pose and pronounced, "The storm is coming. Be brave to face the test of the Revolution." The elevator doors closed.

When we got home, we told Mother everything, including our opinion of Shi-wen Yang. Mother was very distressed, and after everyone else had gone to sleep, I heard her muffled crying in the dark. I gritted my teeth in anger. The next morning, I wrote Shi-wen Yang's name on little pieces of scratch paper and muttered malisons as I flushed each piece down the toilet. I had learned this ritual from a novel; it was said that the victim of these curses would die within three months from a debilitating and painful disease.

Of course he did not die from this, but in the late 1960s, Yang's powerful position in the Communist Party was not enough to prevent his chastisement by the Red Guards. He was sent to the Ox Ghost Reeducation Ranch and was still there in 1970, when the Check In and Look Out Movement began. When his case came up for reevaluation, the investigators were eager to hear Father's side of the story. One group wished to exonerate Yang, while another wished to condemn him further. Both visited Father repeatedly, demanding that he write out confessions concerning his dealings with Yang. From late 1970 to mid-1971, Father received 201 visits of this sort, each averaging three hours.

The investigation focused on the genesis of Yang's Revolutionary career. Yang stated in his résumé that when he arrived in Yan-an in 1939, Father and S. Jiang encouraged and facilitated his joining the Revolution. After the liberation of Shanghai in 1949, a page from Yang's diary stated, "This morning, in the East China Economic Research Institute, I was very happy to meet Jin-ren Tan. We haven't seen each other for ten years. We shook hands for a long time, and I thanked him for taking care of my parents all those years. I also told him that if he hadn't bravely and selflessly offered his help ten years ago, I wouldn't be where I am today."

After the Anti-Rightist Movement ended in 1958, Yang was promoted three levels to the job of minister. In a report entitled "I Give My Heart to the Communist Party," he mentioned his early history. "I joined the Revolution because I hated the Guomindang. The Guomindang's local secretary saw that I had a good reputation with the local young people and that I was their natural leader, and tried to get me to join them. I naturally refused. They sent three spies to my dormitory to kidnap me. I could not overpower three of them myself, so I broke the lamp in my room and jumped out of the window and escaped. After many, many hardships, I finally arrived at the sacred heart of the Revolution, Yan-an."

Everything Yang wrote later referred back to this propagandistic essay. The story grew in excitement and intrigue, painting a picture of a model young intellectual who chose to become a Revolutionary fighter. He expunged the most important people in his past from this record. As a member of the leading class, he thought himself invulnerable, never expecting that in the Grand Cultural Revolution, his confidential files would be opened and his private diary confiscated. He had not imagined that Jin-ren Tan, a man he had left behind long ago, would play an important role in his fate.

Father's anti-Revolutionary status meant that favorable comments would not be considered, but damning evidence would be. He would not have to lie or even emphasize certain events over others; the simple truth would be sufficient. Discovering how a soldier was led to the Revolutionary path was no less important than discovering the identity of a newborn baby's father. Yang came from a "bad" family, analogous to a child born out of wedlock. This detail was of enormous importance.

After the first few interviews, all of us knew what was desired. We suggested that Father oblige the investigators by telling them what they wanted to hear. Even though Yang had not helped us, Father refused to cooperate. Promising to do his best to keep the interrogation visits short, Father agreed that we could signal him by coughing if his answers grew too long.

Father became excited every time he discussed the anti-Japanese war, and he let his words flow freely. The investigators listened to these patriotic stories with keen interest, but upon their completion, they resumed their cold, accusatory tones. We "coughed" constantly, but Father would not or did not hear. He plunged ahead, passionately describing the most rewarding period of his life and the history of simple Chinese men and women on whose shoulders was placed the burden of their country's survival.

△△△ Professor Hu, I may have mentioned this before, but of all the poets of the last two thousand years, Father and Grandfather Pu most respected the indomitable Tao Zi. I often think that although Tao Zi said in one of his poems, "Since the whole world is always against it, why should I bother to pursue my will?" he himself never gave up his ideals. He spent all his life studying hard, writing poems, and fighting against the dark side of society.

Father in a way was the same. He often exhibited a pessimistic attitude toward this world in his later years, but at the same time, he pursued his ideals even harder. He knew that it was only a dream; although he would get no reward, he refused to surrender the ideals that gave him peace of mind.

From your letter, I know that after you graduated from the university, you were assigned to Wu Han to teach, and you were sent to the countryside later. You do not know, therefore, all of the details about Shanghai during the Grand Cultural Revolution, and I am glad, because I think my letters as a result will hold more interest for you.

Sincerely,
Xi-ou Tan

 By late 1971, the young intellectuals in the countryside, whether originally Blacks or reclassified Red Guards, had long since lost any enthusiasm they might have possessed. Their dreams were destroyed by years of heavy physical labor, and poverty, petty thefts, drunkenness, and knife fights became commonplace. At the height of their power five years earlier, few Red Guards thought of the lonely border regions where they were now being reeducated as worthwhile places to carry on the Revolution. The city-bred students were helpless in the countryside; the boys could do less work than peasant women who already had several children. They were assigned to impoverished, backward communes where people garnished their meals of steamed rice with only salt and hot pepper. Even rice was considered a delicacy in places where people subsisted on thin yam and corn gruels. When the students first arrived, the peasants found themselves with more mouths to feed but no increase in supply. Chairman Mao had declared, "The lowly are the most intelligent; the elite are the most ignorant," but the students learned only feudalistic, selfish, narrow-minded attitudes from the peasants, instead of simple kindness.

The students also had to cope with the abuse of power by the PLA officers who had been appointed "political directors," a position of almost absolute authority. While a person could be put in prison indefinitely at their word, a favorite could avoid any hard physical labor and easily obtain the consent needed for marriage or sick leave. Many young women were raped by these officers and their sons.

Parents did all they could to help their children in virtual exile, including satisfying the "local emperors," the cadres of the communes. If there was a chance that their children would be reassigned to local factories or schools, the parents threw good money after bad attempting to bribe those who made the decisions. The local cadres grew ever greedier, and parents who were unable to satisfy them could only ask their children to return home to save living expenses. Those who did had no rights and received no rice, fuel, or cooking oil allocations, and the extra financial and political burden often led to dissension within the family.

Canton Kiss Up had no problems wherever he went, since he had spent a fair amount of money procuring a grandmother. After rising to the level of "barefoot doctor," he was sent to a large Shanghai hospital for six months of intense training. Within a year of her marriage to a peasant, Slab-Tongue received the most precious fruit of Chairman Mao's instructions: a little Slab-Tongue. Although Lard Bucket Lin was a large, tough woman, even she found life unbearable in the isolated regions, and after only ten months, she followed Slab-Tongue's example of marrying a peasant she had known for less than a week. While female intellectuals had the option of marrying peasants, few farmers wished their daughters to marry a man too weak to push a plow. Perhaps the Relocation Movement had been designed to solve the unemployment problem in the cities; why else would such marriages, which ensured that the young intellectuals remained in the countryside permanently, be encouraged?

Relocation of the graduates in 1972, my brother Chi-kai's year, depended on their siblings' situations, since assignments could offset each other. A family with a child in a remote countryside had the right to place another child in a Shanghai industrial position. If one child had an industrial position outside Shanghai, the next child could be assigned to a Shanghai suburban agricultural post. Sick people were not required to make any contribution to the work force. Bitter parents of students in the classes of 1968 and 1969 complained that the new policy was unfair. Young intellectuals who had returned from the countryside told their younger siblings, "If I hadn't gone to the countryside in the first place, you wouldn't have received such an easy job in Shanghai!" Families with very young children planned for the future, never guessing that that the policy would change in less than five years, when the Gang of four was deposed.

Stories of reactions to the new policy swept Shanghai. A seemingly typical, happy family living near Uncle Fong's had a son and a daughter, aged sixteen and six, respectively. The new rules dictated that the brother should be given a job in a Shanghai factory and the girl later sent to the countryside. Not wishing their daughter to be away from home, the parents secretly visited the Relocation Office and begged that the children be allowed to exchange places. Outraged when he discovered the plan, the son murdered his sister and then poisoned himself to punish his parents.

One neighbor had identical twin daughters. In an effort to keep the twins together and in Shanghai, the parents applied for a divorce. Believing that each would retain custody of one twin, they planned on taking advantage of the "only child clause," which allowed parents to keep their one child with them in the city. However, before it would hand down a ruling on their request for a divorce, the court decreed that the parents had to choose which daughter would go to the countryside. Blaming each other for the plan's failure, the parents fought until each truly wanted the separation.

The Relocation Movement policy meant that Chi-kai would be sent to the countryside. This naturally would have a profound effect on our family, but when we had almost given up hope, unexpected help arrived.

16

Dear Professor Hu,

Vice Chairman Lin Biao's directive that all city-dwellers move to the countryside in preparation for World War III was unofficially revoked when his plane crashed mysteriously in Mongolia in 1971, so the order for our whole family to leave Shanghai was rescinded. As Jian-nan's and my hospital records thickened steadily, our status as "sick young intellectuals" was solidified, and we were permitted to remain in the city despite the Relocation Movement. Rei-qing occasionally had to visit her farm, but several doctors in the country hospitals came to her aid by extending her sick leave, which left her free to study at home. By the autumn of 1971, Rei-qing and I had completed the equivalent of a core college curriculum and moved on to advanced topics, such as the theory of microwave radiation. Jian-nan's interest in physics increased constantly, and he often made "wish lists" of physics texts for us to look for when we scoured used-book stores or solicited help from private connections. He wanted to learn about measure theory, Lie group theory, and time, space, and gravitational field. I knew that finding the books would be difficult, as I had never even heard of some of these topics.

We rose at four each morning to begin the day with calisthenics. Then we cleaned Angel Cave and the little backyard before breakfast. Professor Wang's son had a job as a lifeguard at a middle-school swimming pool, so my brothers and I went there each day at 6:30 to swim for an hour. Then four of us studied for eight or nine hours. After dinner we studied more. Before retiring at 9:30 at night, each of us completed a calligraphy project consisting of ten page-size characters.

We also had an hour each day of "scientific activities," which included photography, even though we had little money to spend on developing solutions and materials. Using an old soap dish as a housing, we built a crystal radio and glued a piece of copper wire to the ceiling for an antenna. When the Runt saw it during one of his searches, he believed it to be a telegraph used to transmit state secrets to the United States and Taiwan.

Each Saturday, we "published" a family newspaper called *The Cocked Bolt*. The title, from a saying of Confucius, described our pent-up energies and talents. The four two-sided pages included comics, poems, scientific propositions, and miscellaneous bits of information. Our circulation of one was Father, who would comment on each article and award his own version of the Pulitzer Prize each week. After he finished, we all shared snacks of gruel with sugar and fried dough. The next day, we went to Uncle Fong's to hide the newspaper.

For my twentieth birthday, Father wrote me a poem:

> *My child, already twenty years you have seen!*
> *But your birthdays were lost in this terrible rain.*
> *Were it not for the concern of your Aunt and your*
> *   Queen,*
> *How could we so honor your real mother's pain?*
> *What makes my four angels rise before dawn?*
> *To be the first of four is what spurs them on.*

The good times did not last long. Chi-kai turned fifteen that autumn, the age at which all were required to go to the countryside. Jian-nan was truly sick and I pretended to be so, but this would not affect Chi-kai. The policy stated that since Rei-qing held a Shanghai suburban agricultural position, Chi-kai had to be assigned to an industrial position outside the city.

Representing my parents, I attended several meetings called to explain the new relocation policy. Chi-kai told me that he looked forward to the prospect of a new life as a worker, even if he were sent to an electric power plant in Lin Bao, two thousand miles southwest.

His dream was like the one I had had at his age: work hard, live frugally, and send most of the wages home to help the family become financially independent. Even so, Chi-kai did not find his name on the long lists of those assigned to remote industrial locations. When he questioned a teacher who worked closely with the relocation program, he received only a vague answer. At first, I thought that the policy was fair, despite its shortcomings. It seemed clear what Chi-kai's assignment should be, but two months passed before the teacher regretfully told him, "It isn't possible for you to get a remote industrial position. No factory wants someone with your family background."

"Then where can I go?" he asked.

"You have only one option: the remote countryside."

I talked with the leader of the Nan Yang working-class squad but received no satisfaction. All the way home I cried for my brother, already without motherly love, who soon would be sent to work in the fields for the rest of his life. I remembered how Chi-kai had kept smiling even when his schoolmates hit him with rocks and sticks the day Father had been chastised, and I recovered my courage. I decided to go to the district director and secretary that same afternoon.

At the information desk in the District Administration Office, an old man sat warming himself at a stove. Looking at my worn clothes, he turned up his nose and sneered, "Can anybody walk in and say they want to see the director?" Realizing that the old man would only turn me away, I knew it was useless to explain the importance of my case. I decided to catch the director as he left, hoping that we could talk as he walked to his bicycle, thereby taking little of his time. It was bitterly cold and almost pitch-dark at 5:30 when the office closed. I stood in front of the gate of the building, watching the people leave. I did not know how I would spot the director and the secretary in the crowd.

The streetlights came on and the wind picked up. By eight o'clock I was numb with cold, listening to my stomach growl. Looking up, I noticed a building with every window glowing with warm, friendly light. I thought of the Queen, Uncle Fong, Dr. Wei, the gaunt old man in the hotel—everyone who had helped me out of difficult situations. I continued to scrutinize the people trickling out of the administration building and was wondering how long I would have to wait, when I heard a familiar voice in a Shan Tong accent calling, "Xi-ou Tan!" By concentrating on the main entrance, I had missed this person's exit from another door, so I was taken by surprise.

It was Teacher Peng, looking as if he were enjoying a comfortable life after his release from the Ox Ghost Ranch two years earlier. Wearing a new navy-blue "Mao" uniform and black cotton shoes, he carried a stylish black briefcase. "Who are you waiting for?" he asked brightly.

"The leaders of the district!" I replied sharply, almost blaming him for my failure to find the director.

"Which leader? Director Liu or Secretary Chang?" His voice developed a concerned tone.

"Both of them!" I snapped.

Looking at his watch, Teacher Peng said, "Xi-ou, go back home. It's late. They're still in a conference inside. They won't be done until midnight."

Excited, I said, "They're in the middle of a meeting? Good!"

"I still think you should go home," he said seriously. "Whatever it is, you can take care of it tomorrow." Glancing back at the nearly dark administration building, he pursed his lips and said, "I'm here on loan to the District Investigating Committee. My office is the third room on the second floor." When I did not turn my eyes away from the main entrance, he laughed and said, "All right. I'll leave. Just take care you don't catch cold." He walked into the darkness, shouting over his shoulder, "Remember, the third room on the second floor!"

I waited a few more minutes. The wind blew Teacher Peng's words to me, and suddenly I realized that he had been trying to tell me something. I gradually understood and went home. When I told Father and Rei-qing, they both felt that it could do no harm to consult him about Chi-kai's assignment. Rei-qing said, "I think Teacher Peng wants to help us. Remember when you took him your test results? He wrote that you were suffering from 'advanced' arthritis. That wasn't trivial."

When I went to the District Administration Office the following day, a Saturday, a different old man guarded the information desk. Since I knew Teacher Peng's name and office number, I merely filled out a visitor's form. He was reading documents in his office and did not appear surprised to see me. Smiling, he asked me to follow him out onto the adjoining balcony. He listened carefully to my story and wrinkled his forehead in thought.

"Xi-ou, do you remember Master Lin, who used to be a member of the working-class squad in our school? He's fat and jolly, a bit like a Buddha."

"Yes," I said in surprise. "He left a long time ago, didn't he?"

"That's right," agreed Teacher Peng. "He went to work at the District Relocation Office. Your brother's school is in his jurisdiction." He leaned heavily on the railing, his body slant accentuated by the years of hard physical labor at the Ox Ghost Ranch. "Now, just go to the Relocation Office. It's where the Working-Class Entertainment Club used to be. See Master Lin and tell him that Teacher Peng sent you. Tell him I want him to look into this matter more closely."

Thanking him, I quickly left his office, far more hopeful than I had been the day before. District leaders had the authority, but lower-level administrators such as Lin and Peng had the real power in individual cases. I contemplated the statement: "Tell him Teacher Peng sent you." Was he throwing his weight around to make Lin take a greater interest in the case or was he merely acting like a teacher, referring one of his former students to another official for further indoctrination?

The reception room of the Relocation Office had been a reading room for the Entertainment Club. Covering the walls were slogans, propaganda posters, relocation status reports, and doctored production reports. The room was filled with middle-aged couples, probably parents, and a few innocent teenagers.

A fourteen-year-old seventh-grade boy was asking to be allowed to join the Construction Corps. "Look," he pleaded, "I've stolen our identification book from my parents. Please give me a certificate right away that says that I've already been admitted. That'll mean that the Public Security Office will change my status."

The receptionist said, "Listen, young comrade, don't keep bothering me like this. Come back in two years. You're too young to go to the countryside. Besides, you need parental approval to change your status."

This seemed reasonable to me, but the boy shouted back, "You're destroying the Relocation Movement! You're preventing me from following Chairman Mao's instructions! You're anti-Revolutionary!" No one paid any attention to him. Bitterly, I thought that it was unfortunate that the boy had been born so late. In the beginning of the Cultural Revolution, he would have made an excellent Red Guard.

When my turn came, I asked the receptionist if I could see Master Lin. Still trying to get rid of the troublesome boy, she saw this as her chance. She stood and led me through several doors to his office.

Master Lin listened with concern to my story: "It's a pity. You came a little too late. We filled the industrial quota last Saturday. That includes placements both inside and outside the city, but I can see if there are any spaces in the Shanghai suburban countryside. Write down your brother's name, school, and class." As I wrote everything in my neatest characters, Master Lin pulled out a tobacco pouch and began rolling a cigarette. The meeting was over, but before I could leave, Master Lin said, "Write a letter in as much detail as possible about your brother's case. Address it to 'Working-Class Squad, Relocation Office.' "

Nodding my thanks, I left the office. I went to the District Administration Office to tell Teacher Peng what had happened, but he was in a meeting. Father and Rei-qing were impressed by my meeting with Master Lin. Father said, "I would rather have him on a suburban farm than in a remote factory. We'd still be able to keep an eye on him, and he'd be able to visit home every two months."

As Chi-kai brooded over the remote industrial position he believed was rightfully his, Rei-qing and I drafted our letter. Desiring to keep Teacher Peng involved in the matter, I took a copy to his office that afternoon. When he still had not returned to the office by 6:30, I surmised that he must have gone directly home after his meeting. Because Master Lin had said to mail the letter as soon as possible, and because I was afraid the Shanghai suburban quota would soon be filled, I decided to go to Teacher Peng's home early the next day, a Sunday.

I looked for Teacher Peng at an address given to me by a former classmate. After two frustrating hours, I decided that the mission was hopeless: Even Neighborhood Committee offices were closed on Sunday. Exhausted, I started for Kang-li's apartment, a few blocks away.

Reaching into my pocket, I found the rosary that Kang-li had given me.
She had taught me the "Ave Maria," and I chanted it repeatedly as I
made my way to her apartment, depressed.

The roads were crowded with window-shoppers, but I ignored
both the displays and the people as I trudged along. When I turned the
corner onto Kang-li's street, I saw a three-year-old girl with unusual
arched eyebrows playing around a French parasol tree. Looking more
closely, I saw Teacher Peng near her, tying his shoelaces. Afraid that he
would be swallowed suddenly by the mass of people, I sprinted to the
tree and pulled out the letter. Unwilling to tell him that I had spent
hours looking for him, I commented, "What a coincidence it is, running
into you here!"

While Teacher Peng read the letter, I deduced that the beautiful
young woman standing behind him with a baby in her arms was his
wife. I looked at her shyly. Recalling the wall poster at the start of the
Revolution and the photograph that Xiao-yi Wu had discovered under
Teacher Peng's pillow, I fervently hoped that this woman was the
"bourgeois wench." At any rate, she appeared to be worth all of
Teacher Peng's suffering. He finished reading the letter and said, "Very
good. Go ahead and mail it. I'll call Master Lin on Monday or Tuesday
and see how everything turned out."

Seeing that the business was concluded, the young woman stepped
forward to introduce herself. When she heard my name, she said, "I
have heard my husband speak of you so often! You must come to our
house for dinner soon!"

△△△ The plans were successful: Two weeks later, Chi-kai
boarded the final bus that took the young intellectuals to the suburbs
of Shanghai instead of the remote countryside. Our financial situation
was still difficult, but Rei-qing and I were far more capable these days.
Even I, a relatively poor seamstress, was able to make a pair of cloth
shoes for him. His simple luggage was neat, well made, and clean.

Leaning his head out of the window, Chi-kai waved good-bye to
us. I could see that he was miserable, and understood. Life was cruel
to him, and if it were nothing but an endless series of blows, what value

did it have? I stared down the road long after I could no longer see the bus decorated with red silk flowers. Rei-qing put her arm around me, saying, "Even though we had to go through a hundred times more effort than anyone else to make this much progress, still, we're making progress. So many people have helped us. Don't you think we're lucky, Xi-ou?"

△△△ Professor Hu, Rei-qing was right. Besides Kang-li, I was lucky enough to meet some other outstanding Chinese intellectuals who offered me great help. I often feel that without them, life would have made me cynical and cold. It is now Saturday night. Since I finished all of my errands today, I can write a longer letter tomorrow. Take care.

Sincerely,
Xi-ou Tan

 As I ate dinner last night, I watched D.C. Follies, *a television show featuring puppets that represent famous people, usually politicians. Two of them on this particular show were Richard Nixon and Henry Kissinger. Kissinger had secretly visited Beijing in 1971, and in 1972, Nixon visited China, the biggest event of the year.*

Instructions concerning the visit were relayed through the nation's chain of command, from the Central Committee down to the lowest Neighborhood Committee. All citizens were required to state publicly their feelings about this monumental event at special meetings and to understand the Central Committee's directive: "Don't be too warm to Nixon, but don't be too cold. Don't look up to him, but don't look down on him, either." Along with the rest of the young intellectuals, I attended several meetings at the local Neighborhood Committee office to prepare for the visit.

Work squads were organized to clean the streets and stores and remove outdated wall posters. Residents were told to stay home unless absolutely necessary. The Shanghai People's Militia patrolled the streets to ensure that no class enemies perpetrated any violence or anti-Revolutionary actions during Nixon's stay in Shanghai. A group of young intellectuals conspired to block Nixon's limousine and hand him statements exposing the true nature of life, but one of them informed the Public Security Office and the rest were jailed.

Nixon could not have known the depth of the damage his visit would cause our family.

17

Dear Professor Hu,

Chi-kai left for the farm in November 1971.
Within a month, it was announced that U.S.
President Nixon would be visiting Shanghai in January 1972, the same month in which Mother was to be
released from prison. Everybody was required to attend various meetings to prepare for the visit. Although I went to dozens
myself, I can only recall one.

A retired adult-school teacher, the most intellectual of the Neighborhood Committee cadres, was presiding. First he explained the
Central Committee's directive word by word to the people jammed into
the large room. When he finished, he became excited: "I believe that
Nixon's visit to China is a clear indication of the victory of Mao
Zedong thought in foreign policy. The U.S. imperialists are coming to
us. They're the ones who want to visit our great leader, Chairman Mao.
Chairman Mao isn't going over there! It's like a wife visiting her
husband's mother. We all know the mother doesn't visit the daughter-in-law! We'll never let ourselves be cheated by the U.S. imperialists.
Don't think that just because Chairman Mao is talking to him means
that Nixon is a good man. Just one example will convince you otherwise. Do you remember hearing that Nixon is bringing his 'first lady'
with him? Do you know that 'first lady' means his first wife? We
Chinese refer to such a one as the oldest wife. American leaders have
several hundred wives."

The audience, composed primarily of housewives with an occasional young intellectual like me, hissed in rage. Two young intellectuals sitting near me winked and snickered to each other, also aware of the correct meaning of "first lady." I heard them whispering, "How many wives has Chairman Mao had? I'm going to write to Comrade Jian-qing and tell her to have this fool up here thrown in jail—according to his interpretation, Comrade Jian-qing is the fourth or fifth lady at best."

Over dinner that night, I recounted the retired teacher's absurd argument to my family. Jian-nan laughed until he choked on his rice. When he regained control of himself, he sang a rhyme he had been taught in kindergarten:

> *Smiling American back-stabbing dogs!*
> *Gobble the world for their own just like hogs!*
> *What they don't destroy with guns, bombs, and tanks,*
> *They steal and hoard in tall Wall Street banks!*
> *They ignore the sick and tortured men's screams,*
> *While they further realize their imperialist dreams!*

Rei-qing smiled, saying, "Keep it down!"

Pretending outrage, Jian-nan said, "What? You object to my singing a Revolutionary song? If Nixon knocked on the door and begged us for a bowl of rice, I'd sing this song right in his face!"

Everyone laughed except Father. After thinking for a while, he said, "Bettering the relations between China and the United States will not just have a profound effect on global affairs; it will also bring about changes in national policy."

"For better or worse?" I asked.

"It's hard to say," he said, putting down his chopsticks. "For years I searched for a rationale behind the Grand Cultural Revolution. When Lin Biao's plane crashed, I came up with some theories. The newspapers said, 'Great Leader Chairman Mao has a grand plan in mind, and every event that occurs is part of his great strategy,' but after Lin Biao betrayed him, it was clear to everyone that Chairman Mao really wasn't in control. I think that the Cultural Revolution was due mostly to infighting in the Party's Central Committee. People are always going to struggle for power. Going to the extreme of having a revolution to ensure the victory of a faction was unprecedented."

"But all this jockeying for power was among themselves. Why should they get ordinary people involved?" Rei-qing asked.

"Look at history," Father replied. "In all countries, in all ages, it's always the common people who suffer most during any conflict between leaders. The Chinese people tolerate this oppression, but maybe people of other nations won't. Remember how we once discussed what Mencius said? 'It is the water that floats a boat and carries it from place to place. But it is the same water that can overturn it.' I believe that there will be a time when the people will stand up for themselves, but when, and whether I will live to see it, I can't say."

The exchange made me think of Du Mu's poem "The O Fang Palace," a protest against the extravagant, lecherous lifestyle of Emperor Qing. It had these lines:

> His subjects enraged but silenced from fear,
> The king grows more wicked with each passing year.

It struck me that although the people were terrified of the emperor's power in the Qing dynasty, they at least felt anger. People today were afraid to even show it. Du Mu continued with this couplet:

> Blame not the invaders for destroying your nation,
> Long ago it rotted, before the invasion.

If we thought we had had trouble during the visit of the ousted Cambodian royalty, I was sure it was a picnic compared to what we would face for the leader of a superpower. Anticipating spot searches, we sent out all manuscripts and other possibly incriminating documents and turned out our lights at seven each night. The Runt himself often participated in midnight searches of our home, even frisking Father. Insults like this were harder to bear as we grew older, and this was the worst since we had moved to Angel Cave. We hated Father's tormentors and felt guilty for being unable to protect him.

△△△ Several months earlier, we had received a letter from the Baskct Bridge requesting heavy work clothes for Mother. She was to be transferred to a labor camp. The mimeographed letter did not mention Mother's or our family's name; only the address singled us out. Rei-qing and I immediately went to the Basket Bridge to find out more. A scruffy, middle-aged cadre met us. "My mother was sentenced to seven years in jail," explained Rei-qing. "The time she spent in prison awaiting trial was to have been taken off her sentence. She should be released in January, in forty-two days! Why are they sending her to this labor camp?"

"January of this coming year?" the cadre murmured. Folding his arms, he said, "It's precisely because she is being released soon that she's being sent there."

"Why?" we chorused.

"Nixon is coming! After January, the Nine Classes of Blacks will be denied access to Shanghai," the cadre said. Kang-li had told us that Shanghai had been subdivided into regions based on economic prosperity. Any area that might possibly be visited by Westerners would be off-limits to the Nine Classes. Kang-li's home was in a relatively wealthy section, but because of her contacts, she was in no danger of being evicted, despite her borderline status.

We received another letter from the Basket Bridge in December. To facilitate the transition to the labor camp in the remote province of An Hui, Mother had been sent to a farm in the Shanghai suburbs. We would be allowed one visit. That very afternoon Rei-qing and I bought clothes and snacks for Mother, using every penny we had saved.

We rose at dawn the next day and boarded the bus to the farm, arriving before noon. It was cold and overcast, and in the distance, we saw dim shapes moving in the cotton fields. As we ran toward them, they noticed us and stopped their work. One picker gave a piercing cry, and others joined in the lament. Out of the random wailings, I picked out our names and ran in that direction. I had never considered Mother old, but now she appeared ancient. For the first time I noticed scars that the long prison term had left on her pale forehead. Her bright, beautiful eyes were red and tearful.

I had no sooner entered my mother's embrace when a uniformed guard appeared in the distance, shouting, "One-oh-seven! What are you trying to do? You made everybody start crying. You want to cause trouble, that's what I think!" The guard approached us clumsily, his new, thick uniform in stark contrast to the thin, old work clothes of the prisoners. The crowd around us dispersed even as the guard spoke.

We showed the guard our letter from the Basket Bridge giving us permission to visit. After satisfying himself that the letter was authentic, the guard took the three of us to a room where we could talk. "If any of you start crying, I'll terminate the visit immediately!" he warned.

We huddled together on the floor and the guard left. For the first time in seven years, we could freely discuss what had happened to the family. Mother told us more about her life in prison.

"I'm a Christian now. Aunt Y-jin led me to the Lord. When I first learned that I couldn't return home, I couldn't accept it. But I prayed a lot and gradually calmed down. Even this morning, I was thinking that although I don't know when they'll transport me, it wouldn't be so bad if I had to spend my whole life right here. This farm is right beneath the She mountain, and nearby there's a big Catholic church. I had heard that in the beginning of the Grand Cultural Revolution the church was destroyed by the Red Guards, but yesterday my fellow inmates pointed it out to me in the distance. I could barely make it out, but seeing it made me feel at peace. I didn't expect that today, when I saw you, I wouldn't be able to control my feelings."

Mother held my hand tightly as I stared at her face. She was still beautiful, and her beauty renewed my strength. We told Mother about our sufferings of the previous years. Occasionally she would ask questions, cry, or comment, and we were moved by the details of her prison life and the courage she had acquired. Furiously, I asked, "Mother, do you know why we're still kept apart? It's because Nixon, that stinking rotten egg, decided to visit China!"

Rei-qing said, "Well, Father said that Nixon's visit isn't an isolated event. He thinks many foreign delegations will visit. It doesn't look like there will be a definite date when you can come back to the city."

"It's all right, children. It doesn't matter. I've already thought this through. The work of men cannot change what is happening. We can only accept it. Opening the doors to our country is good. There will be exchange with the outside. This oppression cannot last much longer. Our personal fates are always linked with the fate of our nation. There's nothing we can do."

"That's what Father said, too. He said that perhaps our relatives living in America will try to get in touch with us."

Mother's eyes shone: "Really? What else did he say?" She was hungry for details.

People looked in as we talked. Some were prisoners, some were guards. When we heard whispers that it was lunchtime, a sickly girl with short, thin hair peeked into the room and said, "Aunt Y-yao, will your girls be staying for lunch?" Mother smiled and said, "Go ahead. You can have my share."

The girl was not much older than I. "Who's that?" I asked. "Why's she trying to mooch your rice?"

"That girl's very clever. They say she used to be a Red Guard and that she beat one of her teachers to death. She was an orphan who had been adopted by a childless couple of PLA cadres, and they insisted that she be jailed for killing her teacher. She arrived here the same time I did. Every day she complained that her adoptive parents were too honest. 'After all,' she said, 'my classmates killed lots more people than I did, and nobody put them in jail!' She hadn't gotten off the bus before she started an affair with a male prisoner. When they were caught, the guards held a public meeting to chastise them. She was scared to death and tried to kill herself by eating pesticide, but they took her to the hospital and pumped her stomach. She was released just a few days ago, so I put something aside for her at every meal."

I could not respond. Mother continued, "I really thank your father. If he weren't taking care of you, how could you have grown up so well and learned so much in these seven years? He's a much better parent than I am. In so many ways, life on the outside is far more difficult and dangerous than inside."

Afraid that Mother would start crying, Rei-qing changed the subject: "Mother, in a letter you once asked us to bring you as much sugar as possible. We brought five pounds today, but why do you want so much?"

"It's not for me," Mother smiled. "There are two nuns here who don't have families, so no one brings them anything. They both have hepatitis, and doctors say sugar helps control it. I'm going to give it to them."

The three of us had an endless number of things to discuss, but it was already sunset. The guards did not chase out Rei-qing and me, but Mother's cellmate came to warn us that we might miss the last bus to the city. An attractive young girl peeked in and quoted a famous poet:

> To meet one another is such great strain,
> And parting leads only to greater pain.

"She used to be an actress," Mother said. "She fumbled one of her lines during a performance and was branded an anti-Revolutionary. She tried to kill herself twice, but somebody saved her."

In the few short hours of our visit, Rei-qing and I had seen two girls our age confined in prison, sacrificial lambs of the Revolution. Their experiences had been different but they had one thing in common: Both, in the flower of youth, had despaired of life and tried to end it.

On a cold but sunny January day, President Nixon arrived in Shanghai. The newsstand on Huai Hai Road where my friends and I met to exchange books and notes was on the route of Nixon's motorcade. I went there to get a newspaper early; the area had not yet been cordoned off. The old man who usually ran the newsstand had been replaced by a young man and a young woman, most likely undercover officers. I paid for the paper without incident, but as I headed back to Tien-ping Road, I was accosted by a plainclothesman.

"Halt," he commanded.

Hundreds of seemingly ordinary pedestrians had suddenly joined hands to prevent people from entering or leaving Huai Hai Road. All attention was fixed on the tallest structure in our district, a nine-story building from which many people had jumped in the early part of the

Cultural Revolution. Several families living there had invited me over for meals, but I had always refused, frightened by my strange foreboding about a place where so many people had met their death. The once-bright red walls had faded until they looked as if they were covered with dried blood. Traffic on the street stopped, as at least twenty uniformed policemen ran toward the building, blowing whistles and shouting through megaphones.

The cause of the commotion was a milk bottle. It had fallen from a windowsill on one of the upper floors, shattering on the street. An investigation committee, assembled on the spot, questioned many witnesses and issued its findings: The west wind was the culprit. To prevent another such occurrence, however, families with windows facing Huai Hai Road were ordered by the Shanghai People's Militia and the Public Security Office to remove all objects from their sills.

At ten o'clock I went out with my basket on the pretense of going to the market. No one was sitting at the end of the lane watching, since Madame Couvre was still laid up with her broken femur. I headed for a grocery store across the street from the newsstand on Huai Hai Road.

"You! Where do you think you're going?" someone shouted before I was within ten feet of Huai Hai Road.

"I need a refill of soy sauce," I explained to the two men sitting on the sidewalk, holding up an empty bottle.

"Things are about ready to start. You can't pass," one of them said. When I asked for more details, they shooed me away. Realizing that the moment had arrived, I did not pursue the matter further. I stood on my toes to get the best possible view of Huai Hai Road. It was almost empty, but a few people still ambled about, almost certainly militia members.

I remembered the first time Mother had sent me to this same store to buy soy sauce. I had been no more than seven, and when I returned triumphantly clutching my bottle of soy sauce, Mother kneeled in the middle of the road, her arms outstretched to receive me. Now I was an adult, and Mother was old. She had served the prison sentence that had kept us apart, but we were still separated.

△△△ Some people did benefit from Nixon's visit. Since China wished to improve relations with the United States, people who had connections overseas were treated much better than ordinary citizens. One such person was Professor Li, one of Uncle Xiong's relatives, who had stock in his family's company in the United States.

Uncle Xiong's son, Tao-ran, went to visit his aunt and uncle one day, and there met his aunt's brother, Professor Li. Professor Li had ·taught German at a university in Beijing, and his experiences during the Grand Cultural Revolution were tragic: His wife had committed suicide early on, and he himself had been confined to an Ox Ghost Ranch for eight years. When he was originally sent to the ranch, the fact that he had a large amount of stock in an American firm owned by some of his relatives had counted against him, but with Nixon's visit, it became a reason for release.

With no family left in Beijing, he made long visits to his sister in Shanghai. Years of little contact with people made him agoraphobic, but staying home was intolerably boring, since his sister and brother-in-law had destroyed all their books in fear of the Red Guards. There was nothing for him to do except play with his sister's two grandchildren. Tao-ran thought of Rei-qing and me and asked Professor Li if he would be interested in helping us with our English.

Professor Li hesitated: "Tao-ran, don't get involved with these things. I've just been released, and I don't want to be thrown back. If I do this, I could be accused of using Western bourgeois culture to pollute the minds of young people. A foreign language, by nature, is anti-Revolutionary. It's like poison. It's not that I don't want to teach; I'm just scared of being sent back to the ranch."

Tao-ran laughed: "A foreign language bears no marks of class distinction. It's only a tool. Chairman Mao's quotations have been translated into dozens of languages. You can always say that you're teaching foreign languages in the service of the revolution." He stopped smiling and continued gravely, "Professor Li, I'll personally vouch for the integrity of these two sisters. They'll never betray you. I'd stake my life on it. They're both very intelligent. Just point them in the right direction. They'll follow through and learn something that will benefit them their whole lives."

Professor Li reluctantly agreed. Rei-qing was still in the country-side, so I went to visit him by myself, bringing a college-level English text. He chose random paragraphs for me to read aloud and quizzed me on grammar.

"Did you learn all this by yourself?" he asked.

"This book, yes, I did read this by myself, but in school they taught us the basic rules of English pronunciation and grammar."

"What other languages have you studied?"

"Japanese and Russian. I borrowed a language record and text-book recently to study German, but I haven't made much progress."

Professor Li grew excited: "I don't really know Japanese and Russian. I think you have a good understanding of English, so I don't see any point in teaching you that, but German is my specialty. *Wir wollen nun Deutsch lernen!*"

So I studied German with Professor Li for two hours each day. It was only a coincidence that I had begun studying German in the first place: Kang-li always kept me in mind, and when a patient had wished to please her by lending her a language book and records, she accepted them for me. It had not been part of my independent-study plan, but I never let any opportunity pass. Since I could not keep the materials long, I copied the textbook day and night into the notebook I had made by sewing used envelopes together.

Since Professor Li had come from an affluent family and had learned languages while sightseeing in Europe, he sometimes forgot his caution and told his colleagues vacationing in Shanghai of my progress. Teaching gave his life new purpose, and as he grew more energetic, he lost his fear of venturing outside. When his month's vacation with his sister was over, he prepared to return to Beijing. He wanted me to come over even the day before he left, so I bought him a photo album as a going-away present. When he opened the door for me, I saw a strange man standing behind him. The face of the tall, thin, gray-haired man showed signs of edema, and his broad forehead and deep-set eyes made him an imposing sight.

Professor Li said, "This is Professor Shan, my colleague in Western

linguistics. We just finished talking. Would you go and wait in the
sitting room? I'm going to walk Professor Shan downstairs."

Smiling shyly, I did as I was told. Both professors returned several
minutes later. Professor Li said, "I'm leaving tomorrow morning, but
Professor Shan is staying another two weeks. He has offered to spend
them working with you."

I was immensely pleased, and amazed that a professor would offer
to give private lessons to a stranger, especially under such unpredictable
political conditions. For no pay or acknowledgment, he was still willing
to teach me. For years I had dreamed of having a teacher, and now a
professor from one of China's most prestigious universities was standing in front of me, waiting for my answer. "Yes! Yes, I would like that
very much!" I said, my voice cracking with excitement.

He carefully wrote his address and full name, Qi-tai Shan, on my
notebook. "Tomorrow afternoon," he said coldly. "One-thirty sharp.
I'll be waiting for you." Professor Li walked him downstairs, and I
reflected that I had discerned no humor in Professor Shan's face the
entire time I had seen him.

The next day, Professor Shan and I went to the train station to bid
farewell to Professor Li. While Professor Li was making some last-
minute arrangements, Professor Shan and I waited silently. Finally, he
asked, "Where were you born?"

"Shanghai," I replied, grateful that he spoke first.

"How old are you?"

"Twenty-two."

"Do you have any brothers or sisters?"

"One sister and two brothers."

"What do your parents do?"

I paused: "They're peasants. They can't read or write." I half-
expected to be struck by lightning for telling such a lie. If I had told him
the truth, he might have been terrified to get involved with such a
family, and I would lose my opportunity. After all, who would want
to teach an anti-Revolutionary whelp? I blushed and looked down,
fidgeting nervously.

"Very well," Professor Shan said, smiling for the first time. "You
are the daughter of illiterate peasants."

△△△ Professor Shan had also agreed to teach one of Professor Li's former students, a young man named Y-si Tian. Small talk was not one of Professor Shan's favorite diversions, so when Y-si and I arrived, class began immediately. We listened to him lecture for three full hours, until his wife, an elementary-school teacher, returned home. She would pull a newspaper from her bag and hand it to him, a signal for us to leave.

I awoke early every morning to work on the long assignments until it was time to go to class. Although Y-si seemed far more fluent than I at first, our positions reversed within ten days. He was too busy with his marriage plans to do the assignments, and on the eleventh day of class, he went to his home in Zeng Ru and did not come back. Although I was convinced that I had a talent for languages and worked quickly, Professor Shan never praised me. Whenever I wanted to say, "This assignment is too long—I won't have time to do it," I reminded myself that this was a once-in-a-lifetime opportunity, swallowed the words, and resolved to do my best to complete the work. I finished the equivalent of a year of college-level German by the time the two weeks were over.

"Tomorrow I am leaving," Professor Shan said flatly, closing his textbook. He ended the class thirty minutes early. It dawned on me that he was suffering from severe fatigue. His face was more swollen than normal, his eyelids drooped, and even his hair seemed whiter.

"Professor Shan, you are exhausted!" I gasped.

He ignored this. "In attaining this level of competence in German, you now have a basic understanding of the language. This will make your future independent study easier."

"Can I learn from you further by correspondence? You could send me homework, and I could do it and then send it back to you. You could correct it and send it back to me."

"Certainly!" he said without hesitation. "But for a while I'm going to visit some other cities, and I won't be back at school in Beijing for about another month—say the middle of March."

△△△ Y-si rushed back to Shanghai the next day to say good-bye to his teacher. He did some shopping for his long-awaited wedding and invited me to his home in Zeng Ru. "My whole family's heard of Xi-ou Tan and everyone is dying to meet you!" he said gaily.

"Even if you hadn't invited me, I have been wanting to meet your parents, anyway. You told me that your father knows a lot of scientists, especially physicists. I'd like to bring one of Jian-nan's papers and have your father forward them to an expert."

"Absolutely! No problem!" he said enthusiastically. "Father has the highest respect for people willing to study. He's a physician and has treated lots of important people. He has many contacts and cares about young people."

I spent three days at his parents' house in Zeng Ru after his wedding. One purpose of the visit was to give them one of Jian-nan's papers, but I also wanted to acquaint myself with this extraordinary family. From Y-si's descriptions, I had developed a mental picture of each family member that I found to be almost exact. I was able to talk to them, especially his parents, as if we were old friends. Although the couple worked ten hours a day at the hospital, they still treated me like an honored guest. Sun Tian, Y-si's father, spoke with me at length, discussing the political environment, their ideals, and their attitudes toward life. I told him all about my family.

"Xi-ou, honesty is the most precious of all virtues, but it's not a good strategy in everyday life. Are you so honest with everybody?" Sun Tian asked, sitting up in his cane chair.

Shaking my head, I said, "No, I almost always lie about my family's situation, because the Rightists, anti-Revolutionaries, and the Nine Blacks have become the untouchable caste. But Father taught me, 'Never lie to a real person.' That's my guide."

The wrinkles on Sun Tian's forehead softened: "You are like a water lily. It grows in the mud, but it stays clean, wholesome, and beautiful."

The family listened for three nights to my stories of our family's trouble since 1957. The night before I left, Sun Tian picked up an elaborate terrarium from the windowsill: "My child, can I ask a favor of you?"

Mrs. Tian misunderstood her husband and said, "What do you want Xi-ou to do for you? She's only visiting us and you want her to carry this somewhere for you? Y-si's brothers go to the city often enough. Anything you want moved, you can give to them."

Smiling patiently at his wife, Sun Tian continued, "Could you take this to Mr. Tan on Tien-ping Road and say this comes with my best wishes and highest regards?"

I did not know what to say.

"When I saw how pure and honest you were, my first reaction was fear that you would suffer at the hands of those who lie and cheat. I was relieved to hear your father's rule. My child, you cannot wish to harm people, but you should take care of yourself. You need a sixth sense these days to tell you when you are in danger. But still, you must guard and cultivate a small piece of land inside yourself—and never pollute this space under any circumstances. This is the only way you can keep your integrity while allowing the tree of your life to grow and blossom."

On the morning I left, I got up early and thought about his words. Sun Tian came up to see me in the living room and I reminded him about Jian-nan's paper: "Working with my brother is a struggle for us. He's too fast. Last year, he proposed this concept of periodic fields. My sister and I found it incomprehensible, so he told us to learn quantum mechanics, quantum field theory, and Lie algebra. My sister and I couldn't keep up with him. That both learning and doing original science are trivial to him makes me uncomfortable. On the other hand, I'm his sister, and I know his situation better than anyone else. No one ever gave him any advice, but the book 'wish list' he gave me was so specific that I could almost always find exactly what he wanted in used-book stores. His phenomenal abilities make me think that maybe there's something to his theories."

"It's possible," Sun Tian broke in. "I believe such geniuses exist. It's a different kind of genius than the picture of Chairman Mao that Lin Biao painted. It's similar to what Jian-nan wrote Big Brother Wu, that wherever there is sunshine, the violets blossom. I'm going to mail this paper to my friends in the Academy of Science and ask them to referee it. After that, we can decide how to help your brother further."

Before they left for work, Y-si's parents gave me a warm invitation to visit again soon. I found it hard to say good-bye.

△△△ I gave Father the present and enthusiastically described Y-si's family to my own. Father was sad that he had nothing to give in return, but he said he would write a poem for Sun Tian. Rei-qing then recalled that a letter had arrived from Professor Shan. She pulled it from a hiding place and handed it to me.

> Comrade Xi-ou:
> I have finished correcting your homework and have sent it back by registered mail. The pace of your learning is abnormal, much too quick. While I was in Shanghai, I urged you to be quick because then I wanted you to have a basic grasp of the language while I was still there, but now you should slow down. To progress, you must alternate between periods of maximum alertness and maximum relaxation.
> From now on, you may mail me one homework set every week.
>
> Regards,
> Qi-tai Shan

The letter was dated March 16. Professor Shan had said that he would not arrive in Beijing until the middle of March, so he must have started correcting my homework as soon as he arrived there. I felt like the luckiest person in the world: the finest family, friends, and master teachers. What else could I possibly want? So there, Runt, Couvre, Alley Cat. . . . I have the love that people have given me.

△△△ Professor Hu, studying German was the turning point of my independent-study program. If Kang-li was my first teacher of life, then Professor Shan led me to enlightenment. I could not pay them a penny then, and now I do not think that I would ever be able to pay them enough. You were educated at proper universities, so perhaps you cannot understand my feelings.

Nixon's visit meant that my mother had to spend even more time in prison, but because of it, I was able to study German with a real professor. Of course, nothing could compensate for not having my mother with me, but I like to think that something good can come out of every bad thing that happens.

Sincerely,
Xi-ou Tan

When I first arrived in the United States, I related all of my experiences to an uncle I had never met before. He said, "You're still young. Try to forget these terrible things." I told him that I wanted to remember them, and that I wanted to write them down for future generations. After that, I often had the desire to write, but I always was too busy with my studies and research. By writing to Professor Hu, I was not only helping a distraught man, I was also fulfilling a desire that had lain dormant too long.

As I looked through some of the things I had brought with me from China, I found a letter that my brother Chi-kai had written in 1972, the second spring that he was at the farm. The local Agricultural Administration had announced that the ten communal farms in the area would be sending the young intellectuals back to the city factories. The farm system was to be used as a training center; those who had been there longer would be sent back to the city and new students would be brought in. Chi-kai's letter ran in part:

This evening the farm administration gave the alarm that five hundred mu of cotton needed to be treated with pesticide. At ten o'clock at night, we newcomers, along with several high-school students of the classes of 1966 and 1967, went to the cotton fields to spread the powder. We carried the containers of powder on our backs and stood in a row at one end of the fields. The wind was blowing against us as we walked across a field so big we couldn't see the other end of it. The pesticide powder was extremely poisonous, so at first we used masks and protected our hands by pulling our sleeves down over them. We were afraid that the chemical would still pass through our clothing and into our bodies. However, the weather was so hot we couldn't worry about it too much. We had to do it at night so the dew would make the pesticide stick to the plants. There was so much land to cover that everyone became a "powder man." The pesticide got into our throats, making us cough and feel nauseous. Everyone had swollen eyes. The powder mixed with sweat and dew and stuck to us in little balls that stung our skin. We had welts all over, even on our scalps. We didn't finish the field until sunrise.

The older students, who have been here for three or four years, would soon be permitted to return to the city, so, to make sure of that, they worked harder than any of us. This made us newcomers suffer. I felt sleepy the whole night. I was scattering the powder, then I was sleepwalking. Everybody was really angry at these older students and called them names. They used to bully us, since we were smaller and couldn't do as much physical labor as they could. Now they're very kind to us, because you have to have the whole group's approval to be sent back. It's called "back-to-back" discussion. If someone who wanted to go back received a bad comment from one of us, it would hurt his chances. However, even after all that, they're not that afraid of us, since the key people they have to be friends with are the Party secretaries, the old peasants, and the young intellectuals who are Party members. They say that everybody who is eligible is preparing gifts for these people. They know that the money spent on the gifts is wasted, but they'll try anything they think might possibly help.

The married people are really upset about this. They can't go back, because it would increase the population of the city by too much. The couple would have to be separated. There are a lot of married couples here, and some of them already have children. We even have a nursery now. . . .

Reading through these old letters helps me work through my feelings. The new policy to which Chi-kai had referred allowed Rei-qing to come back to the city. The amount of money she was paid on the farm was small compared to what she could earn in Shanghai. However, money was only secondary: With Rei-qing employed in the city, it would be far harder for us to be rooted out.

18

Dear Professor Hu,

Rei-qing was allowed to return to the city in
1973. Because she could read and write Japanese,
her file was picked up by a large Shanghai steel
factory that was negotiating with a Japanese firm. The
recruiter showed her file to the director of the Mao Zedong
Thought Propaganda Team, with the comment that it would be
inappropriate to allow someone with such a family background to be
involved in meetings with foreigners. Waving his hand in the air
broadly, the director dismissed this idea. "Comrade, don't forget our
Party's line about class struggle: 'We remember your roots, but we look
to your actions.' We can reform her. With invincible Mao Zedong
thought as our guide, there is nothing we can't do!"

The director was greedy for Rei-qing's skill. Because he was in
charge of the indoctrination program, he had no superiors to fear, and
the political timing for such a move was right. Lin Biao's mysterious
death and Nixon's visit to China had a significant impact on both
Chinese domestic and international politics. Now that China had been
opened to international markets, finding a capable interpreter for the
steel factory was a matter of top priority.

Her head held high, Rei-qing stepped into the Shanghai steel
factory. She would have stood out in any crowd, despite her simple
standard attire. Her coal-black hair was cut like a soft helmet about her
head, her cheeks and lips were high in color. Her broad forehead and
marblelike complexion marked her as a striking beauty.

The secretary in charge of production, the Propaganda Squad director, the chief engineer, the head of the technical department, and sixteen others sat with her at the huge negotiation table. In spite of their different backgrounds and ages, all wore the same Mao uniform. The Japanese negotiators at the other end of the table wore well-tailored suits and shiny leather shoes. Their interpreter was a young man, not yet twenty-five. He had majored in Chinese at a prestigious Japanese university, and his fluency was remarkable.

The white-haired chairman of the Japanese firm participated in the talks, although he spoke no Chinese. He had heard that the Cultural Revolution had shut down all the schools, ceasing development in science and technology, and this meeting would reveal to him the status of the Chinese steel industry.

The director of the Propaganda Squad was even more nervous than Rei-qing. Rei-qing spoke slowly to the Japanese for the first ten minutes, but her pronunciation and vocabulary were adequate for the task. She was less experienced than the Japanese interpreter, but she kept a clear head, gradually gaining confidence. Before the meeting was over, no language barrier existed.

At the third meeting, the Japanese asked the chief engineer of the Chinese factory a simple engineering question. Unable to answer, the man nervously stammered, "I don't know . . ." in the Shanghai dialect, which the Japanese interpreter did not understand. Rei-qing cleverly translated the remark as a joke, and everyone laughed.

When the first stage of the negotiations had ended, the Japanese chairman of the board was so impressed with Rei-qing that he presented her with a gift. "Miss Tan," the old man said, bowing as he gave her one of the best calculators available, "you did an excellent job. I hope that we will be successful in our negotiations and that before long, we will see you in Tokyo."

A daughter's success is a father's pride. Many years of Father's persistent work had turned Rei-qing into a well-educated, capable woman. She reported to us her observations on the differences between the Japanese and Chinese engineers: "The Japanese people really knew what they were doing. Our engineers are lazy and don't want to be responsible for anything. I remember once hearing the chief engineer brag about how well he tailored his wife's and daughter's fashionable clothes during the Revolution. He wasn't even embarrassed to admit that he spent all his working hours designing clothes! I don't think he should have wasted so much time like that when his mind was trained for tailoring steel."

"This sort of thing is a real tragedy for the country," said Father unhappily. "Child, you did right at your meeting. You should always pay close attention in the future so you can continue to save face for our country. Thirty years ago, we Chinese wiped out the Japanese invaders. Now they come again, but this time with the world's most advanced technology. This could be even more threatening. My generation fought the Japanese on almost every inch of our land. Your generation has to fight them, too, but unfortunately, China is still in the weaker position."

Because of Rei-qing's outstanding performance, the Propaganda Squad and the party secretary decided to induct her as a Party member. The Personnel Department sent a man to the local Public Security Office to investigate Rei-qing's neighborhood record.

The Runt objected to the idea of Rei-qing as a Party member. "All Tan's children are anti-Revolutionary whelps who support their father. That dog once wrote an anti-Revolutionary treatise as thick as this," he said, holding his hands about two feet apart. "He wrote it all under his children's protection. And you want to allow these people to join our Party? We just don't agree." When the investigator asked to read this treatise, the embarrassed Runt had to admit that they had used it to wash the windows.

The personnel man went to the Neighborhood Committee next, asking the still-limping Madame Couvre about Rei-qing's behavior around home. Without wasting any time on thought, Madame Couvre said, "The Tan children are all very bad. It's difficult for me to express, but I'm sure about how I feel about them. It's not acceptable for them to rebel."

"What do you mean?" the investigator asked, smiling to himself.

"I remember a good example!" answered Madame Couvre excitedly. "Last year, on our great leader Chairman Mao's birthday, they had the gall *not* to eat a long-long-life noodle for him! They bullied me because I was limping, and they thought I wouldn't check on them. But I went anyway, and I took the top off the pot with my own hands. There wasn't a single noodle to be seen!"

Neither the Runt nor Madame Couvre impressed the investigator. The next step for Rei-qing was an interview with the Party secretary, who told her that because of the results of the investigation, she would not be asked to join the Party in the near future. She hid her elation, saying, "I am so far away from meeting the requirements to be an advanced member of the Proletariat that I must work hard to improve myself. When I feel that I have met them, I'll apply on my own." For once, she was grateful to the Runt and Madame Couvre. The respect for the Communist Party after the Grand Cultural Revolution was lower now than ever. Rei-qing wanted only to continue working hard and be her best "anti-Revolutionary whelp" self.

△△△ Tao-ran and Rei-qing had been neighbors since childhood, often playing together until he was sent to boarding school. Only on holidays, when he and his parents visited us, did he have any opportunity to be alone with Rei-qing. For many years, they met occasionally, and the only times they went anywhere together were when they took messages from his parents to Father. Rei-qing always took me along and invariably sandwiched me between them. Rather than speak to each other directly, they often relayed their comments to me. I did my best to bring the two together, reporting every detail to Father.

Tao-ran was a striking, mild-mannered man with highly regarded technical abilities, so it was not surprising that several girls secretly stalked him. A professor's daughter boldly wrote him a love letter that he left unanswered. Tao-ran's parents had never stated that they wanted him to marry Rei-qing, but he suspected it and also thought that she would be an excellent partner. While her beauty did not go unnoticed, he was most impressed by her intelligence, kindness, and common sense.

Our difficult family situation was always on his mind, and he admired our persistent devotion to our independent studies, even under the worst imaginable conditions. Although at times he believed our efforts useless, he still zealously sought out books and journals for us, and he donated spare radio parts or chemicals for our projects. Outside of work, Tao-ran was bored, since virtually all of his former classmates were already married. Attention from female colleagues only embarrassed him, and his usual response to a woman's compliment was to smile and look down. When the boredom became unendurable, he tinkered with electronic devices. He often wondered whether he was waiting for Rei-qing to show her intentions, but he could not decide when to make his move. Rei-qing was a highly independent woman. It confused him that the two of them—from such different backgrounds and living under such different economic conditions—were drawn together.

Not until Rei-qing returned from the farm in 1973 did the situation resolve itself. Both families were pleased with the match, but when it came down to the details, Rei-qing was hesitant. "Sister, are you afraid that you don't really love brother Tao-ran?" I asked when we were alone.

"I didn't say that," Rei-qing replied defensively.

"Then why are you so hesitant?"

"I'm thinking . . . is it necessary to get married?"

"Why not?" I asked, surprised.

"Our parents are still having problems. How can I be selfish and start my own family?"

"Dear sister," I said warmly, "marriage is a new challenge in which people learn how to accept each other, deepen their mutual understanding and solidify their feelings. It's important to learn how to cultivate one another and the shared interests. These things are challenges, but they don't stop you from sharing our parents' burden. The only difference now is that one person's burden can be shared by two. And one person's happiness can be shared by two."

Rei-qing was silent as I continued, "Brother Tao-ran graduated from college when he was twenty-one and has been working in a factory for the last twelve years. If our parents hadn't been involved in Uncle Ji-wang's case, Uncle Xiong would have suggested that you two get engaged back in 1966. They've helped support us for the past ten years, without ever saying anything snide. Brother Tao-ran waited all those years for you, and he deserves a happy ending. He and his parents truly have good hearts. Unless you don't love each other, I don't see any reason why you shouldn't marry him."

△△△ The wedding was scheduled for November. In mid-August, I fell ill with strange symptoms. My test results were normal, but I simply did not feel like studying or doing anything else. Rei-qing took me to several hospitals, with inconclusive results. Kang-li's brother, a respected neurosurgeon, asked Kang-li and Rei-qing a battery of questions. After thinking for a few minutes, he asked, "Has she recently undergone any stressful events?"

"Absolutely not," Rei-qing answered. "She has a lot of emotional strength. She suffered more at the beginning of the Cultural Revolution than most people could stand. And she has a strong will and personality, too. For example, she learned four years' worth of college-level German in seventy-nine days."

"When was that?" asked the doctor, with a quickening of interest.

"Just a few months ago. She's very energetic. She only sleeps one or two hours a night and doesn't show any fatigue," Rei-qing answered proudly.

"That's the problem! This is also a form of stress. She's demanding too much from her brain, so it went on strike. Madame Curie, by asking too much of her brain, started to sleepwalk."

He jotted down something on a piece of paper and gave it to Rei-qing, saying, "These are the most ordinary tranquilizers available. You can buy them at any drugstore without prescription. I think that as long as she doesn't overwork herself, she'll be back to normal within three months."

I was fully recovered within three months, and Father wrote a poem with a line for each of the one hundred days I spent in bed.

When my homework arrived at Professor Shan's home each Wednesday afternoon, he read it through once carefully and then corrected it with a red pen after dinner. He would mail it back the next morning, so that I would be sure to receive it by the following Saturday afternoon. He received no homework assignments during my illness, but, accustomed to mailing me something each week, he sent me instructions on how best to study. Rei-qing wrote him of my illness, but he still sent me a letter each week. Although we had spent only fourteen days face-to-face, he spent fourteen months correcting my homework.

I finally wrote him a letter, saying that I regretted letting down so many people, including myself. I enclosed a copy of Father's one-hundred-line poem. One line read, "A strange person falls to a strange illness," and Professor Shan referred to it in three of his letters. He had not forgotten that I had told him my father was an illiterate peasant. From the poem, the childless Professor Shan glimpsed the deep love and expectation a father has for a daughter. Seeing Father's gift for poetic imagery and remembering my lie, he must have smiled.

I regretted that my illness had drawn attention from Rei-qing's wedding. The preparations were simple, and only a few good friends and relatives were present, but when Rei-qing should have been preparing for it, she was spending her free time going to the hospital to get medications for me. She was so caught up in her job and in taking care of me that some of her friends did not learn of the wedding until it was long over. Even after she was married, Rei-qing had some delicate situations ahead of her.

When our family was going through its most difficult times, several men who were Rei-qing's old classmates ignored her. Now that we were having moderate success, they reappeared, professing love. Through her job, Rei-qing had meet a young mathematician working at a university where his father was president. He fell for her after several meetings, and although he never said anything about it, Rei-qing soon sensed it.

"You have to continue your working relationship with him. Why don't you let me bring him some wedding candy?" I asked, trying to be helpful.

When I went to the president's European-style house, I found him watering the flowers in his large garden. I told him that I wished to see his son, and he chivalrously escorted me inside. A servant took me to the Western-style sitting room, where a huge mirror hung on the wall opposite the door and a fire roared in the fireplace.

Molière could have been describing this same salon as Harpagon's. I was surprised that the Red Guards would have allowed any intellectual to continue living so extravagantly, but I also knew that the president had been protected by Premier Zhou En-li from the beginning. Following the political winds, he had applied of his own accord to go to the countryside and the factories to use his expertise to serve the working class. Praising his ability to mix with peasants and workers, the newspapers called him a model for the intellectuals to follow.

Seeing the luxurious home of this "model intellectual," I recalled the poverty of those peasants and workers. Ah-di had lived next to a ten-member family that had only four plastic rice bowls among them. They shared the bowls as they ate; each person just reached in with his hand.

The mathematician appeared, scattering my thoughts. I handed him the wedding candy and told him the news. Shocked, he murmured, "She's married! So soon . . . it's impossible . . . how come I didn't know?"

"The wedding was very small and simple," I explained. "We didn't invite many people. My sister and my brother-in-law have known each other since they were children."

"Is that so? Very well, very well . . ." the mathematician replied mechanically. He stared into the flames in the fireplace for a few moments, and then asked abruptly, "How many sisters are there in your family?"

"Two," I answered. "Just Rei-qing and me."

"That means that between you and your sister there are no sisters, and that there are no sisters older than you and she." The mathematician was so confused, he seemed to have forgotten the definition of the number two.

"Yes, only two of us," I smiled. "My sister and brother-in-law say that you are welcome to visit their home any time. Here's the address. I have to go now."

Perhaps the mathematician had learned a lesson from being too timid with Rei-qing. He began to chase me, writing me three letters in one week. He said that he would use his father's influence to get me a job teaching German at the university. When Rei-qing read the letter, she told Father, teasingly, "It seems he only likes women from the Tan family. Last night, he came to my home and said, 'It would be ideal if your family had a daughter older than Xi-ou. But I like her a lot. She has the wisdom of someone much older.' "

"Xi-ou, what do you think of him?" Father asked.

"Well, I've thought about it," I answered seriously. "If his father had enough influence to save you and Mother, I'd marry him tomorrow. Unfortunately, he hasn't. Besides, I haven't finished my education, so I'm not eligible to fall in love."

△△△ Professor Shan had a severe liver problem that forced him to return to Shanghai for treatment. So we resumed our German lessons, meeting each Monday, Wednesday, and Friday. If I had the afternoon shift at the scarf workshop to which I had been assigned eight months earlier, I went to his home in the morning; when I had the earlier shift, I bicycled there directly from work.

We knew each other well after our year's correspondence. When I discovered that he had a degree in electrical engineering and had only recently begun teaching languages, I was amazed at his intellect, but I felt my own intuition about him validated: He was precise because he was a scientist at heart.

"Strictly speaking, you're my first German student," he said casually. "I was transferred from the Academy of Science to the Language Institute in 1964 because there was a shortage of language professors. Many were needed to teach diplomats and their wives. I was sent to the countryside for two years before I was to start teaching, because the school building was still under construction. Then the Grand Cultural Revolution officially started in 1966, and I never had the opportunity to teach in a classroom."

"But you have such a command of the language," I said, astonished.

"German is my first language. The parochial school I attended after kindergarten required us to speak German. Because of this, I have a hard time writing Chinese well."

"Then, not only can I study German with you, I can learn science, too!"

I showed him all of my independent study material: the textbook I had hand-copied; my problem sets, both finished and unfinished; my notes; and the outlines I had made of the material I wished to learn. "This is what I've been doing lately. My two books on microwave theory are graduate-level texts from the United States. I have problems understanding some of the material, and I don't have anyone to ask about it. Sometimes I think I understand, but when I get to the problem sets, I can't do any of them."

Professor Shan asked me to leave my materials with him, promising to take a closer look at them. At my next class, he said, "I don't think it's a good idea for you to learn microwave theory on your own. A student needs a laboratory. Since you can't conduct any experiments, it will be hard for you to comprehend the theory. Besides, microwave techniques are mostly important in military technology. It's highly unlikely that you'll ever have the opportunity to do research in this field."

"I don't care if I never use it. I'd like to learn it now."

Raising an eyebrow, he said, "The purpose of learning is to apply knowledge. Even Confucius said, 'Am I a gourd? How can I just be hung on a wall and left unused?' A person's life is short, so spending time learning something you will never apply is a waste. It's easy to learn a particular subject, but the most important thing is to train yourself to pick up a subject faster than other people and at a moment's notice."

"What should I do?" I asked, at least temporarily convinced by his arguments.

"Learning a foreign language is one possibility," Professor Shan replied. "When your German improves, I'll teach you French. You must constantly review your calculus and general physics. When you have a solid foundation, you'll be able to face any challenge."

I nodded and he continued, "Any endeavor requires us to push ourselves, but not into a corner. When I was young, I often went to the Beijing Opera. The actors and actresses who wore themselves out in the first act were not the best members of the cast. The best ones used only about 60 or 70 percent of their energy in the beginning. As the opera progressed, they gave increasingly more of themselves. By the time the curtain fell, they had given everything to the production. When people thought back on the opera, they could still feel its power, thanks to these actors. We have all wasted a lot of time in our lives, but that, too, is part of life." He paused. "Do you know why I first decided to teach you?"

I had often wondered but had reached no firm conclusion. I shook my head.

"Because you're such an idealist. In this world, there are too few souls that have not become contaminated with pessimism. Child, try to keep this precious part of your personality intact no matter what life brings you."

Just as I decided to accept Professor Shan's advice to modify my independent study plan, our friendship faced a new challenge. I received a strange letter in a woman's handwriting. The name in the return address was "Anger," and I was shocked. The first line read, "I am chastising Qi-tai Shan; he is inhuman." I forced myself to read the letter, which was from Mrs. Shan. She said that Professor Shan was mistreating her, that he never wanted to talk to her. His health was failing, and after each of our classes, he would lie motionless on his bed for several hours, exhausted. She hoped that I would quit my studies and never return to the Shan home. She asked me to call her at work so we could meet and talk face-to-face.

Confused and remorseful, I showed the letter to Father, asking his advice. He said, "You're an adult. You have the ability to think independently." Seeing how upset I was, he continued, "It's useless to waste energy crying over this. I can't make decisions for you for the rest of your life. Besides, life is an art. My decisions might not be the right ones for you. Try tackling this problem on your own. Be brave."

I reread the letter, slowly and carefully. I had to admit that Professor Shan's health was indeed bad, and I felt that I was partly to blame. I thought guiltily of how puffy his face had been recently. He had returned to Shanghai for treatment, but I had completely forgotten that Professor Shan was also "Patient" Shan. On top of our regular German studies, I had asked him for problem sets for reviewing my math skills and requested that he read Jian-nan's paper.

I could not sympathize with the rest of the letter. Mrs. Shan's only example of her husband's mistreatment was that he did not appreciate the fact that she cooked three meals a day for him. Mrs. Shan claimed that my German studies were affecting their relationship, but I almost always finished my lessons before she returned home from work. The few times when class had lasted until she arrived home, she had graciously asked me to stay to dinner. Matters had to be much more complex than Mrs. Shan was admitting, but one thing was certain: I was only a catalyst for the problems they were facing.

Since I had a great deal of pride, I decided that I would not continue studying German at the Shan home. Relieved that I had analyzed the situation and reached reasonable conclusions, I went to the public telephone and called Mrs. Shan. We agreed to meet that same evening at seven o'clock in front of the door to the City Lights Cinema.

I did not wait long before I saw Mrs. Shan passing in front of the theater. "Mrs. Shan," I began, "I've decided to do what you asked. I won't come to class anymore."

"Xi-ou, it's not that I don't like you. It's because of him that I have to ask this. He hasn't smiled at me since we were married three years ago. He has some mysterious other woman in his life."

"I don't want to hear about it. I'm returning your letter. Let's pretend this whole thing never happened. I've already written to your husband saying that for personal reasons, I can't study with him any longer." Mrs. Shan snatched the letter from my hand and stuffed it into her purse.

On the third day after the incident, Rei-qing came home from work early to tell me that Professor Shan had stopped by to speak with her: "He came to the factory before it opened this morning and waited by the gate with your letter in his hand. He asked me if you were ill again, but I told him the truth. He didn't say anything for a while. Then he asked me to tell you that you would be receiving a letter very soon from Mrs. Shan. She'll be asking you to study with her husband again."

"Sister, what did you tell him?" I asked nervously. "If he knew what Mrs. Shan wrote, he'd be very angry. It isn't going to be good for their marriage."

"I'm not that silly," Rei-qing said with a smile. "I only told him that you had received a letter from his wife asking you not to study with her husband. I said I didn't know what was actually stated in the letter."

Five days after I had met with Mrs. Shan, I received another letter from her, requesting me to resume my studies as soon as possible. I decided that the next Monday would be a new beginning. Neither Professor Shan nor I mentioned the incident. Mrs. Shan smiled graciously at me the next time we met. I studied even harder, realizing the price Professor Shan must have paid to keep me on as a student.

△△△ That same month, February 1974, we learned Rei-qing was pregnant. Mother had been sent to a reform farm in An Hui province and was now much farther away from us than she had been at Basket Bridge. I asked my coworker "aunts" at the scarf workshop how I could best help Rei-qing. I was very shy at first, not knowing how a well-bred young woman could bring up this subject in public. But I pushed myself for Rei-qing and her unborn child's sake, not wanting her to suffer because of the absence of our mother.

I decided that Rei-qing's health depended upon a strict diet whose basic element was eggs. The family ration was ten a month, but I figured that Tao-ran's family contribute some of theirs, too. This would give her almost two hundred eggs to eat during her pregnancy. Nutrition experts today would be aghast at this regime, but it was the best I could do. I had had a personal policy of standing in line no longer than fifteen minutes—even if it meant that I had to give up that month's ration—but when Rei-qing became pregnant, I waited longer than this and quarreled with people who cut into the lines.

I felt fulfilled and somehow strengthened by being able to take care of my family and friends. My capital was my youth and health. When Grandfather Pu developed pneumonia, Rei-qing and I negotiated through the hospital's "back door" to get him the necessary care. When Father played matchmaker for a friend's thirty-six-year-old daughter, I became his representative and chaperoned the couple's dates. I helped the woman choose her wedding dress and was her maid of honor.

△△△ On the way home from work one day, I met a school-mate two classes ahead of me and discussed with her the importance of independent study. I took her home and showed her some of the books I had hand-copied. She had stopped studying five years earlier because of work, but now she became my student. My most frequent guests were the neighborhood children, who came for help with their homework.

△△△ Professor Hu, fifteen years have passed and Rei-qing's son is now fourteen. I have received so much from so many people, and I try very hard to give as much back. Unfortunately, I can never do enough. I hope I am helping you in some small way; please write and let me know.

Sincerely,
Xi-ou Tan

 It was not until 1974, five years after Chairman Mao's "Newest Instructions," that the "sick young intellectuals" received their work assignments. This meant that the economic independence for which I had yearned would be coming. We were assigned mostly to small workshops owned by Neighborhood Committees, which paid only seven-tenths of a yuan per day. No sick leave was offered.

Most of these workshops were created in 1958 in response to Chairman Mao's call to "liberate the female work force." In the years since their establishment, no one new had been sent to them, and the middle-aged women who had begun working there in the late 1950s were ripe for retirement. Most were married to workers, so their families were generally illiterate. The poorly made equipment was designed for the simplest of tasks, such as sewing buttons, or making cardboard boxes or artificial flowers. But in these workshops, the old aunts I worked with would give me an education of an entirely different sort.

19

Dear Professor Hu,

As soon as I found out that the sick young intellectuals would be getting their work assignments, I thought about the small workshops owned by the Neighborhood Committee. They resembled sewing circles more than factories, with three or four women sitting on stools gossiping as they worked. Afraid that I would be assigned to one of them, I applied for a job in the kindergarten, also owned by the Neighborhood Committee. Although I had no experience caring for children, I loved them and had no doubt that I was fit for the job. Shocked when the request was denied, I went to the Neighborhood Committee office to learn the reason.

The woman in charge of local assignments stared at me in amazement.

"Do you think members of the Proletariat want an anti-Revolutionary whelp indoctrinating their little children?"

Although grossly insulted, I did not give up. "In that case, what kind of job do you think would be suitable for me?"

"We also own a dining hall. I'm sure they can put you to work frying rice or washing dishes there."

"I'm deeply moved by the trust you're placing in me! Aren't you afraid I'll seize this opportunity to poison my class enemies?"

Shock flooded over the woman's face. This struck her as a whole new danger, and she added a large question mark next to the words "dining hall" under my name.

In the end, I was given a job hemming silk scarves for export. Each worker sat in a bamboo chair and had a pole to which to attach unfinished scarves with clothespins. The better workers used their left hands to extend the scarves fully and their right hands to sew the hems in about fifteen minutes. The work was mindless, and since there was no machine noise in the background, the environment was ideal for gossip.

Three aspects of the job made it intolerable. I despised gossiping, but there was nothing else to do; I hate sewing almost as much, and even at my best, I could not sew half as fast as the others; and the detailed work strained my eyes, making it difficult to study later in the evening. I had no legal or moral right to refuse this job, since it would bring a marginal income that could at least pay for the food I ate.

I was placed in the smallest of the five workshop rooms. Three women sat around a small table covered with silk cloth, silk thread, and scissors. As the supervisor introduced me to my coworkers, I realized that the empty bamboo chair was to be mine. "You will be working with Aunt Shi, Aunt Wong, and Aunt Zhang," she said, pointing to each in turn. "And what is your name?" she asked me.

"Just call me Xiao [Young] Tan."

The supervisor turned to leave. As she reached the door, she shouted, "Sai-ping Zhao! Get the bicycle cart ready to ship out the completed goods!"

"All right," came a meek response behind me. Startled, I turned to see a middle-aged woman almost hidden in the corner of the room. She, too, was sewing, and she held the scarf she was working on less than two inches away from her thick eyeglasses. She calmly finished it as if she had not heard the order. I deduced that she was the workshop's token class enemy.

The three women I worked with were friendly, and even though I learned much more slowly than the other newcomers, they were patient. The youngest of the three, Aunt Wong, even gave me some of her own finished scarves to fill my daily quota. Aunt Shi, the oldest, was garrulous and energetic. When she heard the wind blowing outside, she would chant this rhyme:

> One side charcoal, one side brick,
> Balanced on string will weather predict.

During Indian summer:

> October it's time to prepare for the cold,
> But a lazy young bride might persist and protest,
> "Feel the warm weather, summer's not old!
> It's far too soon to start building a nest!"

When it was bitterly cold outside, she would sing, unaccompanied:

> If you're cold, it's your matter,
> You're too bare or too thin.
> But we're all hot together,
> Since you can't peel your skin!

Aunt Wong objected, saying, "What do you mean you can't do anything about heat? This is the age of the machine! There are fans and refrigerators and air conditioners. If you're rich, you just go out and buy them, but if you're poor, you'll just have to sweat with the rest of us."

Aunt Zhang had her own protest: "Everybody is poor now. No one can afford to buy those things. Everybody has to suffer summer and winter the same way." Everyone stopped stitching to applaud Aunt Zhang's shrewd assessment of the current economic situation.

"Aunt Shi, where did you learn all this wisdom?" I asked. "Can you tell me more?"

It was raining hard outside. Beaming with pleasure, Aunt Shi cleared her throat and sang:

> If the clouds are moving east,
> Then it's gale force at least!
> If the clouds are moving west,
> Just be sure to wear a vest.
> If the clouds are moving south,
> Rain will be up to your mouth.

> *If the clouds are moving north,*
> *It will flood all the earth!*

I gave the thumbs-up sign of approval: "Wonderful! Can you teach me any rhymes about how people should behave? Manners and things?"

"Of course," said Aunt Shi, putting down her sewing to devote full attention to her student. She chanted:

> *A person leaving home goes way down in price,*
> *While the value of goods will rapidly rise!*

"I don't think I understand," I said, confused.

"Isn't it obvious?" said Aunt Wong, "Look at this scarf. Here in China, you couldn't get a penny for it. But when they export it, they sell it for a fortune!"

Aunt Zhang shook her head: "No, that's not it. According to my son-in-law, after Nixon visited China, many, many foreigners came to Shanghai. They were treated so well! They got huge lobster dinners. When's the last time you even *saw* a lobster, at any price? So these foreigners, when they left their homes, they became more valuable!"

I begged Aunt Shi to sing another one. She peered at me for a few seconds, opened her mouth wide, revealing teeth missing, and sang me this selection:

> *A pig and a monkey do well not to wed,*
> *And a lamb and a rat shouldn't share the same bed.*
> *A rooster will run when it hears a dog howl,*
> *And a horse can't endure the sight of a cow.*
> *A snake and a tiger will bite, claw, and tear,*
> *And it's almost the same with a dragon and hare.*

Aunt Shi was going too fast for me to absorb anything, and Aunt Wong and Aunt Zhang giggled at my confusion. I did not know that this was the "Song of the Twelve Bitter Enemies of the Chinese Zodiac."

"The most important things for a matchmaker to know are the birth years of each person in a couple and whether the animals of those years are compatible. If they form a pair that are enemies, that's the end.

A marriage between the two is impossible, and the matchmaker has to start over," Aunt Shi explained.

Aunt Wong and Aunt Zhang laughed again—not only at the song itself, but also at my naïveté and my earnest interest in the meaning. Hearing the laughter, the triple-chinned supervisor at the other end of the hall screamed, "Who's the chatterbox down there? That's not going to make the young intellectual learn how to sew a scarf! Maybe you'd like to do your laughing in the remote countryside!"

Renowned for her quick hands and sharp tongue, Aunt Shi was never scolded directly. She continued in a loud whisper:

> If you're pretty by birth, then your beauty is true,
> But if it's makeup and wigs, they'll be laughing at
>   you!

This time, we tried to suppress our laughter.

△△△ I told the family these rhymes over dinner. "This Aunt Shi seems to know a great deal," Father said, nodding his head. "Do you know what she was referring to about the brick and charcoal balance? More than two thousand years ago, in the Jin dynasty, our ancestors knew this principle. They hung pieces of coal on one side of a balance and pieces of brick on the other. When the humidity rose, the charcoal absorbed water and became heavier, which told them it would rain soon."

"But Aunt Shi can't even write her name!" I said, astounded.

"Knowledge and literacy don't always go hand in hand," Father told me. "Many people can write beautifully but are really quite ignorant."

△△△ Sai-ping Zhao, the class enemy of the workshop, could not share in the laughter of her coworkers. She ignored us and sewed with her face buried in her work. Occasionally she lifted her head to thread a new needle. I stared at her almost as a challenge, trying to get a response or at least her attention, but she acted as if she did not notice. As I grew more familiar with my coworkers, I became unafraid to address her openly as Aunt Sai-ping. However, whenever I spoke to her, Sai-ping Zhao looked around, as if she thought I were talking to a different person. Concluding that I was only adding to the poor woman's psychological burdens, I gave up trying to make her think better of herself and to help her feel that she was a part of the group. Although I was curious about Sai-ping Zhao's past, I did not ask, believing that it was wrong to inquire about such things, especially if the person were a fellow Black.

Sai-ping Zhao lighted the workshop's coal stove every morning at ten and boiled enough water for everyone's morning beverage. An hour later, she would collect our food from us, steam it, and serve it to us for lunch. One day, when Sai-ping Zhao left her seat at ten, Aunt Shi said, "Did you see how red and swollen her eyes are from crying? Her mother is dying."

"She's almost eighty, isn't she? What's she dying of?" Aunt Zhang asked with genuine concern.

"Intestinal tuberculosis. She's had it for years," Aunt Shi sighed. "Sai-ping Zhao has no money to buy medicine."

Aunt Wong broke in: "How could she have money? The factory deducts half of her salary to pay for the heating coal we use! They're using blood money to buy the coal. I refuse to use any of the hot water she makes or have my lunch steamed here."

"Doesn't she have any children?" I asked timidly.

"She has a son who was relocated to a remote countryside area in the Southwest. He barely makes enough money to feed himself."

"What about her husband?" I persisted.

No one answered, and I repeated my question. Aunt Shi lowered her voice and said, "Her husband fled to Taiwan with his first wife. Zhao was his second wife. He left her behind."

Aunt Wong whispered indignantly, "What? Second wife? She was from a good family! She could read and write; she had an education. She was forced into that union! I heard that two months after they made her get married, the man took off. Are you trying to put the blame on her for not being able to keep him?"

Sai-ping Zhao had finished lighting the stove and returned to her seat, so Aunt Wong's last question went unanswered. I glanced toward her to see the woman's swollen eyes for myself.

⋀⋀ That night, Rei-qing and I looked through all of our medical books until we found a section on intestinal tuberculosis, which listed the medications used to treat it. I telephoned Kang-li to make sure that these were indeed correct and to inquire about dosage. Then we went to the drugstore.

Rainy season in Shanghai meant a nearly constant drizzle, so Sai-ping Zhao had no choice but to keep the stove inside the workshop, just outside the restroom. She lighted the kindling and put the coal on top, but since the wood was wet, it produced a great deal of smoke. She fanned the flames with a large, dried leaf. When I approached her, she motioned me back. "It's too smoky. You'll choke! Come back and use the restroom in a few minutes," she said, coughing.

I gave her the medicine and told her that the proper dosage was written on a piece of paper in the bag. I shoved twenty yuan and the bag into her hand and went back to the workroom. Instead of concealing her emotions in front of her coworkers as usual, Sai-ping Zhao was crying openly when she entered the workroom. Those who knew nothing of her problems assumed it was due to the smoke from the stove. The more informed thought that she was crying over her mother's illness. Only I knew the real reason for her tears, and deep inside myself, I wept with her.

⋀⋀ Individual salaries at workshops owned by the Neighborhood Committee were calculated by the number of hours worked, so days off were unpaid. All four of us children now were bringing in some form of income, and our money was budgeted carefully. I thought it a waste of my life to work at such a lowly job for such a pittance, since my time was better spent studying, but, as an adult, I had some responsibility for the family's income. Consequently, after I earned enough money to pay for my own food each month, I took the rest of the time off to study, so mine was the lowest salary in the workshop.

As we returned from the workshop's accountant with our wages one payday, Aunt Shi announced that she wanted to give me one yuan [or "kuai"]. Aunt Shi was thrifty—she would not take time off even when she was ill, and would divide even a single feng into two feng if she could. Confused, I asked, "Why do you want to give me money? You don't owe me anything."

"How much money did you get today? Tell us so we can all hear," Aunt Shi commanded playfully.

"Twelve kuai and six jiao," I replied obediently, wondering what was going on.

"And adding one kuai makes what?" Aunt Shi asked, arms akimbo.

"Thirteen kuai and six jiao," I answered, even more confused. The group burst into hearty laughter, and I blushed in confusion. Embarrassed, I asked, "Are you laughing at me because I haven't been here much and didn't get much money?"

The laughter increased. Finally, Aunt Wong wiped the tears from her eyes and said, "A turtle's shell has thirteen pieces. Four legs and a head and a tail make a total of six things coming out from under it."

Light slowly dawned. "Kuai" meant "yuan," but also "pieces," and "jiao" signified either "ten feng" or "appendages."

"By giving you one kuai, Aunt Shi will be making you a whole turtle!" said Aunt Wong, still laughing at the pun.

I could not have laughed harder at myself. I always felt slow and ignorant in front of these aunts. They spent so much time gossiping, but they had a true sense of justice and remarkable intuition, full of understanding and wisdom.

Something that occurred at about this time helped me to gain some of the knowledge they possessed. Kang-li had to be rushed to the hospital for an emergency operation on a goiter and I stayed at her bedside for two nights. When I went to visit her one evening after work, I found her sitting up in bed entertaining the hospital staff and patients with her jokes and stories. As I entered, she began introducing me: "This is my daughter. She's beautiful, isn't she?"

To my embarrassment, everyone said they agreed, noting similarities in our bone structure and coloring. The crowd dispersed, giving us some privacy. Kang-li reached out and pulled me close to the bed, saying, "I disturbed your sleep with my coughing last night. You wiped the phlegm from my mouth, not even worrying about getting your hands dirty. I couldn't have expected that of a flesh-and-blood daughter. I can't even begin to tell you how much I owe you."

Rubbing my hands gently, she said, "It's getting cold. You should use lotion to keep your hands from getting chapped. If you don't like the perfumed kind, you can get some that's unscented." I nodded silently, and Kang-li continued, "As soon as I'm out of here, we're going shopping. I'm going to buy some fabric so I can make you a new overcoat. Yours is too small and thin."

I started to speak, but Kang-li cut me off, mimicking me: "This coat's too warm already. I certainly don't need another one!" I laughed at her accuracy.

We chatted for a while, and then I went to get some hot water for Kang-li's bath. It was the beginning of winter, and hot water was in demand. A crowd of patients' relatives had gathered around the broken water heater, quarreling with the repair crew over when it would be fixed. I waited more than an hour to get two liters.

Hearing the laughter from Kang-li's room as I returned, I thought of her kindness toward others, which created a constant stream of visitors. An old woman, a stranger to me, sat at the foot of Kang-li's bed. A group of nurses and patients listened to their conversation. I was shocked to hear Kang-li say to the old woman angrily, "I just got out of surgery and you've already chased me to the hospital! What would you have done if I'd been dying?"

⚠⚠ Kang-li had once told me about an uncle who had been a diplomat in northern Europe. His habit of frequenting bordellos made him lose both his career and his family. Kang-li's family lived on the floor above him after his return to China, but her mother never allowed her children even to look in on him. Just before the Liberation, he brought a strange woman to live with him. He died several years later, leaving the uneducated, unskilled woman without financial support. She moved back to the countryside to lead an impoverished life. As the woman grew old, Kang-li began sending her a monthly stipend. With the emergency operation, Kang-li had had no time to put that month's money in the mail, and the panicked old woman came to Shanghai in search of her.

The old woman dropped her head, speaking quietly: "First, I went to your home, but no one was there. I found your brothers, but they made me come here." Kang-li's two brothers were chief surgeons at nearby hospitals, and their wives were doctors. They led secure, peaceful lives in the midst of chaos, but, unlike their sister, they had never sent the old woman a single feng. Only too happy to get rid of her, they had sent her to Kang-li without a moment's hesitation. Kang-li snapped, "This visit cost you the whole month's living expenses that I would have sent you if you'd only waited. Next time, write a letter first to see if I'm dead."

The old woman sobbed softly, trying to hide her tears and embarrassment from the surrounding crowd. Was this the same Kang-li Soong I had revered as a queen? This old woman had every reason to be ashamed of her past, but now she was a poor, helpless, lonely old woman. Kang-li could easily afford the money she gave her. Why had she humiliated the woman in front of all these people over a few yuan? Although it was unwise of her to come to the hospital asking for the money, Kang-li's cruel statement blew the incident out of proportion. I thought of how often my family had relied on the kindnesses of those more fortunate than we. How many times had we come close to a similar situation? Fixing my eyes on the floor as the blood drained from my face, I felt the hot-water bottles turn to lead.

"Xi-ou, what's the matter with you?" Kang-li asked, concerned. Glancing at her from the corner of my eye, I put down the hot-water bottles and left.

For ten days I tried to reconcile Kang-li's behavior with my image of her. When Rei-qing asked me to go with her to see Kang-li, I refused, not knowing how to face her. Unable to undo the knot in my stomach, I knew I could not act as if nothing had happened. Rei-qing brought reports that Kang-li missed her "adopted" daughter. We had seen each other daily for more than three years, and she did not want this to change. I went to see her within a month, but it was a year before the friendship was completely healed.

△△△ Professor Hu, it was only then that I realized that people have many dimensions. We all have shortcomings, but Father was right when he said I often took an extreme view of a person, making him or her a god or a devil. My Queen had snapped at that old woman only because she was ill. My coworkers at the scarf workshop helped me to see that people have many sides: At first, I hated the way they gossiped all the time, but they showed themselves to be basically good people, and even though they were not educated, they had a great deal of practical wisdom.

I keep trying to improve myself, and I feel that these long looks at the past help me. I hope that you, too, are benefiting from them. Take care of yourself, and write back soon.

Sincerely,
Xi-ou Tan

Professor Hu's last letter made me want to go back to classical poetry. I made a point of reading a few poems each day, delighting in them as I rediscovered them. Of all Ci poetry, I most like the later work of Li Yu, the last emperor of Southern Tang, but his best works were written after he was captured by those who later formed the Soong dynasty. This poem, describing the sorrow of separation, goes to the tune of "Joy at Meeting":

> Alone, I climbed to the western attic,
> In the heavens, the hooklike moon hangs high.
> A vast yard of lonely parasol trees
> Stretches underneath autumn's clear, cool sky.
> As I watch, a sorrow tears at my heart,
> Unable to cut it, I leave it whole.

It worsens if I try to force neat rows,
The inexpressible taste fills my soul.

Another poem is sung to the tune of "Beautiful Yu."

When end the autumn moon and spring flowers
For one with so many memorable hours?
As the east wind shook my attic last night,
I thought of my lost land, drenched in moonlight.
Yet stand marble steps and carved balustrade,
But my love's rosy youth did long ago fade.
You once asked me how great was my sorrow,
'Tis an endless river with eastern flow.

This was his last poem. When the Soong emperor overheard it, he
ordered Li Yu to drink poison.

20

Dear Professor Hu,

In your fourth letter, you told me that you
did not like to write, but I still want to hear from
you. You have read a great deal of classical Chinese
literature, and you have also suffered. These two things
can make you an excellent writer. All literature must be written
with blood.

Scarves had not sold well in 1975, so our workshop
was closed and I was reassigned to a larger workshop, more like a
factory, that produced machine parts. The noise deafened me before
I even stepped across the threshold. The Neighborhood Committee
cadre introduced me to a short woman operating a lathe: "This is your
supervisor, Ah-liu Hong. Ah-liu is the workshop monitor."

"Supervisor Ah-liu," I said respectfully, bowing to the tiny
woman. She winked at me, her smile crinkling her face like a chrysan-
themum. "Don't be so polite around here." She had a Su Zhou accent,
and the gold from her front teeth glittered in the bright light of the lathe
lamp as she spoke.

Political files followed a person everywhere and were available to
any Party secretary. Ah-liu was already familiar with my family background from the factory's Party secretary and from the other workers,
who knew all of the neighborhood gossip. Even so, she was extremely
friendly to me for the first two weeks, and I was elated to have such a

kind supervisor. Then her attitude toward me changed. She stopped teaching me how to operate the lathe and snapped at me for no apparent reason.

The Neighborhood Committee created the honor of "model worker," to be elected by his or her coworkers as an example of someone who lived by Chairman Mao's ideals. Although she was nearly illiterate, Ah-liu was the one chosen from our division. Because of her popularity, I assumed it was my fault that we stopped getting along.

Many different jobs were done at the workshop, and most people had to master several machines. Ah-liu was in charge of assignments, and I learned how to use six different machines within a month. One day, I was put in charge of a machine that cut long tubes of steel into shorter ones. The friction produced a great deal of heat, so a thin, white cooling solution was trickled down onto the blade and the steel tube as soon as the two touched. The machine was old and the steel hard, so each time the blade cut into the metal, the whole apparatus vibrated, producing a thunderous noise. Dirty oil and cooling solution spattered my face.

"Xiao Tan"—["Young" Tan]—"come here and sign this. It's for your glove, soap, and rice coupons," said Ah-liu, smiling at me for the first time in months. The workshop's policy gave each worker a pair of work gloves, hand soap, and coupons for six pounds of rice. Flattered by Ah-liu's smile, I took her proffered ballpoint pen and circled my name on the list.

Ah-liu, who seemed in an exceptionally good mood that day, stood in front of my machine for twenty minutes chatting with me. We talked first about the rice coupons, and she told me that everyone in her family, including her two teenaged daughters, had an enormous appetite. She said she never had enough of the coupons, since her daughters were growing very fast. She also mentioned that it used to take only three pairs of unraveled work gloves to make a pair of pants for the girls, but now it took five pairs.

"Oh, I didn't realize the work gloves were so useful!" I exclaimed.

"Didn't you know that you could use them to make sweaters, too?" she inquired, smiling.

As she spoke, I looked up at the clock on the wall, worried that I would not be able to finish the day's quota. Sensing my concern, Ah-liu put the glove, soap, and rice coupons on my tool cabinet and said, "I'm leaving now. Stop by my machine later to talk, all right?"

Nodding, I resumed work. That day, I decided to take my whole lunch hour at home. Rei-qing no longer lived there, and Jian-nan and Chi-kai also had jobs, leaving Father alone in Angel Cave all day. Sometimes he would forget our admonitions to stay in bed and get up to answer a knock at the door. It was usually the Runt, the Neighborhood Committee, or some other group investigating our family. Father was usually insulted or ordered to write extra confessions, and we could only tell him that it was his own fault. He protested, "I'm alive, and I'm not deaf. When someone knocks on the door, I answer it. I feel guilty if I ignore it."

Not realizing what psychological damage Father had suffered during these ten years of confinement, we did not understand his behavior. He felt discarded by everyone, since it was dark before we came home to eat dinner beneath the dim, six-watt light. Seeing us talking, laughing, eating, and studying filled him with peace, despite his worry about growing old.

Rei-qing and I were sensitive to changes in Father, but we could not always identify the reasons for them. When we were working or running errands, we missed him, and we seized every possible opportunity to spend even a few minutes with him at home. Rei-qing lived with Tao-ran's family in the northernmost part of Shanghai, but she moved back to the Angel Cave for her pregnancy so that she could be with Father and not be pushed around on public transportation. After her son was born, she visited Father every day, despite her job at the steel factory in the eastern part of the city.

I was glad to go home each day to heat lunch for Father. The day we received our glove and rice coupons, I had a flat bicycle tire, so I had to walk home in the blazing sun via my treeless shortcut. I would have enough time to heat the meal but not to eat it. As I turned down a small lane, I heard someone following me. I spun around to see Aunt Chai, who had been working on the machine next to me that morning.

"Aunt Chai, why are you in such a hurry today?" I asked, without slowing my pace.

"You . . . you . . . this afternoon . . . are you going to talk with Ah-liu?" Aunt Chai panted.

"Why would I want to talk with her?" I asked, confused.

"Don't you understand what she wants?" queried Aunt Chai. When my expression did not change, she said, "I didn't think you did. Ah-liu was asking you for your glove and rice coupons this morning."

I was shocked, yet I believed her. "Why? Everyone gets coupons. If she wanted mine, why did she ask me to sign for them? I thought something was strange when she told me about making pants for her daughters. We only get one pair of gloves a month. Where does she get the extras for making pants?"

Aunt Chai snorted: "Ah-liu doesn't make them herself! All the kiss-ups at the factory do it for her. At the first breath of cold air, the whole family's winter wardrobe was made—from overcoats to new pants to wool socks and cotton shoes. Now that the workshop has a new group of young intellectuals assigned to it, Ah-liu is even more materialistic. Expensive vitamins and health foods just flood toward her home! There's a shortage of electric meters in Shanghai, you know. She didn't want to share a meter with other people and have their usage averaged in with hers, so she got someone to get one illegally and install it at her home—free, of course."

Ten days earlier, Ah-liu and I had been working on the same machine when one of the new young intellectuals whispered to her, "I bought it."

Ah-liu stood up with a huge grin on her face, and they disappeared down a narrow hall between the two storage rooms. Ah-liu returned ten minutes later, beaming. Before the workday ended, she asked me how we calculated our electrical expenses each month.

Each dwelling housed several families who all shared the same electric meter, and whenever the bill was due, there were always arguments about how much each family owed. I told her that those who had meters paid their own bills, plus twenty-four feng for the cost of running the meter. The rest was divided among the other families, based on usage.

"Do you have your own meter?" she asked. I nodded.

"What brand?"

"I don't know. It's very old, older than I am."

Two days after that, there had been an assignment meeting. The healthy, twenty-six-year-old young intellectual who had had the clandestine meeting with Ah-liu was assigned to quality control, the most envied position, along with Aunt Fu, a woman who limped.

These incidents all came together now as Aunt Chai mentioned Ah-liu's meter.

"Do all the workers give their coupons to Ah-liu?" I asked.

"No, not me," Aunt Chai said proudly. "You can tell who gives and who doesn't by the job that person has. If it's hard work, they don't. Those with the easiest jobs do. The young intellectuals generally do. Most of the older people have families to raise, so they need their coupons for themselves."

We kept our voices low. An old Chinese proverb says, "The walls have eyes and ears," and the small lane was close to the machine shop. "There are at least ten young intellectuals in our workshop. Why does Ah-liu need so many coupons?" I asked angrily.

"She uses what she wants and sells the rest to the peasants on the black market." The wind swept a lock of hair across Aunt Chai's face. As she pulled it back and fixed it in place with a hairpin, I noticed for the first time that her hair was streaked with gray. She gently chided me, "Xi-ou, you do too much. Those who don't give Ah-liu any coupons always get the hardest work. No one works as hard as you do. You don't need to be lazy, but it isn't worthwhile to ruin your health."

"Aunt Chai, why are you taking so much trouble for me?"

"I think you're much more naive than the other young intellectuals," she said sincerely. "They don't need my advice. They learned these things very quickly, like the woman who limps. She had brought Ah-liu bottles of vitamins and cod liver oil. People from the outside think Ah-liu has a good heart because it looks like she's taking care of handicapped people by letting one of them do quality control. Actually, Aunt Fu once had a severe seizure, but Ah-liu still assigned her to some of the heaviest work. Aunt Fu was being punished for never giving Ah-liu anything."

When I was a child, I heard a story about a man learning to be a butcher. First he saw a cow. After a while, he saw a mass of bones and organs. Finally, he saw only separate muscles and bones that came together in a single frame. My first impression of the machine shop was that everyone was united and devoted to Ah-liu. After talking with Aunt Chai, I began to see through the façade of people's behavior. I recalled how Father had praised Aunt Shi for her bounteous wisdom in spite of her illiteracy. Although I was only just beginning to know her, I had a strong feeling that Aunt Chai would become a significant person in my life.

△△△ Work, study, and Father kept me so busy that I had little time for socializing. Because of my political background, I did not believe that men would find me interesting, so I never took my male coworkers' approaches as anything more than an interest in friendship. Still, I liked anything that was beautiful, so I especially noticed one good-looking man who liked to come and sit by my machine. I was attracted by his appearance, but not by him as a whole. His father was a famous physician, and although his family suffered a great deal at the hands of the Red Guards during the early years of the Grand Cultural Revolution, they were soon out of danger, just like Kang-li and Sun Tian. Every society needs doctors, so this man could have become educated if he had so desired. However, I saw only vanity in his large, beautiful eyes, and only empty words passed his perfect lips. What a pity, I thought. His limbs are strong, but his head is weak.

One day, he stopped his bicycle in front of mine in the street. "Xi-ou Tan, you take life too seriously. Will you treat me a little better from now on?"

Startled and angered, I shouted, "Let me go! If you have something to say to me, do it at the workshop!"

I pedaled away quickly, pursued hotly. I shouted again for him to leave me alone, and finally he turned back. I did not stop to think that even a person with a weak head has feelings that need to be respected. He must have planned this encounter for a long time, but I did not recognize the courage it must have required. At that time, falling in love seemed a sin to me. I did not want to allow my feelings to make me behave irresponsibly, nor did I think I had acquired enough skills or education to make a marriage work.

My girlfriends had different thoughts. Whereas I took time off to study after I earned enough to pay for my food, my friends fought for overtime and spent their paltry wages on gew-gaws to make themselves attractive. It never bothered me that they did everything possible to attract male attention, or even that they laughed at my simple clothing, but I did get angry when they tried to take me for a fool.

First one of them claimed that she needed to ride to the drugstore to buy medicine for her sick mother. Then another asked to borrow my bicycle so she could go visit her grandmother who was in the hospital with a broken leg. And so on. Believing them all, I could not refuse these requests, and I paid the extra money to squeeze onto a crowded bus to go to my German lesson.

It was not long before I discovered that the girls were using my bicycle to go on dates. They were all dating the same boy to play a trick on him. Impressed by their own cleverness, they boasted that they would do it again. I decided to get revenge. One day at work, I told them casually, "I can predict your future just by looking at your handwriting."

"Look at mine," they screamed, vying with each other for my attention. They all wanted their fortunes read, but no one wanted to be first, so they shoved one another in front of my machine.

I predicted that one girl's boyfriend was in love with someone else. Another girl would have a son with a speech impediment. A third's boyfriend, who was a Navy officer, was to die at sea. I spoke glibly, paying little attention to what I was saying, but the girls believed every word.

Soon I was the workshop fortune-teller, and the girls told me all their secrets to assist my "powers of prediction." Soon the game had gone too far; I had had my revenge, and it was time to stop. "Ah-liu is scolding me," I said to the girls, trying to chase them away from my machine. "If I can't get this month's job done, I'll be the one with the difficult future, not you."

"Let me help you," someone suggested.

△△△ I was stopped in the street again, this time by Lu-yu, one of Ah-liu's "noble ones." Before my fortune-telling skills had been revealed, these people had not condescended to speak to me. "Xi-ou, please tell me my future! I have an important decision to make," begged Lu-yu.

"I was just making . . . no . . . I don't know how to predict the future," I said. I had started to say that I was only making fun of the girls who had taken advantage of me by using my bicycle, but I stopped. The girls deserved to live with their pain for a few more days. Thinking me a fool, they had lied to me repeatedly and forced me to spend the little money I had on buses.

"Xi-ou, help me once, just this once, please," she entreated me.

The next day, Lu-yu bribed Ah-liu to let her pull a stool up to my machine so we could talk. Uncomfortable and impatient, I ordered shortly, "Tell me quickly what it is you want me to predict and write something on this paper so I can see your handwriting."

"All right. Let me start at the beginning. I met a man, Xiao Wong, who also works in a factory owned by the Neighborhood Committee. I fell in love with him, but my parents don't approve because he doesn't have a good income. Mother wanted to introduce me last month to a man who works at the same place she does, but I refused. My parents nagged me about it for a long time and finally told me I was a cheap tramp. The next day, I went to see Xiao Wong and told him how I felt about him. He ignored me, but I still went to see him several times after that. He called me a tramp, too. I cry all the time now. I want to die. What reason do I have to live?"

I thought the whole story banal, but Lu-yu could not finish it because of her tears. Uncomfortable, I decided to cut short the conversation: "Lu-yu, no one's future can be predicted on the basis of handwriting. We're acquaintances but not good friends. I think it would be best if you talked about this to some of your close friends. They might be able to help you decide what to do."

She grabbed my arm. "Xi-ou, you're so different from other people. Other people try everything to get information out of me so they can tell the whole world. But I want to tell you, and you don't even care enough to listen," she sobbed. "I don't have any close friends. You're the only person I can talk to. Won't you help me?"

I hardly knew Lu-yu, and we rarely spoke to each other in the workshop, even when we walked by each other. Now she was threatening suicide, so I could not sit by and do nothing. I asked, "What makes Xiao Wong so self-assured?"

"He's very capable. He can make furniture, tile floors, and install plumbing. He built a small shed in his backyard with his own hands. He's a good cook and a great tailor. He can even knit; that's how practical he is!"

I smiled: "He is a wonder! But even though he can do a lot of things, there are other things in this world that are more important. Why concentrate only on him? Don't you think learning to do some things yourself will help you feel good about yourself and make him respect you?"

I did not sleep well that night. In the morning, I wrapped up two textbooks and took them to the workshop. When no one was watching, I gave them to Lu-yu. "Being a good lathe operator requires some knowledge of geometry and trigonometry," I told her. "I don't have a text for solid geometry, but after you finish learning trigonometry, I can borrow one for you. The radio broadcast for this English text has just begun. Before coming to work, I went to the bookstore to buy this for you. I hope you'll start studying. Since you're on the day shift, you can listen to the broadcast in the evening."

"Can I ask you if I have any questions about these?" asked Lu-yu with new hope in her eyes.

"Of course," I said. I hoped that by studying, Lu-yu would learn self-respect. Although I did not know her well, I did believe in the power of knowledge.

"Oddhead" was about Rei-qing's age. He was indeed odd-looking and had an unusual personality. It was said that he never brushed his stained teeth, and sometimes, when the rest of us were working, he burst out laughing inexplicably. Clever, and good with his hands, he was permanently assigned to repair machinery. People claimed that machines listened to whatever he said. Between repair jobs, he sat on a huge stone outside the factory, facing away from the rest of us. Bandages served as knee patches for him, and his socks did not match. When anyone spoke to him, he stared silently at the speaker with tiny eyes behind thick glasses. It took a host of compliments, which he pretended not to hear, to prompt him to action.

Ah-liu was hard on all the other workers but was careful not to offend Oddhead. The thirty-year-old machinery constantly broke down, and no one else could fix it. If he was unsuccessful, it was set out with the trash. I had almost no respect for Oddhead, because I disliked the way he treated people. Aunt Chai told me that he had an affair with a neighbor's wife and became unbalanced when he was discovered.

One day, I had a problem with my machine and reluctantly asked Oddhead to repair it. He usually made people wait a long time for his services, but this time he brought his tools immediately and scattered them all over the offending machine. He disappeared, and although I waited until the end of the workday, he did not return. Not daring to leave my machine, I waited in vain the entire next day as well. Ah-liu came by at the end of that day, snarling, "You lazybones! All you do is eat and sleep! You never do any work!"

"The machine is broken and the mechanic hasn't returned," I defended myself timidly.

She clutched my arm and dragged me outside, screaming, "Are you dead? Can't you go out and look for him?"

Oddhead was sitting in his usual spot on the rock. Turning to him, Ah-liu pasted a hideous smile on her face and asked in a saccharine voice, "Would you possibly know what the little problem with her machine could be?" He did not respond, and Ah-liu repeated herself twice. Oddhead yawned, "It has caaaanncerrr."

Ah-liu was dumbstruck, and I covered my mouth to hide my laughter. The dismissal bell rang marking the end of the shift. Oddhead fixed the machine in a matter of minutes two days later. "Did you have enough free time?" he asked in a rare flight of conversation.

Suddenly realizing why he had abandoned the machine, I replied, "I don't think this is such a good way to take time off. I didn't enjoy it all that much."

"Next week, you are going to be assigned to the copper-parts job. That's the cleanest, lightest job there is."

"I doubt it. I'll never be that lucky," I said with disbelief.

"I thought you knew how to predict the future." Oddhead's eyes filled with sly laughter. "Why don't you predict your own?"

At the workshop meeting two days later, I was assigned to the copper-parts job. Copper was not shipped in grease as iron and steel were, and it was much easier to cut. Six blades and two drill bits were used in the complicated procedure required to make the copper parts. Sharpening each of the different blades took skill, and reinstalling them in the machine was tricky. I thought that Ah-liu had chosen me for this job because of its technical difficulty. I was unafraid of the job, and since this machine and Ah-liu's were in different rooms, she would not be able to keep such a close eye on me. Of course, I was pleased.

This new job put me on the afternoon shift. On the first day, Oddhead came up to me and said, "Well, was I right? Your luck has changed."

Not knowing how to respond, I just smiled. Oddhead continued, "I realigned this machine you're working on. If you have any problems with it, just come and ask." I thanked him politely.

The afternoon shift stretched from two in the afternoon until eleven at night. At five, the day shift left. The machine was in excellent condition, so I had turned out an entire carton of the product by six o'clock.

"Why are you working so hard?" Oddhead asked, pacing with his hands clasped behind him.

Smiling, I said nothing.

"This is a new product," he observed. "You're the first person to make them. No one knows how many a person can make, so whatever you do will be used as a standard. If you keep going like this, people who can't work as fast will curse you for it."

I had not considered this. "What should I do?" I asked.

Oddhead walked away, laughing. "Relax and enjoy yourself."

The next day, the blackboard showed that I had made three hundred of the copper items. The woman who used the machine on the other shift, "Pockmark," was a few years older than I and had more formal education. During the time our shifts overlapped, I quietly related Oddhead's advice about making too many, emphasizing that the blades and drill bits needed to be installed by the mechanics. I mentioned that it was extremely time-consuming to get the blades back in place after sharpening.

Pockmark implied that she understood, but the blackboard indicated that she had made 1,250 items. I made 450 the following day. The record for the next three days read, "510 vs. 1,300, 510 vs. 1,450, 500 vs. 1,680." Oddhead saw that I was worried and suggested, "Can't you remove all the drill bits and blades before you leave tonight? Let her try to install them herself."

I nodded. The blackboard the following day read, "500 vs. 0." Pockmark had still not finished installing the blades by the time I arrived for work. The next day, she used the blades as I had left them, and the record became "500 vs. 1,840."

"I think Pockmark wants to become a Model Worker at my expense," I told Oddhead.

"You just have to let her install the blades herself. I bet she'll never turn out more than two hundred a shift."

"But I can't remove the blades and bits every day. Copper is soft, and anyone with common sense would know there isn't any need to sharpen the blades every day," I said, discouraged.

Oddhead closed his tiny eyes in thought. "I've got it," he whispered. "You know the stone that sharpens the blades? Use it against the slope of the blade instead of along it. The blade will lose its edge, but nobody will be able to tell. No one can work for very long with a dull knife."

Oddhead showed me how to practice the maneuver. When I started the machine again, the blades and bits were so dull they barely marked the copper. The clever idea was successful, and the stunned Pockmark soon became subservient to me.

When I told the story to Father, he smiled and asked how the country's productivity would ever increase.

"But I won't make a penny more if I work any harder," I said, justifying my actions. "Of course, if I don't do as much, I won't get paid less, either. That's the advantage of our Socialist system."

Father stopped smiling and said seriously, "No. That's the short-coming of our Socialist system. I have understood this only since I left the academic world."

△△△ I found Oddhead intelligent and not very odd after all. I encouraged him to study calculus, and soon he developed an independent study plan of his own. He began washing, dressing more respectably, and treating people more kindly. He came to my station each day for half an hour, usually to chat about calculus, but occasionally we discussed national politics as well.

These conversations soon became grist for the gossip mill. Sometimes I overheard what others said about us, but I refused to let their narrow-mindedness destroy the friendship. People watched Oddhead's behavior with particular interest because of his reputation. I reminded myself that especially for this reason, I needed to keep our friendship intact. Suppose he did live up to these people's expectations and made a mistake? Then it would be very important for me not to let him down. He has already become a better person. Everyone can be opened; the problem is finding the key.

Professor Hu, I believed for a long time that I had discovered the keys to Oddhead and Lu-yu. Later, I was proved wrong. I will tell you these stories in another letter.

I still look forward to another letter from you.

Sincerely,
Xi-ou Tan

21

Dear Professor Hu,

In your letter, you described how painful it
was to lose your best friends. Death is no stranger
to me, but I have always feared it. I have noticed that
many families in the United States have cats and dogs, and
I think that this is good. Not only does it encourage children's
loving instincts, it also helps them understand birth and death.
My adolescence was spent in a troubled time. As a Chinese saying
goes, "If you turn the nest upside down, how do you expect an egg to
survive?" We heard constantly of people committing suicide or dying
some other way, and my family was always in danger. We had no
trouble speaking of death, but the first time I felt the pain was when
Grandfather Pu died.

In 1975, Chun-pu Chu died, and the master lay in quiet
repose on his bier. He reminded me again of Tao Zi, who had left his
post in the artificial world of serving the emperor to move back to
nature and the ways of peasant life. Death returned him to his eternal
home, free at last of earthly existence.

Rei-qing had visited him on August 4, eleven days before he died.
When he expressed his concern for her health during her pregnancy, she
told him, "The baby's due in about a month. My father and Tao-ran's
father want you to choose the name."

Grandfather Pu promised happily: "I can barely remember giving you your name, but I remember naming Xi-ou as though it were yesterday." He stroked his long white beard. He smiled, saying, "Shiou Tan, Xi-ou Tan."

"Father and Mother always joke that you gave her that name because she was ugly when she was born," said Rei-qing. "Is it true?"

The old man laughed: "I decided on that name before she was born. If she had been a boy, he would have had the same name. Both you and your sister have one very attractive feature: broad foreheads. 'Before your arrival, your head will hit the temple.' "

Grandfather Pu was in high spirits. Before Rei-qing said good-bye, he handed her a paper wall hanging: "I made it this morning. Give it to your father for me."

The hanging bore a poem by Tao Zi.

> You visit but once your best years,
> And morning cannot help but wane.
> Work hard while you can, and with care,
> For time you can never regain.

Father was excited by his mentor's gift: "Master Pu's work is like a warrior's sword: The older it is, the more it glitters. His writing is as fine as the best-tempered steel."

I was studying at home four days later when someone came to tell me that Si-qi was calling me on the public telephone. Grandfather Pu was very ill. He had contracted uremia three days earlier, compounding his pneumonia. He was sent to an emergency room, where he lost consciousness. It was the hottest day of the summer, and the workers and city-dwellers were suffering from heat exhaustion. The emergency room was packed, so the hospital was trying to move Chun-pu Chu out. Si-qi wanted our help.

I ran home, told Father the news, and then rode my bicycle to the public telephone and called Rei-qing. I asked her to call Uncle Xiong, whose cousin was a cardiopulmonary specialist. He could at least make sure Chun-pu Chu would get a bed in the emergency room. Next, I rode to Kang-li's hospital and asked her to assemble the best doctors for consultation.

Drenched with sweat, I pedaled toward the hospital where Chun-pu lay. As the sun beat mercilessly through the still, heavy air, I became light-headed and lost control of the bicycle, swerving all over the road. Running alongside a cement wall, I tore open my left arm. Huai Hai Road was as crowded as ever, even in the stifling heat. I tried to calm myself. Passersby ignored me, lost in their own worlds. The smell of sweaty human bodies and the loud sounds of summer in the stagnant air combined to make me nauseous.

Finally I reached the hospital. Unable to find the emergency room, I approached a custodian who was watering the floor of the lobby to cool the building. His back was turned toward me, and when I started to speak to him, I froze. It was not a strange male janitor, it was Si-qi. "Aunt Si-qi, what are you doing here? Why aren't you with Grandfather Pu?"

"I have to have a good relationship with the hospital staff. This is the most important thing to do right now," she answered nervously. Sweat covered her forehead, and her thick glasses were fogged. Pity for the woman swept over me, for although Si-qi still loved her father, she was too afraid to let it be known.

When I reached the emergency room, Chun-pu's breathing was labored, his eyes almost shut. An intravenous tube fed his arm, and Grandmother Chu stood gently fanning him and crying. He had not regained consciousness since coming to the hospital.

I suggested that she go home and rest for a while, but the artist's loyal wife refused to leave his side. Mother and Father had often told me stories of this couple's harmony, especially during the anti-Japanese war, the most difficult period of their lives. Thanks to them, I was able to understand the Chinese folktales of married couples who were so completely devoted that they vowed that although they were not born on the same day, they would die on the same one.

The cardiopulmonary expert had contacted the hospital to get a bed for Grandfather Pu. A very pregnant Rei-qing arrived in the evening, and although we spoke no words, we both knew that this would be the last time we would see him.

Ten beds were squeezed into about thirty square meters. A middle-aged man in a cadre's uniform was visiting the patient in the bed next to Chun-pu, and I saw the cadre eyeing Chun-pu's pale, emaciated face and long, flowing beard. Even in mortal illness, Grandfather Pu possessed the air of a great artist. The cadre stole over to the bed and grabbed the patient record. When he recognized the name, he shouted, "Aha! Chun-pu Chu! Chun-pu Chu!" When the cadre left, I hid the patient record, wanting Grandfather Pu's peace not to be disturbed.

He did not open his eyes again. The wall hanging of Tao Zi's poem was his last accomplishment, his hope for all who would come later.

△△△ Through much pain, a new life came into being.

Rei-qing's baby was born a month early, possibly because she had had no chance to recover from the grief of Chun-pu Chu's death. When I heard the good news, two lines from "The Song of an Old Tree," which Father had written when he was young, came to mind:

> *Where you burn down the tree,*
> *Our protector is born!*

My heart raced as I went to the hospital to see this strange, tender, pink new life. I was more nervous about seeing this innocent new baby than I would have been to see an Army general. In a matter of hours, I had gone from being a sister to being an aunt.

Some believe that people are born either wholly good or wholly evil. I believed that my new little nephew must have been born entirely good. Holding him in my arms, I patted him gently. He was not yet accustomed to light, and he cried when he was hungry or wet. When I placed him in the bath, he screamed and grabbed my blouse, clutching tightly to keep from drowning. Smiling lovingly, I looked down at the little bundle of humanity I held in my arms and thought of his future. Given love, he would return love. Given clothing, shelter, and food, he would become responsible. Given an education, he would become useful to society.

The child needed a name, Grandfather Pu's unfinished task. The child's two grandfathers were still grieving, but they did share the joy brought by a newborn baby. The Buddhist saying, "One side is happy, the other side sad; they are one" eloquently expresses the loss and gain of life. The friendship of these two men had become stronger by weathering stormy times, and it seemed like only recently that they had toasted their new acquaintance. It had been thirty years, and now they were both white-haired grandfathers.

Uncle Xiong arrived at Angle Cave to discuss with Father the important subject of naming their grandson. "You name him," he suggested modestly.

"Your choice is mine," Father replied sincerely.

One would think that these two intelligent, knowledgeable men, so well versed in classical Chinese literature, would have no trouble finding a good name for their grandson. But with Chun-pu's promise left unfulfilled, they were caught unprepared by the premature arrival. Since neither would assume the task, they unexpectedly turned to me.

Blushing, I said, "I've never thought about a formal name for him, but I do have a nickname in mind. Rei-qing ate almost two hundred eggs, *dans*, during her pregnancy. I think we should call him Dan-dan." The two grandfathers heartily approved the nickname, but the child still did not have a formal name.

Finally, Father said, "Ju-jin, Dan-dan's birthday is so close to the day that our Master Pu died. What do you think about the name You-pu?"

"Excellent! 'You' has three meanings. The first, meaning 'younger,' can refer to him as 'young pu.' The second means 'another,' so we recognize him as a 'second' Pu. And it also means 'to protect,' and we look to him for new hope for protecting the future. It expresses our feeling for Master Pu, and the hopes and dreams we have for our grandson. Yes, let's call him 'You-pu.' "

I prepared the red paper and brush pen, and the two grandfathers worked together to make the birth announcement. When I saw "You-pu Xiong" and "Dan-dan" appear on the paper, my heart skipped a beat. I committed myself to a special relationship with my nephew. The family now had a "new protector" through whom to look to the future.

△△△ A year and a half passed.

It was January 9, 1976, and I was working the afternoon shift at the machine shop. That morning, I wrapped my head and neck in a large muffler before bicycling against the cold wind to Professor Shan's home. A technical difficulty produced a jumbled burst of sound and static from the loudspeaker system outside the Jin Jiang Hotel. As a dirge began, I pulled my bike up to the side of the hotel to listen. The volume decreased, but I understood the words: Premier Zhou En-li was dead.

It was no surprise, since the premier had not taken part in any diplomatic activities for quite some time because of poor health. I told Professor Shan the news, and the two of us sat together quietly, not knowing what to say. Premier Zhou was considered the most humane of all the government officers, and he treated intellectuals with respect. Rei-qing and I had invested a great deal of energy in our En-lightenment plan. Although we had sent a village's worth of letters to Premiere Zhou without receiving an answer, I still felt a connection with him that I did not feel with any of the other leaders.

Later, at home, Father pointed to the radio and said angrily, "The health of a prime minister of such a large country ought to be public knowledge! The Party has been lax in its duty to the people. It has isolated itself from us. Rumors fly in all directions, and in the end, all they can do is lamely read us an obituary when one of the rumors comes true."

When I went out to buy Father a newspaper, I saw people already wearing black armbands. My own workshop distributed them to each employee. Several days later, women began wearing white flowers in their hair. The flowers were made of various materials and came in an assortment of shapes and sizes. Each woman wore hers differently, taking advantage of the rare opportunity to set herself apart. Rei-qing commented, "Only Shanghai citizens would do this! I heard that the people of Beijing reacted very emotionally to the passing of Premier Zhou."

On April 5, a huge crowd gathered in Tiananmen Square to pay tribute to the memory of Zhou En-li and show their anger with ten years of oppression and dictatorship. All were arrested. Aunt Chai's son was on a business trip to Beijing that day and saw the memorial service. He told his family and a few close friends about the bloody suppression of the masses but maintained to others that he had been ill and shut up in a hotel room all day. Everyone in the workshop was ordered to turn in a report listing his or her hour-by-hour activities that day.

Zhu De, the chairman of the National People's Congress and the former commander of the People's Liberation Army, died that July. An earthquake the same month killed 200,000 people in Tang Shan. Several old aunties in the workshop insinuated that the Communist Party would not last long. They claimed that Premier Zhou and Chairman Zhu De were beings from a twilight world and that their existence corresponded to huge stars in the sky, which would soon die also. The rumor was that the disastrous earthquake of Tang Shan, so soon after the two men died, was an omen of the impending doom of Communist power. I worried about the safety of the old aunties, but my mind was filled with contradictions. Although eager for change, I knew that it could also bring disaster.

△△△ Oddhead's bicycle caught up with mine one night when our shift was over. As we parted, Oddhead pointed to his armband and said clearly, "I sincerely hope we will wear this until another day."

I understood his meaning and assumed that the PLA men patrolling Kang-ping Road would also. While I wondered if Chairman Mao's death would follow, I was frightened to the core, so I only glanced up at Oddhead and nodded briefly. He added boldly, "That day will come soon."

"That day" arrived very soon indeed: September 9, 1976. At three in the afternoon, a dirge played over the 9,600,000 square kilometers of China. Rei-qing and I were on Kang-ping Road teaching You-pu how to walk. His fat little legs and tiny white leather shoes stuck out of his pale green overalls as he toddled from Rei-qing to me and back again. When the dirge sounded from all directions, You-pu became terrified. He stood crying in the middle of the road, so we picked him up, patted him, and carried him home.

The noon broadcast had announced that there would be an important bulletin at three, but when we heard the dirge, we knew that

Mao was dead. Lowering my voice, I said, "I'm glad we won't have to teach Dan-dan to be a good hypocrite."

Children born during these years were taught in kindergarten not only Chairman Mao quotation songs, which all adults needed to learn, but also Revolutionary nursery songs. The most popular ones were "I Love Beijing Tiananmen," and "Dreaming about Chairman Mao at Midnight":

> I watched my little brother
> Sleeping soundly through the night.
> I saw him smile and waken,
> Although the hour was midnight.
> He tells me that he smiles,
> "For dreams of Chairman Mao tonight."

Parents worried that their children would repeat the slights they heard at home about the government, so they discussed politics behind their backs. Most taught their children to love Chairman Mao for their own protection. There were a few children only five or six years old who were labeled anti-Revolutionaries at the beginning of the Revolution. Through simple curiosity, or by parroting what they heard at home, or testing their own creative power, some of these children shouted anti-Revolutionary slogans: "Down with Chairman Mao!" or "Chairman Mao is a rotten egg!" bringing punishment on their entire family.

How could we teach You-pu the noble concepts of a nation, its leader, and its people? Could we train him to interpret correctly every statement his teachers would make, including the lies, and to accept his self-confined grandfather and his imprisoned grandmother? If he asked, "What kind of person was Lin Biao?" could we say that he was a traitor yet admit that when we were his age, we waved a Little Red Book over our heads every day saluting his eternal health? Would he understand if we spoke openly to him? Would he parrot us, or point out the teacher's lies in class? Telling him nothing was perhaps the safest strategy, but was it being responsible to the next generation? We thanked God that we no longer had these worries.

Even though I had already finished my shift the day I heard the news, I returned to the workshop. It was filled with people when I arrived, but the machines were off, and the only sounds I heard were cries of sorrow. A makeshift table was covered with three large wreaths and several hundred white paper flowers. I saw Ah-liu's long face and heard her ask, "How come that anti-Revolutionary whelp hasn't shown up? She must be at home drinking and celebrating!"

Pretending not to hear, I wormed my way through the crowd to the table and began making white paper flowers. The old aunties who only a day earlier had so secretively begun rumors of Communist power's impending doom were bawling as if their parents had just died.

My workshop held a memorial service in the Neighborhood Committee's mourning room. Ah-hua, one of the most prolific gossips among the old aunties, wore the traditional clothing of feudalistic mourning: a piece of hemp hung over her hair and back, and a white cloth with a red square sewn at the heel covered her black cloth shoes, while several other pieces of hemp fell from her shoulders to her knees. The extra cloth made it difficult for her to move her overweight body, but she managed to climb the steps to the stage. Throwing herself on the ground in front of Chairman Mao's portrait, she wailed like a professional mourner: "Aaaahhhh . . . Chairman Mao . . . how could you so thoughtlessly leave us behind? Aaaahhhh . . . Chairman Mao . . . do something good for us . . . take us with you!"

Several young intellectuals snickered at the ridiculous words, strange voice, awful tune, and unusual dress. Ah-liu, adept at turning her emotions on and off, stopped crying. Jumping out of her seat, she shouted, "Who's laughing? The class enemy is taking advantage of this tragedy! Search her out!" The whites of her large, angry eyes were red as she fixed her gaze on me. This was the second time she had put me in a politically dangerous situation. Bravely, I lifted my head and stared back at her.

I had been too worried about another situation to laugh. The Central Committee had already given the directive that a national mourning period would begin at three o'clock on the afternoon of September 18. This service, the final observance of Chairman Mao's body, would be broadcast nationwide. All Chinese not in Beijing were to pay their respects in front of the nearest public television. The Runt ordered Father to go to the Public Security Office with other Blacks. I helped him write a thousand-word request for a waiver, but I was not sure that the application would be accepted.

When it came time for Ah-liu to pay respects to Chairman Mao's portrait, she sobbed magnificently: "Ah-hua has the deepest reverence toward Chairman Mao of anyone I've ever seen. She cried so sincerely that all of us must take a lesson from her. But the class enemy doesn't give up even at a time such as this! She is already planning new evils. She was just laughing! It was her! That anti-Revolutionary whelp! Did you hear it?"

In the pregnant silence, I made up my mind that as long as Ah-liu didn't say my name out loud, I would be quiet. This was her revenge for the blackmail game I refused to play. Ah-hua suddenly forgot about crying. She was still kneeling, but her back was turned to Chairman Mao.

"I didn't hear any laughter." This was Aunt Chai's voice.

"Neither did I." The echo rippled through the crowd.

One of the young intellectuals who had been laughing mustered his courage and said to Ah-liu, "Aunt Hong, you must be imagining things. None of us were laughing." Taking the kneeling Ah-hua's arm, Ah-liu stepped off the stage in defeat.

It was difficult not to laugh at the feigned seriousness of the old women mourners at the many services, but the threat of an official response to any irreverence kept most people intimidated. At one service, a young man from the workshop next door to mine became bored waiting in line, and he began watching the Party secretary-general bowing to the people. The secretary had been chastised at the beginning of the Cultural Revolution, but when he was liberated later from the Ox Ghost Ranch, he resumed his former position. As the representative of Chairman Mao's family, he received the bows of those who only a short time earlier had chastised him. He was known to some as Comrade "Ji Gen-fa," and although it was not his real name, it was a common one that also meant "bald spot." Watching the bald head reflect the light as it bobbed up and down, the young man from the neighboring workshop burst into laughter. He was arrested and sentenced to ten years in jail.

⚞⚟ "Ah-liu is making life very difficult for us," Oddhead told me that afternoon.

"I'm thinking of writing her a warning letter. I need someone to help me, though," I replied.

"What kind of help?" he asked.

"She's in charge of the day shift next week, and I'm on the afternoon one. If someone put the letter on her tool cabinet in the morning, she wouldn't have any reason to suspect me."

Thumping his hand to his chest, Oddhead said, "Next week I have the day shift, too!"

The warning letter, written in a semiliterate style, exposed Ah-liu's exploitation of the workers. I thought that she would be too intimidated to respond openly but might ease her demands on the workers. To my surprise, she handed the letter over to the secretary of the Neighborhood Committee as if she were the victim. She demanded an investigation, and many meetings were held. Everyone was asked to recall what had happened the morning the letter had appeared. Although I was not there that morning, Oddhead, Aunt Chai, and several of my close friends had the day shift. It did not take genius to pull together the circumstantial evidence. The committee voted to pursue the investigation, but since nothing was more important than properly mourning Chairman Mao's death, the matter was put aside temporarily.

⚞⚟ The political situation took another abrupt turn in October 1976. While bicycling to the workshop, I saw a group of university students parading at the intersection of Kang-ping and Yu Qin roads. Their banners read, "Jiao Tung University," and they were shouting, "Down with Jian-qing! Down with Zhang Chun-qiao! Down with Wang Hong-wen! Down with Yao Wen-yuan!" "Down with the 'Gang of Four'!"

People stopped in their tracks—some smiling, some puzzled, some angered, and some worried for the students. Tears of happiness tingled in my eyes. Ten years earlier, at the same intersection on a hot and stuffy afternoon, a group of Red Guards in mustard-colored uniforms with broad belts across their waists had marched and sung the "Song of the Red Guards."

War with the Japanese took eight years, I thought, but war with ourselves had taken ten. China had experienced the worst of human nature, and our people had experienced insult and torture. Ten years was only an instant compared to all of history, but to a single human being whose life is only a small slice of time, ten years were far too precious to lose. I listened to the quiet happiness I felt inside. Our family had survived. Father had lost his freedom and his health was getting poorer, and Mother was doing forced labor on a farm and could not return home for a reunion, but compared to the atrocities other people had suffered, and considering how many had died or had been killed, we had done well. We were alive and safe.

△△△ When I arrived at the workshop, I sensed a change in the atmosphere. Ah-liu ordered all the machines shut down and told us to march to the Shanghai homes of the Gang of Four on Kang-ping Road and search them. Each member of the Gang of Four had homes in Beijing and Shanghai, and perhaps in other places as well. Everyone complied, pressing out the doors.

More than a thousand workers, students, and peasants were already standing in front of the fence that separated them from the houses. The demonstrators held small, flag-shaped banners with slogans splashed across them, shouting, "Down with the 'Gang of Four'!" Fifty PLA soldiers nervously defended the fence's single gate as representatives of the workers and students argued for entry. Someone inside the gate house came out to negotiate, but the mob did not wait peacefully. The already-scattered PLA soldiers never used their weapons, for, even armed, they were no match for the angry people. The line they had formed broke quickly, and the crowd stormed past.

I was in the middle of the throng. Caught up in the fervor of the moment, I joined in the crowd's angry shouts and threats. Gorky's *Memoir of Lenin* described the workers' attack on the Winter Palace, and although the homes of the Gang of Four were not as grand, and we did not carry guns on our shoulders as the Proletarian workers did, I saw the new Liberation unfold with the same powerful force. Once past the gate, the ecstatic crowd tossed caps and coats skyward.

The head of the PLA detachment shouted through a megaphone, "Mayor Ke's home and family will be left unharmed!" Ke, the former mayor of Shanghai, had died shortly before the Cultural Revolution but had been regarded as Chairman Mao's local right-hand man. The unruly mob ignored the PLA officer, and I followed the crowd first into Zhang Chun-qiao's home.

Inside, I saw Zhang's daughter a few feet in front of me. She was about Rei-qing's age, and her dark eyes looked out anxiously from behind her glasses. Neither of us spoke, and she sat silently on the plush living-room sofa, holding one hand against her cheek. Black cloth flowers draped the frames of two large portraits of Chairman Mao and Premier Zhou. The irony was inescapable, since it was no secret that Zhang had waited eagerly for Zhou's death so he could assume the post. He and Jian-qing had planned for the day of Mao's death when she would take the title of empress.

A man who appeared to be a teacher was interrogating the daughter, commanding her to confess her father's sins to the masses. The invading workers and students, uninterested in confessions, explored the home of the people now in their power. At first, they only looked at the beautiful and expensive furnishings, but then they began the destruction. They broke the hanging lamps with stones, jumped up and down on the furniture, and spit on the walls and floor of the bathroom. The ordinary peasants, students, and workers did little damage compared to what the Red Guards had done to my home, but the same psychology was in effect. Upset, I could not understand why Revolutionaries had to use destruction to validate their cause and prove their loyalty to it.

We found Wang Hong-wen's home, his second residence, already destroyed. He had once been an ordinary member of the working class, but the ten years of the Grand Cultural Revolution had made him a national leader, powerful and rich. This fact infuriated the crowd. Discovering several pairs of leather shoes in the closet, the people spit in them and threw them over the balcony. The crowd shouted with glee each time an item sailed out a second-floor window, seeing their own poverty magnified in comparison with the wealth of the upstart politicians.

Leaving the angry, excited throng, I walked slowly to an empty spot in the grassy garden. I looked up at the sky and prayed silently that the Revolution that had put the nation at peril would soon end. Feeling as if I were the only clearheaded person around, I stood apart from the crowd of people shouting and destroying property. Suddenly, I caught a glimpse of a familiar person and called out, "Aunt Sai-ping!" She was so nearsighted that she could not possibly have seen me, but she came straight toward me. "Yes, Xi-ou Tan?"

I went toward her, surprised: "How did you know it was I who called you? There are so many people here."

For the first time, she looked me full in the face and smiled. "You are the only person who would call me 'Aunt' in public," she said. She told me that she was going to try to get her son home from the remote countryside, and that her mother had responded well to the medication I had given her. I was happy for her, and so touched by her warmth that I cried.

That evening, Rei-qing told the family that on October 6, several days before their Shanghai houses had been raided, the Gang of Four had been caught in their Beijing homes. The news flashed through Beijing and people secretly toasted the capture. Father commented, "The 'People's Revolution' has just occurred and no blood has been shed, no bullets fired. The Chinese people are very fortunate."

△△△ I thought that my family's life would become easier now, but in fact, the opposite was true. The Runt visited more frequently and his verbal abuse increased.

You-pu was learning to talk, and although he only spoke a few words, he understood everything that was said. Rei-qing and Tao-ran brought him to see Father at least once a week. As Dan-dan and Father were playing together happily one day, the Runt barged in. Saliva sprayed from his mouth as he screamed, "Jin-ren Tan, what do you think you're doing? You should be reforming yourself instead of wasting time with your grandson! Your trashy Gang of Four isn't here to support lousy whelps like you! What do you think of your precious Party being flushed down the toilet? Who are you going to kiss up to now? Sooner or later, the Proletarian fist is going to smash you to pieces!"

You-pu did not understand all of the words, but he did realize that a devil was grilling his grandfather. Using the only weapon he had, he screamed. For twenty years, Father had swallowed his pride and borne humiliation like this, accepting unwarranted abuse for the sake of his unfinished work and family. Now a white-haired grandfather, he would no longer countenance this ridiculous censure.

His eyes blazed: "Don't bully me! You're the one who's supporting the Gang of Four! You're the one bullying the people like a fox in tiger's clothing. My patience has limits. Even if my sentence had been a fair one, I finished it four years ago. Who gave you the right to lecture me? Where is the discipline of the Party? Where is the law of the country?"

"What are you talking about? Who is breaking the law here? Nobody's stealing anything from you!" the Runt spit back. No one had accused the Runt of this, but we all knew that each time he came to lecture Father, he slipped small items into his pocket. Angry, he ordered Father to attend a chastisement meeting and also to help build a fallout shelter. He knew that this was in fact a punishment for me, because I had to do all of Father's tasks.

△△△ Father felt dizzy one day two months later, so Rei-qing gave him medicine to lower his blood pressure. After that, we monitored it with a blood-pressure gauge borrowed from Kang-li. Finally, we decided it was time to take Father to a doctor. We put a gauze mask over his face to protect him from the winter cold and escorted him to the Zhong Shan Hospital, where the doctors gave him a complete physical examination. They found nothing wrong, so we all took the opportunity to tour the city.

Father was in excellent spirits that night. If Rei-qing had not needed to rush home to take care of You-pu, we would have gone out to eat wonton. It had been ten years since he had set foot in the dynamic, cosmopolitan city of Shanghai. The changes it had undergone made him feel like a stranger.

Twice we took Father to the movies under the watchful eyes of Madame Couvre and the Runt. Theaters were now permitted to show films other than the eight Revolutionary Model movies, so some were featuring old copies of Eastern-bloc or Korean movies. Tickets were hard to obtain, but Rei-qing and I got two: one for Father and the other for Chi-kai, so he could go along when he was home from the farm.

It was a treat for both of them, but I tortured myself while they were gone. Would Father end up sitting next to the Runt, the Alley Cat, or Madame Couvre? Perhaps the film would be stopped and the lights turned on, and the police would check for identification. I tried to distract myself by working abstruse mathematical problems until they returned.

△△△ Chi-kai's industry and personality eventually won respect for him at the suburban farm, although for the first three years he was bullied by those older and bigger than he. In every society, the strong rule the weak, but here, weakness could be political as well as physical. While Chi-kai could not change his lot in the political system, he fought desperately for achievement in other areas. To increase his physical strength, he asked for the hardest, dirtiest work, even if he could not complete the job.

After a day of hard labor, he was barely able to move. His hands trembled from exhaustion as he held his rice bowl at dinner. Chi-kai paid close attention to the advice of his peasant coworkers, for he took his farm work seriously. Gradually he became adept at growing vegetables and rice, tending cows, and raising pigs. He caught fish to improve the diet of his unit on the farm. Years of such work made him proficient at all the farm jobs in his unit, and the muscles he flexed were impressive.

Farm workers were given five-day vacations every few months, and the young intellectuals were sent to the city to visit their families.

Chi-kai's coworkers enjoyed the city culture by window-shopping and going to the cinema. Chi-kai went home to study. Rei-qing and I checked the algebra and English assignments he had done at the farm and helped him with material he had not yet mastered. His coworkers returned to the farm with their backpacks stuffed with food, but Chi-kai's was stuffed with books.

After his day of heavy physical labor on the farm, Chi-kai would go to the children's day-care center, empty in the evening, to study. He often fell asleep as he worked on his homework, usually not awakening until dawn. The harsh sunshine and twelve-hour days exhausted him, and he often awoke drenched in perspiration. Ignoring the light-headedness he felt when he awoke, he studied until it was time for work.

Jian-nan had once given him a book entitled *How to Repair Alarm Clocks*. On one of his vacations, Chi-kai purchased a broken alarm clock in a second-hand store in Shanghai and repaired it. He hung it inside the mosquito-net curtains around his bed so he could rise thirty minutes before the sun. Each morning, he jogged around the trees forming the windbreak for the fields and then went to the river to wash. He would carry two five-gallon buckets of water to the dormitory and add purification chemicals so the others could use it to bathe and drink. His dormitory was the cleanest one on the farm. It was named a Model Dormitory, and even the women were forced to tour it.

Another year passed, and Chi-kai saw all of his coworkers reassigned to industrial positions in the city. Even those with below-average performances were sent back because they had spent the required number of years on the farm. Rei-qing had been lucky with the new policy, and she was allowed to return to the city as soon as it became official. But matters were more difficult for Chi-kai. The loopholes of the new policy were well-known by now, and those with influence were the first to leave. No clause forbade the return of a Black to the city, but no help was available, either.

Chi-kai's roommate had written me a letter telling me that Chi-kai had saved a woman visitor from drowning. Chi-kai and four coworkers—all older, taller, and stronger than he—had been mending their fishnets by the river. Not far from them, two women attempted to cross the river in a small boat, one at a time. The boat overturned with the first woman in it, but she caught hold of a rope tied to a docking post before she could be swept downstream. Unable to swim to shore against the swift river current, she held fast to the rope while her friend onshore screamed for help.

The four older workers remained where they were. The riverbank was steep and the weather was rough. Saving the woman meant putting his own life in peril, but Chi-kai jumped into the icy water without hesitation. Powerful waves impeded his progress, and when he reached her, he realized how difficult it would be to pull the large, heavy woman to shore. By the time he pulled her up on the riverbank, she had passed out.

The most respected of his four coworkers, a "poor peasant," said, "We should thank young Tan for rescuing this woman. Saving another's life smooths your own path after you die. By tradition, her parents must burn incense and candles, serve a huge feast, and send her to him as a slave. If she had drowned, we wouldn't have the strength to cross this river again."

If a Red had done this, the deed would have been lauded with the hero's picture and story appearing in the newspaper, but for a Black, it was not even acknowledged with thanks. But Chi-kai's name was placed high on the list of those suggested as candidates for returning to the city, and no one objected. He reported this news to us, and we were ecstatic. I waited eagerly for the confirmation from him, but no letter came.

Father and I decided that a visit to Chi-kai would raise his spirits. As a surprise for him, I rose at midnight to bicycle ninety kilometers to the farm, arriving at noon. From Chi-kai's letter, I knew that the small hut at the edge of the river was his. Standing upright in front of the hut was a pole to help the fishermen determine their position when they were out at sea.

I faced the ocean, with the river behind me. A boat floated in the distance on the river; Chi-kai was fishing, having left an older peasant to guard the hut. The walls were made of thin plastic sheets pasted together with seaweed. When I walked in, I was impressed with the hut's tidiness, especially since it was so near the beach.

Checking Chi-kai's bed, I found the linen clean. A half-written letter addressed to us was under his pillow. It was filled with thoughts of frustration and depression, so perhaps he had been reluctant to send it. It also confirmed our conclusion that he had been denied a return to Shanghai. Although accustomed to facing difficulties in my own life, I could not accept the fact that they happened to those I loved. Despite my pity for my brother, I refused to reveal my emotions in front of his coworker.

Within the hour, Chi-kai returned from his fishing. Although it had been muddied by the long ride, he recognized my bicycle leaning against the wall of the hut. His first words were, "You should try out for the Chinese Olympic bicycling team!"

Chi-kai and I walked the bicycle a few meters along the embankment and sat down. Facing the ocean, a silver ribbon rising to the edge of the sky, he told me what had happened since his last letter. His emotions were still close to the surface, but he was no longer in the depths of despair.

"Older Sister," he said firmly, "I'm going to take action. I'm asking to be transferred to Yan Fong's unit, and I'm also going to apply for the Youth League. I'll definitely be in Shanghai next year."

Yan Fong was the same age as Chi-kai, and they had become good friends from the day they met on the farm. People often mistook them for twins. When Yan Fong was twelve, he lived away from home with his grandmother. One day, he received a telegram asking him to visit his parents in Tian Jin. When he arrived, he was handed an axe and was told to break down the door of his parents' home. His father's body lay in the front room, an anti-Revolutionary suicide. His mother had already been sent to a hospital for the mentally disturbed.

That day, Yan Fong made up his mind to join the Youth League and the Party to ensure his future. Although he could have remained in the city after his graduation, he gave up this option to pursue his goal of Party membership. One of his relatives was the Party vice secretary, and with this man's influence, Yan Fong was sent to a suburban farm. He joined the Party and became the secretary of one of the farm units, supervising eight hundred people. He seldom spoke to others of his past, but he and Chi-kai were victims of the same "disease." He told Chi-kai his past and was honest with his thoughts.

"I went to see Yan Fong yesterday," said Chi-kai. "He said he'd send in a request for me to be transferred to his unit after spring recess. I'm going to stay there for a year and help him work out a few of his problems. He'll help me join the Youth League. When my political reputation has improved, I'll have a much better chance of leaving than I do now. Yan Fong set up a series of reforms after he took over the unit, and now the unit has its own set of rules. If you work hard, you are rewarded, and if you do something wrong, you are punished. It practically breaks the 'iron rice bowl.' In their unit, you can't just sit around doing nothing and expect to get paid the same as the others. They planted a lot of trees, so their unit will look a lot different from the others in a few years. Yan Fong wants me to be his adviser."

"Good!" I clapped my hands. "Brother, I wish you success."

It started raining as I was bicycling home. The rain came down harder as I entered the city, and when I crossed the threshold of Angel Cave, the sky was groaning with thunder. It was past nine, but Father and Jian-nan had not eaten dinner. As I sat down to eat with them, the rain was falling in sheets.

As I started to tell them about my visit, we heard a knock at the door. Opening it, I saw an indistinguishable figure, soaked by the rain, under the light. Without asking who it was, I pulled him in and discovered that it was Y-si's brother, Y-xing. I hurried to get dry towels for him, and he pulled out a letter that had been hidden under his shirt. Handing it to me, he said, "Here. My father asked me to deliver this to you in person."

Y-xing's father, Sun Tian, had always been kind to us. I remembered how generous he had been in volunteering to show Jian-nan's paper to his academic contacts. And Father enjoyed the terrarium I had brought back from him. The letter was still warm from Y-xing's body. It read in part:

> Dear Xi-ou,
>   When I saw the country celebrating the defeat of the "Gang of Four," I thought of you and your extraordinary sister and brothers. In the darkest times, you lived your lives with strength and courage. You

fought to master the ability to serve your country. Now
a new light is dawning. It is your turn to be in the center
of it.

My eyes filled with tears, but Sun Tian's encouraging words helped
me forget the exhaustion and frustration of the long, tiring journey to
Chi-kai's farm. While my family did not get to bask in the light
immediately, improvement was just around the corner. I will tell you
about it in my next letter.

Sincerely,
Xi-ou Tan

*The "Great Leap Forward" Movement claimed in 1958
that within fifteen years, China would be more advanced
than the British Empire. Scientists worked around the
clock on impractical experiments, such as proving that a minute
amount of kelp was the nutritional equivalent of a day's portion of rice,
or determining whether or not pulverized fish bone could be used as a
semiconducting material. They obtained no useful results and wrote
reports that could only embarrass them later.*

*History repeated itself eight years later with the scientific absur-
dities of the Grand Cultural Revolution. The most famous incident was
the criticism of Newton's laws of motion. Chairman Mao said, "The
anti-Revolutionary does not disappear from history on its own. It is like
sweeping the floor: if there is no broom, the dust will not disappear."
Three centuries earlier, Newton had declared that "a body with a given
velocity, unaided or impeded by external forces, will continue moving
with that velocity." In other words, if nothing gets in the way, a moving
object keeps moving. One of the groups of the Academy of Science
stated that this was equivalent to saying the dust would disappear
without the broom, and Newton's statement was labeled anti-
Revolutionary. No one dared to point out that the two statements had*

nothing to do with each other. The Revolutionary Mass hung large posters denouncing Newton's conspiracy with modern anti-Revolutionaries to contaminate the minds of the people. No one dared bring up the fact that Newton had been dead for three centuries. The posters, written by many famous scientists, announced that Newton had been a counterfeiter in his later life and had had numerous concubines.

Albert Einstein was next. A countryside teacher declared that he had experimentally disproved the theory of relativity. After gathering data and interpreting his results, he jumped to his conclusion, failing to consider experimental error. A highly respected newspaper ran it as a front-page story with the headline, "Another Victory for Invincible Mao Zedong Thought." The newspaper had gone to press, but at the last minute, just before distribution, someone discovered that the teacher did not understand experimental error. The paper was not released, and international embarrassment was avoided.

Dear Professor Hu,

On a November morning in 1976, I went to the periodicals section on the third floor of the Shanghai Library; in 1973, it had reopened for limited use. As an electrical engineer, Tao-ran had a pass, so I borrowed it and pasted my picture over his.

Father took me there when I was a child. While he looked for references, I would sit, resting my head on my hands and gazing peacefully out the window. I often fell asleep like this, and Father would shake me gently when he was ready to leave hours later. His arms filled with heavy books, he would walk with me to the People's Park, next to the library. Then it was my turn: I played while Father waited. A perfect collaboration.

I had come to the Shanghai Library to look up the components of an expensive prescription medicine that a neighbor had received from a relative in the West. I had no trouble with its English description, but the Latin words were unknown to me. I found them quickly in another text, and my task was complete. Not wanting to pass up a rare opportunity to be in the library, I decided to enjoy the solitude and study instead of going directly home.

Timidly approaching a shelf filled with books bound in leather embossed with gold leaf, I carefully removed one. It was an encyclopedia, and my volume focused on animal cells. The minute print and detailed photographs of the plants impressed upon me my ignorance of the natural world. But I had neither the background nor the facilities to study biology. Even if there had been no Grand Cultural Revolution to impede my education, I would never have done well in the life sciences. I received the lowest grade in my life, a "C," in biology during my first year of middle school for refusing to dissect a frog.

Replacing the book, I searched for materials more closely related to the fields I knew. As I passed through one of the reading rooms, I spied a journal on a table with two Chinese characters, *Kaga Ku,* or *Science* in Japanese, on the cover. I flipped through the first several pages until I came to an advertisement for a book entitled *Quantum Chemistry.*

Quantum chemistry? I wondered why I had never heard of it. I decided to find a book on that subject and learn about it. Searching the card catalog, I found no Chinese books on quantum chemistry. I would have to read Japanese, English, French, or Russian ones. I copied the catalog numbers of the Japanese texts so that Rei-qing could borrow them with her library card. Frustrated, I left the library. When I got home, I wrote a note to Tao-ran requesting him to ask his college-educated friends about quantum chemistry.

Two months later, Tao-ran's friend's friend's uncle's niece's grandfather's old classmate wrote to me—a complicated chain of communication that managed to make it back to me. The response was a turning point. First, quantum chemistry attempts to explain phenomena that classical chemistry cannot. Two large divisions exist within chemistry: experimental and theoretical. Quantum mechanics is the foundation for the latter, which is also called quantum chemistry. Second, unless experiments need to be done, quantum chemistry can be self-taught.

"Then I'll teach myself quantum chemistry," I determined. Professor Shan agreed with my plan, saying, "Learning a foreign language is not an end in itself. A language is merely a tool. It won't help you until you have a place to apply it. If you have both a language and a science background at your disposal, you can introduce new foreign science and technology to China."

My ambitions were higher than this. I did not want only to

introduce new science and technology to China; I wanted to be an expert in my field of study. I began studying the principles of general chemistry and the Japanese text on quantum chemistry at the same time. Between my job and taking care of our home, I had little free time, but I devoted most of it to self-education. Remembering what happened when I studied German, I tried to sleep at least seven hours a day.

△△△ At the machine shop, it had been some time since Oddhead had shown up at my lathe to talk, but I assumed that he was busy with his own life. Aunt Chai told me she had heard that Lu-yu and Oddhead were dating, and I recalled that Lu-yu had recently claimed to be too busy to study English and math with me. I was not jealous; I thought them well suited. It was their prerogative to leave me out of the secret. They would tell me at the right time, and I was happy for them.

It was nearing the end of the Saturday-afternoon shift. Lu-yu had not yet stopped by to tell me if she wanted to meet on Sunday to discuss the next week's problem sets, so I walked over to her machine. She was chatting with Oddhead, so I asked, "Lu-yu, can you come over to my work station when you have a chance?"

She must have known what I wanted, but she eyed me coldly, saying, "Can't you tell me here?"

"Tomorrow afternoon, same time, same place?" I asked hesitantly. I had not told anyone, including Oddhead, that I was teaching her English and math.

"No, I don't have time for that. No." She sounded as if I were the one asking a favor. I left. After discussing the matter with Rei-qing that night, I decided to leave them to themselves. I had enough of my own studying to do.

△△△ The first college-entrance examinations since the beginning of the Cultural Revolution were scheduled for the end of 1977. Graduate-school entrance examinations were delayed several times but finally were scheduled for May 1978, and I registered only for those.

Years of self-education had given me confidence in my abilities, but still I worried.

The "Red Guard college students"—those who had been in college when the Cultural Revolution began and were now between thirty and forty years old—were my competition. Two hundred sixty-five students from all over the country registered for the same adviser that I did. More than ten were research fellows and assistant professors from first-class universities outside the city. If they became graduate students, they could move back to Shanghai.

Ah-liu sniped, "Nine out of two hundred sixty-five! She doesn't have a chance! She never finished high school, let alone set foot on a college campus. She's stupid to hope for so much! As the old saying goes, 'There's only a single step from the ground to the sky.' She might as well be trying to walk to the moon!"

While Ah-liu sneered, even my good friends worried that I had set my sights too high. Some tried to persuade me to take the college test first, yet I was adamant about not becoming an undergraduate. I was taking a risk but subconsciously had something to prove.

Most of my classmates were still in the remote countryside, although the lucky ones were in county or commune factories. They worked all year, barely filling their stomachs. Putting money aside for a visit to Shanghai was a luxury, so they had no opportunity to come and prepare for the examinations.

Although many of them had once been Red Guards, they were no better or worse than people of any other era. Placed in the same historical and political setting, any generation would have made the same stupid, cruel mistakes as mine did, taking the roles available at the time. Many decisions were dictated by family situations, the primary cause for most actions. Ancestral traditions, also important, were the secondary cause. The seed of evil was thousands of years old; the soil, perfect; and the climate, ideal. Many generations had fertilized it, and it took root and grew with the Cultural Revolution.

If the Red Guards had been born into a slave-holding society, they would have become obedient slaves. Born in feudal times, they would have gone to the capital to take exams to become suppressors of the people, as duty would have dictated. Born during a war, they would not have feared dying for their country. I did not despise them for belonging to the generation of the Red Guards. Under a normal educational system, important scientists, philosophers, artists, and writers would have appeared, but before we could determine our own personal philosophies, we were seduced by the slogan of the Revolution, "Knowledge is useless." Swept by the storm of "Abandon classroom study and commit yourselves to the Revolution," all impulses to pursue knowledge for its own sake were strangled. No one knew that the classrooms would be closed for more than a decade and that a whole generation would be barely literate.

I do not know if I would have been a Red Guard who fought, robbed, and chastised others if my circumstances had allowed it. Only by luck did I miss being sent to the countryside. My burdens were still heavy, and I had many reasons to become frustrated and depressed, but the hopelessness of my lot in life never made me lower myself or my ideals. I had survived, holding my head high, and had gained something most of my peers lacked: knowledge.

My greatest assets were my loving, close-knit family and my friends. Father and Rei-qing were the two most important people to me during my childhood. Then there were the people who educated me, Chun-pu Chu, Kang-li, the old man in the hotel, Lao Li in the working-class squad, Professor Shan, Dr. Wei, the Sun Tian couple, and so many others. Perhaps the Runt, Alley Cat, Madame Couvre, and Ah-liu should be added to this list. If I had been made of clay, these would have been the artisans who shaped Xi-ou Tan.

My knowledge gave me an obligation to my peers. People called us the "lost generation," but I could use my meager talents to show the world that there was still hope, that some day we would prove our worth. As long as we had time, we could stand up to be heard. We could recoup our losses and master our destinies.

Armed with these thoughts, I walked into the graduate-school exam. It was a competition among different academic experiences and ages, but for me it was a test of the ability to surmount personal difficulties. Mine had not ended: The afternoon before the first exam, Madame Couvre ordered me to clean the whole lane's sewage, since the "Patriotic Sanitation Inspectors" might be coming to check the neighborhood.

The second exam was held in mid-July, during an extremely hot summer. My ankles were so swollen each evening because of the heat that I used a wet towel and drank cold water constantly to keep cool. Father fell ill at the beginning of July, with symptoms of heatstroke, and he suffered from pain that radiated from his chest out to his limbs. I sat by his side, fanning him with one hand and holding a book in the other.

Chemistry was new to me, and I had difficulty borrowing material on the subject. Two days before the exam, a friend who had agreed to borrow an important reference book for me was unable to get it. Worried, I decided to visit a university in the suburbs and went directly to its chemistry building. In the hallway, I met a middle-aged man, and in conversation, I found that he was a chemistry lecturer. I forthrightly asked for the book. He lent it to me and also explained some of the more difficult problems. I was elated.

When the results of the exams were announced I was number twelve of the fourteen people selected from the 265 who took the first exam. Nine of these fourteen passed the second examination, and I was number three.

Before I could be officially enrolled, however, several problems had to be surmounted. Pei Wu, my adviser and a famous scientist, invited me to his office and said, "You did quite well on the exams. We decided to admit you. But before the admission becomes official, we must work together to accomplish several things. The personnel cadre of the Shanghai Academy of Science visited your machine shop and the Neighborhood Committee. The Revolutionary Mass is unhappy with the idea of your being admitted to graduate school. They think it inappropriate for our country to spend money cultivating you."

I sat in silence. Pei Wu knew all about political survival: He had been one of the famous scientists who had denounced Newton. His rosy cheeks spoke of health, and his clean, well-tailored clothes underscored his financial success. Sighing quietly, I thought about the "Revolutionary Mass"—Ah-liu, Madame Couvre, and the Runt!

Pei Wu looked at my blank face and mellowed his tone: "Of course, their opinion is extreme. We've already admitted you, and this decision is not easily revoked. I notified the press. They'll be interviewing people associated with you. I know you're unusually talented. It's their job to let people know this is the spring of science. It's my job to convince the press to explain that the Revolutionary Mass cannot stop us from admitting you." I was uncertain whether I should thank him for his honesty or whether this was something I had a right to expect.

Pei Wu said, "You did worst on the politics portion of the test— fifty-four out of one hundred. You come from a Black family, too. When we report this to the academy, we'll face some problems. Consider writing a criticism about your background. That way, we can submit something with the rest of your file to appease them." He paused, checking his calendar: "The sooner, the better."

The Gang of Four was ousted and the Grand Cultural Revolution denied. Court cases filed against Blacks were now in the arduous process of reexamination, yet I still needed to confess my anti-Revolutionary background and write a falsehood on a paper that would go in a file to follow me forever. Shaking my head, I said in a low, firm voice, "No, I won't do it."

Pei Wu's eyes grew wide. "Why?" he asked incredulously. "It isn't difficult at all! I can find you an example and you can copy from it."

"I know it's not difficult, but I won't do it," I stated. "Both of my parents have been abused."

Pei Wu looked shocked. Drawing himself up, he said, "Xi-ou Tan, how can you say that? Even though the Grand Cultural Revolution was denied, you must always keep in mind that both your parents were labeled Rightists. The Anti-Rightist Movement of 1957 was rightfully guided by Chairman Mao and our Party."

"I can tell you in detail why and how they were labeled as Rightists," I said confidently. "I investigated their cases myself. My parents were wrongly accused."

Pei Wu stood up and began pacing: "You did very well on the exams, and you would be the only self-taught student in my group. I don't want to lose you." He stopped and faced me squarely: "Will you at least promise that when the press interviews you, you won't repeat what you said about your parents being mistreated?"

"As long as no one asks me to criticize my family," I answered quietly.

"If your father really loves you, he won't be angry with you for what you say about him," he said, softening his voice. I felt two tears trickle down my face.

△△△ The press went to the Neighborhood Committee, the machine shop, and the local Public Security Office for background interviews. Journalists had great authority then: By waving a press card, they could demonstrate the importance of their tasks to any local person. Ah-liu, Madame Couvre, and the Runt spoke ill of me and my family, but they were all harshly upbraided by the press and my coworkers.

As I entered the machine shop one day, I heard Ah-liu boast, "She's different from everybody else here. I saw it on her first day! Why else would I have picked her as my apprentice? She's like a golden phoenix among all of us chickens!" Everyone agreed.

Although I hated to be late for my shift, I did not want to walk in on their lie. But a sharp-eyed coworker spotted me and dragged me to Ah-liu's machine. Smiling until her eyes became little slits, Ah-liu said, "Xi-ou, when you reach the top of the world, don't forget your supervisor. You're so talented. You've saved face for me, since I risked so much in choosing you as my apprentice." Not waiting for a response, she continued, "You still don't have a boyfriend, do you? You have such a pretty face! Some big, famous scientist is going to marry you! Don't forget to send your wedding candy to your supervisor, Ah-liu!"

The press also interviewed Professor Shan, asking him how he was able to find and cultivate a talented youth like me under such conditions. He used no flowery speeches to make his point, and he refused their suggestion that he had wanted to fight with the Gang of Four. He simply said, "Xi-ou Tan is an exceptionally pure and honest person. She was willing to learn and I wanted to teach her."

"How did you feel about her taking the examination for the quantum-chemistry appointments?"

"I don't think she should have chosen that field. It's not compatible with our country's needs. She's fluent in German, has a good understanding of English, and has a reading knowledge of Japanese and Russian. I think she should have tried to enter a foreign-language program. Then she could have translated scientific works that we need and foreign texts that would have helped improve education in our country."

Expecting accolades for me and statements of vengeance for the Gang of Four, the journalists were disappointed: "Did you tell her your opinion before she applied for this position?"

"Of course, but she didn't listen to me. She has the right to do as she pleases, and I respect her decision even if I don't agree with it."

I myself was interviewed three times, but I was irritated by the process and the attention. The journalists tried to trap me into saying that my self-education was motivated by Revolutionary ideals. They wrote that I had begun independent study in direct opposition to the Gang of Four's suppression of education. They asked for my views on Zhang Tie-sheng, who had turned in a blank paper at the entrance examination and then become minister of education. Had I studied harder because I hated this man? Did I take the entrance examination with two hundred Red Guard college-student competitors because I wanted to use this action to criticize the Gang of Four? Knowing that I would be admitted anyway, I answered absentmindedly. When it hit home that I would be leaving Aunt Chai and my friends in the workshop, I felt a little sad.

People constantly greeted and congratulated me, in shops or on the street. Strangers introduced themselves, shook my hand, and told me that they were proud of me. One day, the local Party secretary at work asked to speak with me. She ushered me into a small, windowless storage room, empty except for two stools. We both sat down, and she asked frankly, "Xi-ou, how have I treated you?"

"Very well," I replied sincerely. The wife of an old Army officer, the woman was illiterate but fair. I had had several encounters with her in the application process for graduate school, and I felt that apart from her bureaucratic tendencies, she was a good person.

"I'd like to ask you one thing," she said. "Since this is your last day at the workshop, it won't make any difference to you if you tell me this, but it will be very important to me."

My heart sank, since I knew what the secretary wanted to know. She went to the storage-room door and checked the lock. Returning to her seat, she faced me and whispered, "Do you know who sent Ah-liu the warning letter?" As I shook my head, the secretary continued, "We all know you didn't write it, since you were working the afternoon shift and the letter was found in the morning. But someone must have written it. Tell me who it was. It's been so long that we won't pursue the issue."

I replied emphatically, "Sorry, I really don't know."

"Was it Oddhead? You don't have to say anything, just nod your head."

Ah-liu must have convinced the secretary to ask me these questions. Oddhead and I had stopped talking to each other, so Ah-liu thought she could take advantage of what she assumed was a rift in our friendship.

"Please don't ask me any more questions. I don't have any information for you," I said. "But how come the committee didn't investigate when it happened?"

◿◿ Professor Hu, not long after I left the workshop, Oddhead abandoned the pregnant Lu-yu. She developed a mental problem and sat in front of his house for months, crying. When I went to visit in 1984, I heard that she married a man from Hong Kong thirty years older than she. He has a wife and children in Hong Kong, but when he comes to Shanghai for business, he spends his nights with Lu-yu. I pity her. If she had kept on studying, she might have graduated from college and had a good job by now.

◿◿ Light filled my graduate-school classroom in the University of Science and Technology in a suburb of Shanghai. The professors were not as dramatic as those of the Sorbonne in Paris, and they would never have claimed to have grasped the sun and thrown it away—as did one of Marie Curie's professors—but I greedily listened to each lecture, trying to catch every word. Like the young Marie, I sat in the classroom overwhelmed by feelings of warmth and goodness. It seemed like a dream. All the bitterness and suffering I had experienced was worth that moment.

The downfall of the Gang of Four did produce a "spring of science and technology." Public opinion demanded that talent be sought out and cultivated. As the new hope and life for the people, we, the first class of graduate students, were honored and respected by our peers. We were expected to fill a twelve-year gap of knowledge.

I missed dinner at the university one day to finish writing a paper. When I went to the dining room to purchase some cold biscuits and hot soup, I found myself alone except for an old, white-haired man. After watching me for a while, he came over to my table and asked if he could join me. I nodded, and he brought over his tray. He removed his wallet from a pocket in his blue-gray uniform and took out a card. "I work in the electrical-engineering department. This is my identification card."

Startled by his direct Western manner, I smiled. When I glanced at the card, I was shocked: "Professor Han? Are you the same Professor Han who wrote *Waveguide Theory*?"

He looked surprised but answered evenly: "How do you, a chemist, know about a book I wrote ten years ago about microwave theory?"

I told him of my independent-study plan and how I had read his text. Then I asked him how he knew I was a chemist.

Professor Han smiled: "Do you really want to know? There's a rumor on campus that a woman graduate student in the chemistry department knows four foreign languages but has never attended college. I heard it at a faculty meeting. I thought about asking you to give a talk to the electrical-engineering students about learning a foreign language on one's own, but it seems I should ask you to speak on microwave theory instead."

I shook my head. "No, no, Professor Han, don't ask me to give a talk. I haven't learned microwave theory very well. I spent years studying the theory, but I still don't know what a waveguide looks like."

He looked sympathetic. After thinking for a few minutes, he asked, "Have you had your birthday yet this year?"

Confused, I gave him an uncertain smile. He continued, "I was just wondering. It isn't polite for me to ask, but I hope you won't feel shy about answering an old man's question."

△△△ Since the only other woman in my class was married, I received the attention of more than twenty men. We graduate students shared a single mailbox, and one of those men kept the key. Each Wednesday, I received a letter from home. Someone told me later that every Wednesday the men argued among themselves over who would deliver my mail. Unaware of this at the time, I did not care who brought my letter. Smiling, I would thank the person and then run outside to be alone for a reunion with my family. Each Saturday, I went home to visit them in person.

When I told Father about meeting Professor Han, he asked happily, "Did you tell him when your birthday is?"

I nodded. "He insisted. When he found out that my birthday is two months away, he got pretty excited."

"He wants to give you a present!" Rei-qing sang out gleefully.

Rei-qing was right. When my birthday came, I opened his beautifully wrapped box to find two waveguides, one elliptical and the other square. Each had a pink bow around it. An elegant card, written in a careful hand, read, "Happy Birthday to Xi-ou, and my greatest respect to her father, who has worked so hard and well to cultivate her."

△△△ Professor Hu, you must have a basketful of my letters, if you have kept them all. Why do you not reply? Have I offended you or are you too busy with your work? If it is the former, please forgive me, for I had no intention of hurting you. If the latter, I am happy that you have regained your interest in your work. In any case, please write to me, even if it is only a few words.

Sincerely,
Xi-ou Tan

23

Dear Professor Hu,

The story I am going to tell you happened between September 1978 and February 1979. I was a contented graduate student in the University of Science and Technology, but I missed my family a great deal—Father most of all. Every Saturday morning after the last class, I was the first to rush out of the classroom to catch a bus returning to the city. The buses ran every thirty minutes, but I felt that I sustained a loss each time I missed the first possible one.

Father's health was poor, and he was always tired. The pain he had previously experienced—which spread from his chest to his arms and legs—recurred frequently. He ate less and became gaunt, but his mind stayed young and curious. After Chun-pu Chu died, Father developed more patience with life and people. Forgiving those who had hurt him, he looked with open eyes at those he loved. He knew that this personal welfare would improve with the changing political climate. Former colleagues in the Chinese Encyclopedia Publishing House told him that the personnel department was busy reexamining cases filed against Rightists, and that his name was near the top of the list. The procedure was long and complicated, but it seemed that most people's names would be cleared.

Holding onto hope, we expected Father to regain his health and leave Angel Cave to resume his work. Rei-qing bought him a poster at the Spring Festival entitled "Sunrise Seen from a Cave," a scene in a ballet based on one of the eight Revolutionary Model movies called

White-Haired Woman. The ballet told of a woman who hid in a mountain cave for many years after her landlord raped her. In the final scene, her boyfriend of long ago discovers her and persuades her to leave her hiding place. Her former neighbors and friends come to bring her home, and, as she makes the decision to reenter society, she looks out of the cave, smiling. The sun is rising, and her now-white hair is wrapped in a red scarf as she faces the light streaming through the cave's entrance.

Father knew why Rei-qing had bought this for him. We complained during his first few years of confinement that he was not careful enough about feigning illness; now we worried that he spent too much time in bed. Father began writing his memoirs shortly after You-pu was born and Chun-pu Chu died, although he was unable to explain why. The water of the Mi River in the countryside of his youth sparkled more brightly in his mind than his present surroundings.

Father was happy that Rei-qing was doing well in her interpreting career and that I was doing equally well in school. Both Jian-nan and Chi-kai had taken the first college-entrance examinations offered. Although their results were in the top 4 percent, there was still an unstated policy against the cultivation of Blacks that year, and both were denied admission. By the fall of 1977, political discrimination had been eradicated from the educational system, but this time Jian-nan failed his health examination.

Chi-kai had been transferred to a job in Shanghai but did not repeat the tests, explaining that he did not want to face another separation from Father. People outside the family were shocked, but we supported him. Before he started at the factory, he used the vacation time he had left over from his job in the countryside to visit Mother in An Hui. When he returned, he was assigned to work in the dining room on the morning shift. He did not enjoy the job, but it was flexible and gave him time for his studies.

Father worried more about Jian-nan. He was easily the most gifted of us all, especially in science. The two papers written when he was only sixteen had been given to one of the highest academic authorities in the field. They sat in this man's hands for four months—until he finally sent them back to Sun Tian with a letter that repeatedly quoted Chairman Mao and ended with the sentence, "Young people should be putting their energy into the Revolution, not studying such impractical things as this type of theory." Jian-nan had revered this man, but now the idol had fallen. Severely wounded by his two failed attempts to enter college, Jian-nan refused to take the entrance exams again.

Father worried about our friends as well. Gui-feng and Xiao Zhang had a happy marriage, and gradually her father came to accept it. She had a miscarriage but became pregnant again soon afterward. Her sister, Mei-feng, went to a teachers' college at the end of 1977, and her brother held a good job. Ah-di, married and the mother of a son, was living in northeast China. She contracted bubonic plague, so Father had me send her some precious herbs that friends had given him. Father was also concerned about Yan Fong, who had lost his father at an early age. Father urged him to bring his younger sister to visit.

Father thought that the Revolution encouraged unhealthy marriages. Marriage, like the class struggle, had become tainted by politics, since it was the only way the young could alter their political identification. How successful could be the marriage of Lao Mo's friend, the mathematician named Wu, who had married a woman he hardly knew in order to keep his room in Shanghai? Problems of the parents would be visited upon the children, for a revolution does not affect only one group of people; its effects are seen for generations. Father no longer had the energy to ponder complex questions, however. He had difficulty concentrating, and his thoughts wandered. No longer able to write, he did his best to hide that from us.

Bright and happy during the Spring Festival of 1979, Father looked better than he had in years. He ate, drank, and chatted with the steady stream of young guests. The political atmosphere was more relaxed than it had ever been, and everyone was sure that Father soon would be asked to resume his work at the publishing house. Chi-kai's wages for one month were spent on a winter coat for Father, and when he tried it on, the crowd of young people said that the white-haired old man glowed like an angel. We were fortunate to have real friends.

No one noticed that Father seemed different. The only indication of his degenerating health was that his hand shook as he poured the wine at dinner. The Spring Festival ended on the fifteenth of the first month of the Chinese lunar calendar. Father awoke early, gasping for breath, on the morning of the sixteenth. We thought that at worst he had a cold.

△△△ On February 10, 1979, the sixteenth day of the first month of the Chinese lunar calendar, it was cold and windy, and the sun hid behind the clouds. I needed to catch the bus back to the university, for Pei Wu was going to observe me setting up an experiment that morning. Because Pei Wu was so active in the scientific community, he had not yet had a chance to see me work in the laboratory. At dawn, I heard Father gasping. Jian-nan called Rei-qing, and he and Chi-kai took Father to the ear, nose, and throat clinic.

Although I had studied several medical texts, I neglected to consider that Father had spent the previous twelve years of his life in bed, and that his chest pains had not been diagnosed properly. When the doctor found nothing wrong with Father's throat during a routine examination, he took X-rays. Father was having more difficulty speaking by this time, but we children still assumed it was nothing more than a sore throat. Rei-qing rushed in, and I began to say good-bye, whispering, "Father, I'm going to school to do some experiments. Professor Wu will be there today to supervise me. I'll be back this evening."

He made a series of indescernible sounds but waved his hands to encourage me to leave and catch the bus. I grasped his cold hand, shaking it hard and long. Saucily I mimicked his generation's custom, saying, "Lao Tan, see you later!"

He looked up at me, not responding. A strange expression came over his face, and I was frightened: "Well, Father, I won't go." He gave me an angry look. Tearfully, I said, "All right, I'm going. I'll be back this afternoon."

I wished I could stop the bus and walk back, but the image of Father commanding me to return to school made me behave as a dutiful daughter and remain where I was. Terror gripped me as I walked into the chemistry building. The lobby darkened and my legs wobbled. I nearly fell to the ground, but, grabbing the banister, I steadied myself and raced upstairs.

Pei Wu was chatting with a lecturer in one of the labs on the third floor. "Professor Wu," I gasped, as I burst through the lab door, "I need to take some time off. My father's in the emergency room right now. His situation is cri. . . ." I stopped the frightening word *critical* from slipping past my lips.

"Go home," he said quickly. "Don't worry about what's going on here." As I left, I heard him say to the lecturer at his side, "I'm sympathetic to her father's situation."

When I reached Angel Cave at 4:30, Jian-nan was the only one there. Facing me, his voice trembled as he said, "The clinic said that Father had advanced lung cancer. He's been transferred to Central Hospital. Rei-qing and Chi-kai are there with him. They told me to stay and wait for you, but we should leave for the hospital right now."

My worst fears were realized. I grabbed Jian-nan's hand, and we walked quickly to the bus stop. He told me that Father understood what was said to him but could no longer speak. When Chi-kai had told him that he was taking him to the hospital for a complete physical examination, Father had grabbed the corner of the table and refused to leave Angel Cave. He exerted such strength that it was difficult for his strong, young son to move him, but Chi-kai finally had carried him on his back out to a waiting taxi. As I listened to Jian-nan's halting voice, I burst into tears. We were silent for the rest of the trip, knowing that Father did not have long to live.

Father had passed away at 4:25 that afternoon. His face was peaceful and his body in repose, but his eyes remained partially open, as if he were expecting someone. Rei-qing closed them, remembering that those who were treated unjustly during their earthly lives took their anger with them. The angry promised to die with their eyes open, making it difficult for their families to close them. Father's eyes closed easily. He brought love to his life and carried it with him to his death.

Father lay on the hospital bed as though he were napping. I entered the room fifteen minutes too late. Sitting beside him, I softly called his name. I pressed my cheek against his cool face, trying to warm his life back into him, breathing rapidly to hold back my tears, since children's tears would bring suffering to their fathers in the next world.

I thought I would burst with the secrets I had kept from him: the En-ligh-tenment plan, the love story I was writing about him and Mother for their anniversary, our scheme for bringing his brother from the countryside for a birthday visit. Questions flooded me. Were the six hidden manuscripts in their final form, and to which publishing house should we send them? I wanted to go to the United States for graduate school—should I apply?

Uncle Xiong, Tao-ran's father, arrived just before Father's body was removed from the room. He sat at the head of the bed, sighing and holding Father's cool, lifeless hand. We refused to let the morgue attendant come near Father, but Uncle Xiong calmed us by saying, "Your father has more freedom now than he ever had when he was alive." He wept silently and spoke no more.

Later that night, I could not recall how I had come to leave Father's side. I had not cried when I saw him at the hospital, but now I gave myself over to the sadness. Instead of weakness, I felt its strength supporting me. I saw Father's image urging me back to the university and heard Walt Whitman's poem:

> O Captain! my Captain! rise up and hear the bells;
> Rise up—for you the flag is flung—for you the bugle
>   trills,
> For you bouquets and ribboned wreaths—for you the
>   shores acrowding,
> For you they call, the swaying mass, their eager faces
>   turning;
>   Here Captain! dear father!
>   This arm beneath your head!
>   It is some dream that on the deck
>   You've fallen cold and dead.

The most important person in my life, my idol and closest friend, had fallen cold and dead, but his victor ship was in, the ship of family life was safely anchored. For its captain, the voyage was done.

△△△ Shanghai sparkled. Red and green lights blinked on and off in the windows of the market facing the hospital. The neon sign flashed, "Fine Cakes and Snacks, Fresh Fruit in Season." Neon apples, bananas, and grapes appeared at one moment; cakes, bowls of ice cream, and pudding appeared next. Rei-qing and I used to shop here for Father, to buy the sweet sesame chips and seaweed cakes he loved. We were neither rich nor gourmets, but we scoured the city to satisfy Father's cravings. When he saw that we had bought only the highest-quality brands of these very expensive items, Father initially refused to eat them, but we cajoled him until he did, although he admonished us not to spend so much money on one person again.

Returning home from the afternoon shift at the machine shop, I often found Father reading. Instead of entering Angel Cave, I would bicycle the forty minutes to Huang's Family Store to arrive in time for the late-night opening, when fresh, sweet sesame dumplings were offered for sale. Coming home out of breath, I would rush into the kitchen to start cooking the dumplings. I always kept the broken ones for myself, giving Father those that were whole. We would sit at the table, eating and talking of the day's events. When Father teased me about my impetuous trips to the store, I only smiled and blushed.

Just before Father died, I had been close to making an unwise decision: I had considered leaving school. When I was at the machine shop, I had been able to have lunch regularly with Father and could take time off from work for independent study. Now that I was in school and unable to see Father during the week, I worried that there was no one to cook dinner for him: "After all, family is more important than education." Inevitably I remembered how difficult it had been to get into graduate school, but every waking moment, I thought about all I had left behind.

University life touched my poetic soul. Each day, I heard students reading out loud in the veil of early morning mist and the tap-tap-tap of chalk on the classroom blackboard. I saw silhouettes of students playing sports against the setting sun, and the pattern of lights in the library windows. Others found these scenes commonplace, but they struck a chord deep within me.

My mind wandered back to the poor household we had run for the previous ten years. Although I was ashamed of my home and family when I was an adolescent, they made me proud as I grew older. Love kept each of us from suffering alone, and the hope of pursuing knowledge sometime in the future gave us children the energy to fight during our darkest times. How could I think about leaving the graduate school finally opened to me?

As I passed through the gates of Central Hospital the day Father died, I remembered my indecision about school. It held no meaning now. I recalled an old poem:

> *The tree wishes to stop swaying,*
> *But the wind wants to keep blowing.*
> *A child wishes to care for his parents,*
> *But gone from the earth they have no wants.*

Professor Hu, it has been hard for me to write this, and tears are streaming down my face. I still miss Father, oh, ever so much. Yet life goes on. We must live it for those we loved who have passed on before us. Please keep trying, and remember that I do understand. Write to me if it would help you, and please take care of yourself.

Sincerely,
Xi-ou Tan

 Father had passed away, but Mother still lived. She had been apart from us nearly fourteen years. We were young children when she left, and, in our memories, the image of our beautiful mother was linked with the dismal jail. What sin had she committed that warranted seven years of jail? What further atrocity had she perpetrated to deserve endless labor with other innocent people?

We tearfully drafted several telegrams to her, not wishing to frighten her with the bald truth, but if we stated events too casually, she

*would not be released. We drew up four different versions and sent her
one each day. The first said, "Father is sick." The second was, "Father
is in intensive care." The third said, "Father is severely ill." The final
telegram stated, "Father is in critical condition." The farm would have
no reason to suspect the telegrams were false, and Mother thus would
be prepared for the truth.*

*During the days that we sent the four telegrams, we children and
Tao-ran discussed going to Beijing to get our parents exonerated. Old
Chinese folktales told of ordinary, helpless people going to the capital
to plead cases that were decided unfairly in their home provinces.
Universally understood and artistically rendered in their early forms,
these stories were rewritten by thousands, handed down from one
dynasty to the next, and translated into the local dialect.*

I had once read a play called Yang Nai-wu and Xiou Gu. *Yang
Nai-wu was a handsome, well-educated man who had been childhood
friends with the poor but beautiful Xiou Gu. Trapped by their own
honesty and innocence, they were used as pawns in the battle between
the different elements of society. Through the strength and courage of
Yang Nai-wu's sister, they were freed in the end, but at great cost. When
the sister went to the capital to plead her brother's case, she had to show
her commitment by lying on a bed of nails. Willingness to overcome
physical pain was the evidence of a person's sincerity, and I knew I had
to have such spirit.*

24

Dear Professor Hu,

The evening of Father's death, my brother-in-law Tao-ran and we four children sat in Angel Cave and discussed our next steps. Rei-qing held my viewpoint: exoneration or death. Exoneration would permit Mother to return and she could at least have a peaceful old age.

Tao-ran told us that we would need a "back door," since people all over the country were sleeping in Beijing streets to get a place in line to ask for reexamination of their cases. Rei-qing reminded me of one of the journalists who had interviewed me when I passed the graduate-school entrance exams. His chief editor had gone to the welcoming party that the Academy of Science held for the new students and talked with me for quite a while.

Rei-qing and I made plans to go to Zhen Ru to visit Uncle Sun Tian the next evening. He had quite a few connections in Beijing, and I was confident that he would be happy to help us. The silence of finalized plans filled the room, broken only by the ticking of the clock.

I volunteered to go to Beijing to file the suit. The focus of the Exoneration Movement was currently only on cases from the Anti-Rightist Movement of 1957 and the Cultural Revolution. Our parents' cases fit in the nine-year gap between them, and no cases filed during that period were being brought up for reexamination. You-pu was still a baby, so Rei-qing could not leave, and Tao-ran was not directly related to Father. My two brothers were too inexperienced to do all that was required, so I decided to leave on the evening after the funeral services.

The next morning, everyone except me went to work as usual. National regulations gave a worker three days of leave when a parent died, but since my father was an anti-Revolutionary, his death counted no more than a dog's. Theoretically, the Revolutionary Mass would be celebrating it. I had already told Pei Wu about Father's condition, so he would not expect me back right away.

The morning air was cold, but I did not notice it as I walked toward the Public Security Office. Behind the chin-high counter was the same middle-aged police officer who had been on his elevated platform for ten years.

"I would like to cancel my father's residence registration," I informed him. "He passed away yesterday afternoon."

He looked shocked, but then burst into wild laughter: "Hahahaha, Jin-ren Tan went off to the happy world!"

My face paled. When I opened my mouth, no words came out. My face flushed several seconds later, and I started trembling. Through clenched teeth, I said, "Are—you—really—a—human—being?"

The officer rose slowly from his chair. He had never met Father, but he had seen us bringing Father's confessions to the Runt three or four times a month for the previous ten years. Everyone at the office seemed to know every last detail about our anti-Revolutionary family, including the fact that we "whelps" had entered the factory and the university. The officer's wild laughter had stemmed from his professional instincts, and he stopped, not at all irritated by my accusation.

"Do you need a certificate of cancellation for the cremation?" he asked more politely. But he did not wait for my response. Returning to his desk, he withdrew the necessary forms from a drawer and began filling them out.

△△△ Chi-kai had difficulty renting an auditorium for the funeral service. Many people who had committed suicide or who were killed by Red Guards at the beginning of the Cultural Revolution had been exonerated, and consequently there were a great many memorial services being held. Chi-kai had rented the hall from ten to eleven on the fourth morning after Father's death. It was the only slot available until the next month.

One of the cadres of the Chinese Encyclopedia Publishing House attended the funeral and sent a wreath in the company's name. He had just begun examining cases wrongly filed during the Anti-Rightist Movement of 1957, and although he had never met Father, he considered it his professional responsibility to attend the ceremony. Before the service started, he asked me if the huge portrait of Father hanging in the auditorium was a recent picture of him, but I told him that it had been done by some of our friends from memory, as the Red Guards had destroyed all of our better pictures.

The cadre sighed sympathetically. After a few moments, he said, "The characters on the banner over the portrait must have been drawn by an old man. The calligraphy is so carefully done."

"No, I did them," corrected Rei-qing, surprised that a personnel cadre was interested in calligraphy. Most such cadres had little education and considered calligraphy feudalistic.

"Why are you still using 'Mr.' for your Father? When I talked to you last, I told you that your father's case was decided wrongly and his name would be cleared. You should have used 'Comrade' instead."

"Thank you, but we talked about it and decided that 'Mr.' best expresses the respect the attendees have for our Father." Rei-qing added softly, "You called him 'Comrade' on the ribbons on the wreath you sent. Aren't you afraid of being accused of disloyalty to the Party?"

The cadre started to speak, but then he realized that Rei-qing was trying to tell him something. Looking around, he noticed a middle-aged man and a limping woman mixing with the crowd, scrutinizing everyone who entered. A young student had placed a large wreath in a corner and was signing his name on the register at the entrance. The writing on the ribbons read, "My beloved Uncle Tan will live forever in my heart." The man and woman under the wreath craned their necks to read the ribbons and the signatures underneath. With a sly smile, Rei-qing twisted a Revolutionary slogan: "The Gang of Four do not rest even in their coffins."

Father's face was so peaceful. People made deep bows as they paid him their last respects, and someone even whispered something to him. Several intellectuals took the risk of political backlash in attending the funeral. Kang-li stood in front of the body, her face full of sorrow, as if she were crying for a brother. Uncle Xiong officiated at the service, and one of Father's former Qin-hai colleagues gave the eulogy. Many people brought poems written in beautiful calligraphy to hang on the wall, and half were classical ones. Many others had little education. Aunt Chai and a few other women from my workshop handed out cake and candy as the people left. "Cake" and "happy" are homonyms, and the peasants had a custom that the family of the deceased should give the mourners something to ensure there would be happiness after the sadness of a funeral.

The personnel cadre from the publishing house later became a good friend of ours. He had joined the Revolutionary Army when he was young, but after he resigned, his good character kept him from progressing in his career. He realized that the limping woman and middle-aged man were spying on the people at the funeral. Like himself, the man was wearing the signs of a former PLA soldier, and the cadre felt ashamed that a onetime PLA officer would do such a thing: "I would never have appreciated how good the people were who came to pay respects to your father unless I understood all that they risked in coming. They didn't attend a funeral for an ordinary person; they showed their respect for a great mind."

Ten years had passed since our En-ligh-tenment plan. The situation in 1979 was more favorable, and we also had some people to introduce us to higher authorities.

Two days before Father's funeral, I had gone to the office of the editor-in-chief of one of the Shanghai newspapers. After staring at me for a few seconds, the man took me to the offices of several powerful friends. They wrote letters of introduction for me, and, after thanking the editor profusely, I went home.

Rei-qing and I had also visited Sun Tian. Although as a doctor he had seen many final partings, he wept for the loss of the friend he had never met. Sun Tian wrote me several letters of introduction to famous intellectuals living in Beijing, the highest authorities in the capital. Rei-qing and I tortured ourselves: Why had we not taken these actions while Father was still alive? Uncle Xiong answered, "That's the way things happen. It's different from a tragedy on the stage. If the play doesn't reach its climax, the audience won't cry. When the peak of real tragedy strikes us, it's too late to do anything about it."

△△△ The long, black express train snaked its way through mountains, fields, and cities. I had not slept well since Father passed away, so I tried to nap. When I closed my eyes, I dreamed of Father walking toward me, smiling. He started to sit on a sofa, but when I saw that it was dusty, I stretched out my hand, motioning him to stay standing. He disappeared and I awoke. Opening the window of my compartment, I inhaled the air fragrant with the smell of good, rich earth. Father's life had been full of pain and unjust treatment, but everyone remembered him for his kind smile, not his suffering. I did not understand this, but it was the same way in my dream.

All my life I had longed to visit Beijing. In kindergarten, I learned that Beijing was the capital of the People's Republic, the place where Chairman Mao lived. In primary school, I learned that it was an ancient city with a long cultural history, the cradle of China's 5,000-year-old civilization. Until the Cultural Revolution occurred, I did not doubt that I would attend one of the excellent universities there. Beijing became not only the Red headquarters but also the cradle of the Red Terror and the source of violence and rumors. If I had been able to leave my family when college-entrance examinations resumed, I would have applied to a graduate school there.

Once I arrived, I settled myself in the home of one of Uncle Xiong's relatives, but I did not tell the old woman my reason for visiting the city. I was ready to leave at the first sign of trouble, since I did not want to damage others' lives. Later that same day, I borrowed a bicycle and went to visit a Party theoretician at an institute belonging to the Central Committee. At home I had been told that it was difficult to get in to see him, so I told the guard that I was his niece from Shanghai. Within minutes, I was seated in his office.

The man was at least seventy, but he looked healthy, if a little thin. His long nose was like an eagle's beak, but his eyes were mild. I had heard that he had been placed in a Guomindang prison before graduating from college and that his refusal to write a confession about his

Communist activities cost him several years of confinement. He spent his prison days systematically teaching himself Marxist-Leninist theory, and eventually he became a Party theoretician. After his release, he went to Yan-an, the center of Red power. Prior to 1957, he was highly respected by the Party, but he was exiled to northern China during the Anti-Rightist Movement.

He was allowed to return to Beijing in 1961 but was greatly changed. For either psychological or physical reasons, he had lost his former eloquence. He overcame the problem several months later but was no longer outspoken. By 1978, his name was again in the newspapers. Some thought that he was a political upstart, but the older people knew that he was a star that had very nearly burned itself out. The star that had been fading for twenty years suddenly shone more brightly than ever, but now the eyes held deep-seated wisdom, sensitivity, and empathy.

I had not expected a Party theoretician to be a mild-mannered scholar, so my initial nervousness dissipated. Removing his bifocals, he asked, "How old was Comrade Jin-ren Tan when he passed away?" He had read the letter I gave him four or five times, and now he placed it on his knees as his body sank deeper into his large armchair.

"Sixty-six," I replied, the tears prickling my eyes.

"Sixty-six . . . still very young . . . can still do a lot of things," he said to himself. "Do you have a place to live?" he asked abruptly.

"Yes, I do." I showed him a file of the materials Rei-qing and I had compiled for the exoneration appeal. "May I leave this material with you?" I asked, expecting him to acquiesce.

The theoretician lifted the letter from his knees. "No. Your family's situation has been stated very clearly in this letter. There have been countless cases of mistreatment like your parents' over the years. Exoneration suits are now piled as high as a mountain." He stood, reaching his hand toward me: "Comrade Xiao Tan, I hope you will return to school as soon as possible. But call me before you leave Beijing."

Still feeling the warmth of the theoretician's large hand on my palms, I walked slowly through the institute gates. Beijing is much drier than Shanghai, and all around me, dust swirled up in the chilly wind. Terribly disappointed, I walked my bicycle. The man said he understood Father's situation, so why had he not accepted the file?

The slender white tower of Bai Hai stood in the distance against the gray sky. Sometimes obscured by clouds, it made a striking silhouette against the ominous sky. Beijing was full of architectural wonders and national treasures. Each building, temple, stone bridge, and clock tower had its own fascinating historical roots, but my mind was elsewhere. Mounting the bicycle, I rode to the Sha Tan district to visit a Chinese linguist. I hoped for a miracle.

The man and his wife lived in a huge house with a beautiful, well-kept yard. They huddled next to the stove as he read Sun Tian's letter without emotion or comment. His left cheek occasionally twitched, pulling his eyes closed. "It's very difficult for me to help you with this matter," he said. His accent was from the south, and he continued slowly: "I'm only an unimportant humanist. I don't even have the energy to catch a chicken."

"Uncle Tian told me that he mentioned several powerful people in his letter to you. I was told that you are acquainted with them, and that they may be able to help me," I said.

"This . . . uh . . . Comrade Sun Tian does not know." Everything was silent except for the coal burning in the stove. Finally, the strained atmosphere was broken by laughter from the yard. Jumping from his seat, he ran to answer the door. Three men and two women entered, together with the bitter cold wind. Rubbing their hands together and stamping their feet to warm themselves, they said loudly, "Hmm! You two look so comfortable. This room is so warm!" "Congratulations! Another big article of yours was published. It took the whole second page of the newspaper!" "I heard that you were appointed director! How come you didn't tell us?"

The linguist chuckled. His embarrassment disappeared, and his face smoothed out as he smiled. Feeling awkward, I rose to say good-bye. The guests had noticed me by then, but the linguist did not ask me to stay, and he bowed slightly from his seated position. I kept my eyes fixed on the floor as I passed the guests, and their jocularity lessened.

Unlocking my bicycle parked beneath the window, I listened to the escalation of the noise and laughter from inside. As the snow began to fall in this stranger's yard, I felt a new loneliness. Streams of tears fell to my lips, and my hands trembled as I fumbled with the lock.

"Do you want to come back in and warm up?" The linguist's wife had appeared behind me.

Unable to find my hankerchief, I wiped away my tears with the back of my hand. I turned to the woman and said, "Thank you, I'm leaving now."

"Leave your Beijing address with me so I can get in touch with you if I need to," the old woman said, stubbornly holding the handlebars of my bicycle. Snowflakes fell on her white hair, melting to tiny, sparkling prisms. She must have been outside of the house watching me for quite some time, since her nose was red and she shivered from the cold.

"Thank you." Biting my lip, I turned my face away, unwilling to let my tears intrude on another's happiness. I wrested the bicycle away from her, mounted it, and pedaled down the snowy road. When the snowflakes grew larger and stuck to the road, I got off and walked the bicycle. The buses crawled through the streets. After fighting the snowstorm for two hours, my courage crept back.

When I reached the place I was staying, I wrote a letter to the Party theoretician. After mailing it, I went to visit two other men. One was far less important than the Party theoretician, but his manner indicated the opposite. Several guards were posted in front of his office and bodyguards protected him wherever he went. I had heard that his rise to his current position had been smooth, although some posters had accused him of living too rich a life. For example, in his home were several young, pretty masseuses who were not allowed to do housework, knit, or write for long, since these activities might put calluses on their hands. He was also criticized for not reading newspapers and books. Since he enjoyed life and cared little about his work, he never became a threatening force in any power struggle within the Party. He greeted me with a smile and took the materials I had brought, but he probably forgot the matter as soon as I left. He was well liked because he was so inoffensive, but I did not place my hopes in him.

I then went to visit one of Sun Tian's close friends, a luminary of the Beijing intellectual world. Only his wife was home; he had just gone abroad with a Chinese delegation. I spoke with her for a few minutes and then wrote a note for the man.

The wife examined the handwriting, noting that it was based on the Yan style. Clearly an expert, she described it as childlike in its thick strokes, yet sophisticated in its natural force and energy. My hand-writing lacked the usual delicacy of most women's, and few people had ever spoken positively about it. The old woman's comments reminded me of Father and his training, and I wanted to cry. Instead, I said good-bye and left quickly.

The Party theoretician had written me an enthusiastic letter, ask-ing me to see him before leaving Beijing. We met, but again he refused to take my file. He handed me a letter, instructing me to take it and the court-case materials to a Shanghai linguist. I carefully placed the sealed letter in my book bag. He walked me to the door and then suddenly returned to his desk and produced a bag of chocolates. He handed it to me with a smile, saying, "This is from my granddaughter. She gave it to me for my overnight work." I tried to refuse the chocolates, but he insisted until I took them.

He walked me to the stairway and patted my shoulder: "Try to control your emotions. Keep your sadness in check. Many people have already paid the bloody price for the Cultural Revolution. Only a few of us were lucky. Try to establish yourself in graduate school as your father wishes." His voice was low and serious, and I felt an unspoken tie with him. I told him that I was returning to Shanghai the next day, and that I had a quantum mechanics test to take as soon as I arrived at school. He smiled and nodded, then watched me walk down the stairs. The sun melted the snow on the streets and the icicles glistened on the trees. I reflected on his words as I walked to the train station.

Purchasing the ticket for my return trip, I saw an old woman begging from passersby in the corner of the ticket office. I imagined that she was a widow come to Beijing to file suit for a daughter who had died in jail, and I gave her all my loose change. Before I had gone far, I retraced my steps and placed my chocolates in the old woman's hands. Crying, I left her.

Next I went to say good-bye to the Chinese linguist. When I stepped in the house, he put on a secretive air, asking me to take a seat by his desk. He looked around the room guardedly and lowered his voice: "You're very lucky! One of the guests who was here the last time you visited asked me about you. He said he felt sorry for you. I told him the truth, and he sent me a letter to give you. The woman in charge of your father's publishing house is one of his former students. You can use his name to see her."

The linguist took a tiny key from his pocket and unlocked a desk drawer. Removing a large book, he extracted a sealed letter from between two leaves. He handed it to me, and I recognized the name of a famous writer on the envelope. I remembered a gentleman with a healthy glow and a five-o'clock shadow who had looked at me curiously.

My last important task was to visit a man who had been Father's friend for more than forty years. He had been a famous university professor but was fired in 1957 and now made his living as a ricksha driver. Seventy-four years old, he had no children and had recently lost his wife. We children had decided that if my Beijing visits went smoothly, I would tell him that we would support him financially as we had our father.

The old man wept for some time when he learned of Father's death, so it was my turn to comfort someone. I stayed in his simple room for less than two hours, but I helped him clean it and then prepared his dinner. I was about to leave when I noticed that his overcoat pocket had a large tear. A poor seamstress, I had always despised the times at home when the comforters had to be cleaned and restitched. When Father saw how busy I was, he would quietly bring the newly washed and dried comforters in from outside. Putting on his bifocals, he would stitch away until I came home and angrily took them away from him. Father teased me about the long stitches I always took in haste, and I became defensive and angry. As I sewed this old man's overcoat, I felt that I would gratefully have borne the worst of Father's teasing if only he could have stood there and spoken to me at that moment. Everyone dies and, once dead, is gone forever. It is so simple, yet it took so long for me to comprehend.

During the early part of the Cultural Revolution, Chairman Mao was healthy and had no need of doctors, requiring them instead to treat peasants, workers, and other ordinary people. In the fall of 1976, his health made it necessary to have a medical team always available, so a committee selected about thirty of China's best doctors and flew them to Beijing. Soon after Chairman Mao's death, the names of these doctors were listed in the newspaper. We had been fortunate enough to meet two of these doctors and clever enough to deceive them. The incorrect diagnoses made by Mao's former physicians were still in our patient records, but before we had enough time to savor our victory, Father's death overwhelmed us. We were human, and thus prone to mistakes: When Father was dying, we thought he had a cold.

I had completed my tasks in Beijing, but I felt empty inside. Depressed during the return trip to Shanghai, the final verse of Whitman's poem ran through my mind:

> My Captain does not answer, his lips are pale and
> still,
> My father does not feel my arm, he has no pulse nor
> will,
> The ship is anchored safe and sound, its voyage closed
> and done,
> From fearful trip the victor ship comes in with object
> won;
> Exult O shores, and ring O bells!
>   But I with mournful tread,
> Walk the deck my Captain lies,
> Fallen cold and dead.

Professor Hu, I remember that the Chinese newspaper here announced your friend's death a month ago. One of his American colleagues had already sent the ashes back to China. His wife will come to the United States soon to attend the ceremony at which he would have received an award. He was like the ox you wanted to paint, but in the last part of his life, he had the dignity of a human being. He did what he wanted to do in science, and people could openly pay their last respects to him. Do you not think that all of these things should be a comfort to his friends who are still alive?

I hope you will become stronger and not live life as an empty shell. Please take care of yourself.

Sincerely,
Xi-ou Tan

25

Dear Professor Hu,

While I was in Beijing trying to exonerate my parents' names, Mother came home for a visit and then returned to her farm. I missed my last chance to see her, for Mother died ten days after Father passed away. She missed Father's funeral, for she had not received our first three telegrams. When she read the fourth one, stating that Father was in critical condition, her first thought was that he had died. Even after fourteen years of separation, she knew.

She had not been concerned about Father's health, because our correspondence code used "Brother Ying has been very sick recently" to mean that the political situation had become tense and that the family had suffered. Over the years, father's physical and political well-being had become one. When my parents had separated, father had been a healthy, energetic middle-aged man, and she had kept this image in her mind.

When she received the fourth telegram, she was allowed to return to Shanghai. She had already missed the last bus to Wu Zhou, a town on her way, so she decided to walk home in the dark. Not wishing to believe that her husband was dead, she held onto the hope of seeing him alive. This became her source of strength for the journey.

From Mother's notebook and from the stories many of our friends told us, we were able to know many of Mother's thoughts and feelings during this period. She climbed the mountain road, thinking of the man she had married thirty-eight years earlier—they had been separated for half of those years. The moon peeked out from the clouds. In its cool glow, the road's twists, turns, and steep grades were outlined sharply. Never sure where her next step would land, Mother tripped in the holes and ruts in the road, her eyes flooding with tears when she stepped on stones and dead branches.

She thought about the fairy tale she had never finished writing when Rei-qing was a child. Her right to literary composition had been taken away after the Anti-Rightest Movement in 1957, but she occasionally let her mind wander back to the characters in that unfinished book. The tall mountains surrounded her in the cold, dark night with the distant full moon. From the corner of her eye, the angels and tiny animals from her book came alive to chase away the loneliness that clung to her. She hoped that the little images would not disappear, and she wished that her tired mind could rest in the fairy-tale world she had created.

It was almost midnight when Mother arrived at Angel Cave. The first thing she saw was the urn that held Father's ashes. Mourners filled the room, and she was strangely relieved to have everyone crowd closely around her. Dropping her baggage at the door, she embraced my brothers and sister and our friends. Father had counseled many of the young people who were now here mourning him, and just as they had looked to him as a surrogate parent, they responded to Mother in the same way. Although exhausted and dirty from her journey, she did not appear overcome by Father's death. She called each of our friends by name, recognizing them from the descriptions we had provided on our visits.

Mother had only just learned of her husband's death, yet she graciously acted as hostess in the home she had never seen. Asking Jian-nan to boil water, she began making tea for everyone. From her luggage she produced a large bag of peanuts, a scarce food that Father had loved. She had traded her overcoat for them on the way. She offered the peanuts to the guests, saying, "This was one of Uncle Tan's favorites. Eat them for him and give me peace of mind. If he were here, he would have insisted I offer them to you."

One of the young mourners asked Mother how long she would be in Shanghai. Unthinking, she answered, "Only a day or two," explaining that she had started her journey as soon as she had received the telegram and so had had no time to file for a longer visit. Pleased that her husband's funeral had been formal and well attended, she said that now she would be able to wait patiently until an application for a longer visit was processed.

She was slender and strong, despite the years of prison and farm work, and her skin looked translucent in the light of the six-watt lamp. Her eyes were beautiful in their shallow recesses, her nose straight and strong, her cheekbones high and aristocratic. Her lips were full, red, and gentle. In the dim light, Mother looked to her guests like a goddess from an ancient myth.

The guests trickled home, respectfully bidding Mother farewell. Rei-qing asked, "Do you really want to go back to the farm tomorrow afternoon?"

"Yes. I want to go back as soon as possible, so I can appeal from the farm for the exoneration of your father's name."

"With Xi-ou already filing suit in Beijing, I know we'll be successful," Rei-qing said.

"Yes," Mother replied, "but it won't hurt for me to follow with my own appeal."

Realizing that Mother's mind was made up, Rei-qing began thinking of the food and clothing she could take to the farm. Reading her daughter's mind, Mother said, "I'll be coming home as soon as possible, so I won't take anything extra back with me."

When the guests had gone and the family was asleep, Mother rose to sit in front of the urn that held Father's ashes. She had no tears, only a feeling of emptiness and loss. She cherished the times they had spent together—the good and the bad, the frightening and the uplifting. A stream of pain had flowed through their lives: the anti-Japanese war, the Revolution, the Anti-Rightist Movement, and the Cultural Revolution. There had never been a day without crisis, but the overriding happiness they shared was their four children. She had always hoped for a peaceful old age together when they could make up for all the pain they and their children had suffered.

Mother now had two goals: clearing Father's name and then dying quietly. She had thought that incarceration in the Basket Bridge was preferable to working on the farm so far from the family, but when her fear of Father's death was confirmed, she felt that her whole life had been drained from her. She did not have the feudalistic idea that a widow should commit suicide, but she and Father had become one spirit through their marriage, and now the purpose of her life was gone.

She left for the farm the next day. The authorities rewarded her prompt return with two days off, which she spent writing the appeal. It would have been much more convenient to write it at home, but, unsure of its impact, she thought it best not to risk our well-being. Her roommate helped keep the matter hidden.

The night she finished writing the appeal, she slipped into a beautiful dream. She was a girl again, wearing a long, white gown in a large garden. She ran through the flowers, grasses, and trees, and, as she watched the flying birds, a handsome stranger, the same age as she, approached and lifted her up onto a splendid dark horse. He mounted his own steed and the horses whinnied, leaping into the sky. Turning around, she saw that the young man who had carried her away had become the middle-aged Jin-ren. The ever-smiling eyes looked deeply into hers, full of the warmth and passion of their married life. Startled, she cried his name out loud, "Jin-ren! Ren!"

She awoke. It was only a dream, but she wanted to remember it. Afraid that she would forget it if she moved, she lay motionless for a long time. When she sat up, she reached for a flashlight and wrote the dream down in her notebook. Sister Y-jin, the Roman Catholic nun who had befriended Mother at the Basket Bridge, kept the notebook with Mother's other personal belongings to give to us several months later.

Mother came home quickly, as she had promised, but not alive. She had begged God to allow her to be with Father in heaven as soon as possible. God heard the cries of my poor, exhausted mother. As she crouched by the river washing her clothes the day after mailing her appeal, she was felled by a stroke. She dropped to the ground, never to awake.

△△△ I missed my quantum mechanics test. Cruel reality had struck again. Tears no longer fell from my eyes, but my mind was drained. Mother followed Father; the single soul that was their love flew from the hardships of this earth. Mother had enjoyed the violin concertos written for the love story of Lian Shan-buo and Zhu Ying-tai, a couple who were prevented from marrying by their feudalistic society and so turned into butterflies and flew away together after their deaths. Father and Mother were like two grass plants growing side by side, relying on each other. In a barren garden stretching to eternity, where the land is yellow and the sky gray, a north wind blows, and two tiny grass plants at the horizon grew weak in the cold but sang passionately about the green life they knew existed somewhere, sometime.

I had difficulty understanding why careless, insensitive people are allowed to live so long. When I thought of the short, pain-filled lives of my parents, I could not be at peace. My tears were gone, but every cell of my body wanted to climb to the top of a mountain and scream, scream, scream up to the blue sky and down to the dark earth. I put aside the two letters I brought from Beijing, useless because of Mother's death. I took a leave from school and spent more than a month alone, hardly speaking at all. It could not heal my wounds, but it was long enough to stop the bleeding. I finally packed up my parents' belongings after picking out the best clothes to mail to Father's brother in Hunan. I wrote almost a hundred thank-you notes to friends both in and out of the city, and then a final journal entry: "This is the most pain I have ever experienced. I will never be afraid of anything again."

I returned to school, a changed being.

Five years later, on June 10, 1984, I went to the Shanghai Supreme Court again. I stepped into the building already fifteen minutes late for my appointment. Still, I stopped to notice the surroundings. The Supreme Court building was like an old, long-lost friend to me, and I could not help but feel nostalgic. When I went to the receptionist's desk, a tall, wiry, middle-aged man addressed me petulantly.

"Why are you so late, Comrade Rei-qing Tan?"

"Bus number sixty-six had to stop at the railroad tracks," I replied. The bus had been stopped, but the delay was short and I had arrived at the courthouse twenty-five minutes early. Instead of waiting inside, I went to the banks of the Huang-Pu and stared at the water.

Mumbling something, the man rose and led me to the administrative offices. A quiet younger man—in the curiously fashionable courtroom garb of plastic sandals, T-shirt, and rolled-up polyester pants—followed him, carrying a briefcase. Not until the younger man pulled a stenographer's pad from the briefcase did I realize that the middle-aged one was the local magistrate.

Looking around at the long tables, I realized that we were in the cafeteria. The pungent odor of the caustic soda used to clean the tables brought back memories for me, and I enjoyed it. The magistrate took out a cigarette and rolled it in his fingers for a few minutes before beginning his interrogation.

"Name?"

"I am Jin-ren Tan and Y-yao Bai's daughter," I answered, unwilling to give my name just yet. I handed him the summons from my pocket.

"Comrade Rei-qing Tan," he said, after reading the paper, "I insist that you answer my questions directly. You arrived at this meeting somewhat late. I can only assume that you are not taking this matter seriously."

Rolling my eyes, I took on a comically rigid pose. "All right," I said in my dizziest voice. "My name is Xi-ou Tan. Rei-qing's my sister. She's busy teaching today, so I came in her place."

Appalled at this admission, the magistrate barked, "Why did she go to teach today? I told her to take this summons to the Party secretary in charge of her school to be excused for the day. I find your attitude intolerable!"

"But isn't it all right that I came?" I asked almost flirtatiously.

The magistrate unbent a little. "Please state your name again."

" 'Xi,' you know, the word for smashing something, and 'ou,' like the raven, only you spell it a little differently. But that doesn't matter. That's my name." I almost said, "You know how Madame Mao said we want to 'smash' the legal system?"

It took the stenographer several minutes to extract my name from my lengthy answer. I gave my age and place of birth in a similarly convoluted manner. Knowing that the next question would be where I worked, I decided to dispense with the silly answers. "Has the court rejected the appeal my mother mailed five years ago?"

Ignoring my question, the magistrate insisted that I tell him my place of work. "I'm sort of between jobs right now," I said, with careless unconcern.

"Are you a member of the 'Youth Awaiting Employment'?" He frowned.

"No," I replied with the same indifference, "I'm not."

"Well, what are you?" he asked impatiently.

I sighed: "I'm just a student."

"Where?"

"Princeton University."

Neither the magistrate nor the stenographer recognized the name. "That doesn't sound like a local university," the magistrate said suspiciously.

"No, it's not," I said emphatically.

"Well, then, write down the name of the university, the province it's in, and the name of the city."

I wrote, "Princeton University, Princeton, New Jersey, United States."

The magistrate was astounded. "Oh, you're visiting from the United States. Excellent." He beamed with pleasure: "When did you arrive?"

"Last night."

"Oh, you only arrived last night and this morning you came to the court. You have a real spirit of involvement!"

Without a word, the shadowlike stenographer also smiled in admiration. Looking at my clothes, the magistrate continued, "How long were you in the United States?"

"Four years."

"You don't look like you've been in the United States for four years! You're dressed so simply," he said, expressing the widespread notion that Chinese people who had visited the United States wore loud, unusual clothes to demonstrate their worldliness.

"Your Honor," I said in a truly serious tone, "you know that my father and mother were branded as Rightists and anti-Revolutionaries for more than twenty years. When my father died in February 1979, my mother submitted a request for a pardon to clear his name. She died in mourning, only ten days after his death. Now that they're both gone, it doesn't make any sense to continue the process. The request has been turned down every time it's been made. If you have refused again, I, as a representative of my brothers and sister, have come to withdraw it."

"No, no, no, Xiao Tan, don't misinterpret this," the magistrate said, waving his hand. "I asked your sister to come so I could tell her in person that your parents' names have been cleared. It's even better that you're here instead, so I can extend the warmth and love of the Party to a student who has been studying abroad." Putting on his glasses, he began to read from a document bearing the large red seal of the Shanghai Supreme Court.

As he read, my face flushed and tears welled up in my eyes, but I refused to let them fall. Glancing up over the paper, the magistrate saw my reaction and gave me an understanding look: "I know how you feel. So many people react the same way. When one gets such joyful news, it's easy to be overwhelmed and cry. The Communist Party is always ready to admit when it has made a mistake. When, in any time, from East to West, has any nation been governed with more wisdom and justice than under the guidance of the Communist Party?"

The tears in my eyes had dried while I bowed my head for a few seconds. Growing angry, I slowly lifted it again: "What good is it to clear the name of someone who's dead?"

"No," the magistrate continued, "you're still young and haven't seen as much as we. This is a great, important thing. Those who have left the world before us take great spiritual comfort in the knowledge that they are once again honored by the living. Those still with us can directly benefit from the monumental turnaround of this great nation."

I said nothing, remembering how I longed for this news during my adolescence. I had so often dreamed of my parents' friends rejoicing. Mother and Father could have resumed their beloved work, Father laboring tirelessly through the night and Mother attacking her novels with her former zeal. My brothers and I would walk Father to the publishing house and Mother to the newspaper office each morning.

It had been a long, fruitless wait. Today the document that would have brought so much joy had finally arrived, but now there were no warm, smiling parents, only cold ashes. My parents did not need this comfort to sleep forever. The "monumental turnaround" was no comfort to those of us still living, for when we were faced with being sent to the countryside, and not permitted to attend the university, the document was not there. It had arrived too late—a cruel, ironic end to a tragedy.

I refused to jump up jubilantly to shake the magistrate's hand, and go away to live happily ever after, as had so many other grateful recipients of such documents. The same Supreme Court once reviewed my parents' sentence, only to recommend that the Proletarian Dictatorship censure us. Four years and seven months after my parents had died, I was being told in the Supreme Court—or, rather, in the cafeteria of the Supreme Court—that their shame and suffering were due to a little political misunderstanding that should be totally forgotten.

Emotionless, I finally asked, "Is that all you have to say to us?"

"Oh, I almost forgot to tell you. Since the people on whose behalf this appeal was filed are both deceased, the Supreme Court will not consider any requests for economic compensation." Looking at me, he added, "But if there is any great need or difficulty, perhaps we can make some special arrangement."

"Thank you," I said coldly as I rose to leave, "we have no great difficulties."

The magistrate seemed amazed that everything had gone so smoothly. He had been through dozens of cases like this, and everyone had wanted their tears of blood repaid with every cent they could squeeze from the government. "Xiao Tan, we will be glad to help you in any reasonable way we can," he reiterated.

"Thank you, but we could not touch any such money," I said, trying to end the discussion and moving toward the exit.

"I'd also like the addresses of your grandparents and other relatives living abroad. We will mail them copies of this document in a few days so that they, too, can share in the joy of your parents' exoneration after twenty years."

I raised my eyebrows but stopped what I was about to say. I finally said, "That will not be necessary. My grandparents do not know that my parents are dead. Good-bye."

△△△ I never expected my parents' case to have such an ending: a cafeteria in the Supreme Court in 1984, long after their deaths. My family paid the bloody price for the Revolution. I met Mother's father and stepmother in the United States for the first time in 1983. They passed away in 1986 and 1987. My uncles who went to Taiwan in 1949 came to the United States in the 1960s to pursue their degrees. They are all doing well in their careers, and they helped hide the news of my parents' deaths from their own parents. We pretended that everything was fine whenever my grandparents asked, occasionally sending letters to them with our parents' signatures at the bottom. They were old and did not realize the deception. By now, they have all met in the next world, and all these misunderstandings are clarified.

△△△ Professor Hu, I have not received a letter from you for quite some time. Please write to me soon.

Sincerely,
Xi-ou Tan

After Nixon visited China in 1972, it became possible to correspond openly with relatives abroad, so I wrote to my uncles who taught in the United States. They suggested that I apply to graduate schools in the United States, and the Chinese government's new "open door" policy also encouraged students to do this.

There is an old Chinese saying that as long as the parents are alive, the children should not go far away. I came to America in 1980, but if my parents had been alive, I would not have been so determined to pursue my degree here.

26

Dear Professor Hu,

After my parents passed away, I more seriously considered going to graduate school in the United States. My four uncles had received their degrees from American universities, and two were teaching at the university level. Because of my lack of formal education, they suggested applying to Ivy League schools and other well-known private institutions, since state laws would make it difficult for me to enter a public university. They gave me a list of schools, and I spent my free time filling out forms and collecting letters of recommendation.

I continued to go home from the university every weekend to see my brothers and sister. One Sunday morning in December 1979, I came home from visiting some friends and was surprised to find Pei Wu sitting on one of our makeshift sofas in Angel Cave. Because he took his work wherever he went, he had manuscripts and books on his knees. He had not removed his hat, scarf, and overcoat, since Angel Cave was drafty and the outside temperature was below freezing.

"Xi-ou, Professor Wu has been waiting for you here for almost three hours!" scolded Chi-kai.

I apologized. "Professor Wu, I'm sorry to keep you waiting so long. I didn't know you were planning to visit today."

"I had an urgent message," he said openly. "I can't write you a letter of recommendation to study in the United States."

Stunned, I demanded, "Why not? Just the day before yesterday, you said you'd mail it before the deadline. It's already December and some of the schools have deadlines at the beginning of January. Time is short already."

"I know," Pei Wu said. "That's why I had to bring you this message in person. It's complicated. It's related to Da Ma."

Da Ma and I were two of the nine students Pei Wu had taken in 1978. Da Ma was the first to apply to graduate schools in the United States and had left in the summer of 1979. I was the second student to apply.

"Isn't Da Ma already in one of the state universities in the United States? What does that have to do with me? I only applied to private schools."

"Da Ma did poorly in his classwork in the United States," Pei Wu explained. "He finished college before the Cultural Revolution, but he still couldn't adapt to the American educational system. If he can't, how can you? I think you should give up this idea." When I said nothing, Pei Wu continued, "I'll treat you well. The Academy of Science is thinking of awarding degrees. You'll be among the first to receive a Ph.D. in China. You'll have a very bright future."

Stubbornly, I asked, "Please tell me, Professor Wu, why you can't write a letter of recommendation for me." He avoided my stare and I continued, "You're my adviser. You have the responsibility of writing letters of recommendation for me. I didn't attend college as Da Ma did, but it doesn't necessarily follow that I'll do worse than he. Besides, how I do in the United States isn't your problem. You only have to tell them about my performance so far."

Pei Wu thought for a while and sighed: "All right. Everyone in the international academic world is aware of the accomplishments of several outstanding Chinese-Americans, including 'Dr. Marvel,' who teaches at Da Ma's university. He recently came to a meeting in Shanghai and used his school as an example to summarize the performance of Chinese students in the United States, criticizing Da Ma in particular. I said some very good things about Da Ma in the letter of recommendation I wrote for him. If anyone ever asks, 'Who recommended Da Ma?' the ax falls on my neck. I'd worry less about someone's going to the State Educational Council to speak against me. If anyone tells President Deng Xiao-ping about the problem with Da Ma, that's the end of me.

I did not know how to respond, although I thought that Pei Wu was overreacting. "Dr. Marvel" had not necessarily meant any harm, but it was possible that someone could take advantage of Pei Wu's situation and report him to the Central Committee. Pei Wu had academic and political competitors, so his worry was not unfounded. The recent Open-Door Policy worked to please foreigners, and Dr. Marvel was one. I played with the fringe of my scarf.

"Xi-ou, please consider my opinion. I think you'll have a much brighter future if you stay here. You'll be graduating in several months and you can stay at the Academy of Sciences to do more research. Or you can go to the university and teach. As soon as the degree-awarding process has been established, I'll see that you get a Ph.D. If you're interested in visiting abroad, you can go after you get your degree. It wouldn't be easy for a woman like you to go to the opposite end of the earth and fight for a degree. Can you survive at a first-class university?"

"I can," I insisted.

Pei Wu said nothing at first. The north wind blustered about the house, rattling the windows of Angel Cave.

"Professor Wu, may I ask a favor?" I asked.

Pei Wu looked at his watch and saw that it was already noon. Adjusting his hat, he gave me an encouraging glance. "As long as it is within my capabilities."

"Could you pretend you see no evil and allow other professors to write letters for me?"

Pei Wu smiled. "Don't worry. I'm going to Gui Yang on business next Wednesday, and I won't be back until the middle of January. But," he added, either thoughtlessly or purposely, "if even I am afraid of this threat, who would do it for you? Maybe you can find some old man who isn't afraid of heaven, hell, or Dr. Marvel."

⧓⧓ "That's ridiculous!" spat Rei-qing when I told her the story. "So what if he really is some marvel?" She sighed, "In the Chinese scientific world, Pei Wu's a big fish in a small pond, but he's afraid of being eaten by a bigger fish. I wonder who will conquer Dr. Marvel."

Tao-ran said, "The day before yesterday, Dr. Marvel came to visit my factory. He doesn't even know the details of how a generator works, but people still took notes and passed the information on to those who weren't there. The pendulum swings both ways. China was closed for so long, but now that it's open, we swallow everything that comes our way, regardless of how ridiculous it may be. Perhaps this is a flaw in our national character."

Rei-qing thought for a few moments. "It seems odd that Professor Wu would ask you to find an old man to stand up to Dr. Marvel. Why does he have to be old?"

I told her, "I think he's saying that anyone who believes he still has a future would be just as afraid of writing a recommendation. I could look at the dark side, and say that if he doesn't agree, then no one else would have the fortitude to go against him. Professor Wu's nickname is 'Little Despot.' I never took it seriously. I thought it was just because people were jealous of him, but perhaps he deserves it after all."

Tao-ran smiled. "I've heard my colleagues talk about your adviser. They say he's like the opposite of the Nieng Buo–style dish of Chou tofu, which smells wonderful when you're close but stinks when you're far away! I think many famous people are like that."

Concerned, I added, "Professor Wu is an honorary professor at the University of Science and Technology as well as at several other famous universities. Maybe I'll have to find someone outside academia to help me, someone with nothing to lose."

Rei-qing pondered the matter and then said, "I think I might know someone. Teacher Yang, who writes for the *Scientific Weekly*, has a lot of contacts with professors and scientists in different disciplines. He might know the best thing to do."

Tao-ran and I readily agreed. After we decided what to say to Teacher Yang, I left. It was after midnight by the time I boarded the nearly empty bus to return to the university. Nestled in the corner of my seat and wrapped in a large overcoat, I watched the sparkling city lights pass by.

I thought about Da Ma. It was midday in America at this same moment, and Da Ma would be in class, or perhaps between classes

studying. He and I had not spoken more than ten words to each other.
I had only heard about Dr. Marvel, and the recognition he brought
China, from my parents when I was a young girl. These people seemed
so remote; how could they touch my life like this? A bitter smile crept
to my lips.

△△△ Teacher Yang was vacationing in his hometown, so
Chi-kai volunteered to visit him for me. My brother returned three days
later with a letter of introduction for me addressed to an old man
named Qin-tang Lu. Teacher Yang told Chi-kai, "Tell Xi-ou to see
Professor Lu and ask him if he's willing to help her. American universities generally require three or four letters, but as long as we have one,
we're on our way. I'll be back in Shanghai in a week, and we can get
together then."

I went to visit Qin-tang Lu. The small house with a large garden
was in a quiet neighborhood. He was a very tall man with a strong,
straight back; he looked much younger than his eighty-odd years. His
loud, rich voice was well suited to lecturing, and he struck me as an
open, honest man.

After carefully reading my introductory letter from Teacher Yang,
we talked. We discussed the French Revolution and quantum mechanics, Zhuang Zi's "free and unfettered roc," and the philosophy of
Francis Bacon. I was infatuated with the depth and breadth of Professor
Lu's knowledge. Mrs. Lu eventually interrupted to invite us in to
dinner.

Professor Lu smiled, satisfied with our conversation. "Very good,
very good," he commented. Suddenly realizing that he had been testing
me, I flushed with nervous excitement. He folded the recommendation
forms I had handed him earlier and put them in his drawer. When he
said that it would be an honor to recommend such a highly qualified
young person to an American university, my cheeks flushed again. I was
so relieved that I now had one of my three letters.

Two days later, I received a letter from Professor Lu saying he
wanted to see me as soon as possible. It was dinner time, but I skipped
my meal and rode my bicycle to his home. When I arrived, the family

was eating. They introduced a beautiful middle-aged woman as their third daughter, who taught at a university. In the traditional manner, I called her "Third Auntie." They asked me to eat with them, but I was embarrassed to dine with a family I had known for less than seventy-two hours. But Professor and Mrs. Lu made it impossible for me to refuse.

Professor Lu said, "I asked you to visit because I need to know the correct English spelling of your name and school. My past experience with Westerners tells me that they respect the scientific spirit. Their primary philosophical emphasis is on honesty, with accuracy next in importance. I hope that the letter I'm writing for you meets these standards."

Before I could reply, Mrs. Lu said, "China's policy on education is improving. Young students are allowed to go abroad again. There's less discrimination against Chinese in American universities these days, and people are more friendly. Far fewer women are interested in going abroad for education than men, so you'll have an active social life!"

Professor Lu interrupted his wife: "Xi-ou has to concentrate on her studies. Falling in love is an emotional upheaval. One moment, the world is wonderful, and the next, it flies apart. Many valuable years can be lost this way. You can't have two good things at the same time."

"It will be in Xi-ou's best interests to be happy in both her career and her personal life," she responded.

The old couple began seriously debating the merits of love. Third Auntie made a face, saying, "Both my parents are unusually talented people, aren't they?" We all laughed.

After dinner, Professor Lu said, "Xi-ou, there's one thing I want to ask you. Your adviser just got back from Gui Yang. Will he have enough time to mail your recommendation before January 10?"

Conflict raged in my mind. Professor Lu was retired and might understand Professor Wu's problem, but his daughter was still teaching in a university and therefore was vulnerable. For her sake, I thought I should be honest with him, but a base voice in my mind whispered, "Xi-ou, don't be stupid! As soon as you tell him the truth, he'll realize it was foolish of him to agree to write the letter. Your future will be ruined."

Finally I said, "Professor Lu, I also believe firmly in honesty and accuracy, and there's something I should tell you before you decide to write a letter of recommendation for me. You may wish to reconsider." I described the events that had led me to visit him: Pei Wu, Da Ma, and Dr. Marvel burst from me like water from a broken dam.

There was a long silence. My cheeks were again flushed, but the inner conflict had subsided. Whether or not Professor Lu wrote a letter was not as important as being relieved of the burden of dishonesty. Losing the recommendation because of sincerity was better than regretting any half-truths.

The edges of the windows were frosting, but it was as warm as spring inside. The pot of coal burning in the center of the room emanated warmth, and the water for tea began boiling. A fairy tale I had read as a child, "The King of Golden River," was about an old magician who happily sang, "Lalaleelala, leeleelalala. . . ." I felt like the magician, so happy with myself I could have sung out loud.

Professor Lu and his wife exchanged glances. She rose and took a large photograph album from a cabinet and handed it to me. When I opened it, I was stunned. It was full of pictures of Professor Lu and his family posing with Dr. Marvel.

Professor Lu announced, "Xi-ou, I'm very happy to see that you're so honest. I've had a long relationship with Dr. Marvel. I think Professor Wu's concern is unnecessary. You don't need to beg him again. I can help you get all the recommendations you need."

He lighted a cigarette. He still spoke emphatically, but this time with pride. "Xi-ou, go to school tomorrow and get your transcripts. I'm sure that between those and my reputation, my colleagues in the academic world will be more than happy to recommend you."

I do not remember how I got home that night. I first went to see Rei-qing and Tao-ran to describe the miracle. I ended by saying, "So many people live with high ideals but never see justice done in their lives, and they begin to question the power of truth. I know that whenever I'm afraid to be honest, I'll remember what happened tonight. I'll never again shrink from being true to myself and others."

△△△ Professor Hu, I received several acceptances from American universities, but I chose to go to Princeton for the sole reason that I thought Einstein had lived in the town. Like a barefoot country girl, I put my two hundred books into a dilapidated old suitcase. As I crossed the border to meet one of Father's friends, "Uncle" Kai-ping, for the first time, the strap by which I dragged the suitcase broke. As I pushed the giant case from behind, Uncle Kai-ping laughed in recognition. From the stories he had heard about me, he realized that only I would do something so impractical. He shipped my books to the United States for me and still has my broken old suitcase in his Hong Kong apartment. He says, "Someday, when you're famous, I'll show this to the press."

Along with the books, I brought with me a lot of love, hopes, and dreams of a scientific career. Whenever I remember the jaggedness of my parents' lives—how they suffered and saw no justice done—my heart is torn. Some people say that I ought to try to forget the past, but my family history, written in tears and blood, is inseparable from who and what I am. The "I" of today is the integrated "I" of all that I have been in the past. Until I die, I will not forget. A Turkish poet once wrote:

> *A bullet fired travels*
> *Days and nights through.*
> *I am what I am still,*
> *The same mind and soul.*

I was a child when the Cultural Revolution began, and too happy to worry. In the more than twenty years since then, I have experienced so much change, but inside I feel the same. So many of the changes that the Cultural Revolution forced on people have been reversed, and I see with a painful heart that a new reversal is taking place. Morality is declining, and less value is being placed on love, friendship, motherland, and science. I have entered the "palace of science," and it is beyond the imagination of the little pigtailed girl who stared at the sky and its sparkling stars. However, it is not as noble, fair, or beautiful as

I had hoped. Still, I try to keep my mind uncontaminated and my ideals pure.

Most people think that I am a success and should be happy. Instead, I feel infinite disappointment and loss. The pain I feel now is no less acute than that of my darkest days in China, although I am not sure why. Sometimes I feel so unsatisfied, and an abyss of loneliness opens in front of me.

Professor Hu, although I am still very confused about many things in life, I am firm on one point: helping others. You once asked why I wanted to spend so much time writing to you. It is because those who once received help wish to offer it.

Sincerely,
Xi-ou Tan

 I mailed my letter to Professor Hu in the morning. I had a feeling of completion, even though I still owed him four letters: I had finished the stories about my life in China. When I reached Cal Tech, I checked my mailbox without expectation; it had been nearly two weeks since I had received a letter from him and I had come to the conclusion that he was not going to write.

I was wrong. Mixed in with the junk mail was a thin letter with a Boston postmark.

 Dear Xi-ou,
I have spent the last ten days proving a difficult problem in number theory. It seemed impossible for so many years, but I found the solution this morning. May I use your father's name for my new proof? It is not a monumental achievement, but is important to me.

You knew me a long time ago. The mathematician "Big Brother Wu," Lao Mo's friend in your tenth letter, is I. The letter disturbed me for two reasons. First, I had never known that the real reason for Xiao Mo's death may have been beatings by the Red Guards. Perhaps his sister, Lao Mo, was too cautious, for she never told me this. As the old saying goes, any debt has an owner. Twenty years have passed, so whom should I ask to pay the debt for Xiao Mo's life?

The death of the love between Xiao Mo's sister and me bore the mark of the times. When I was branded an anti-Revolutionary, my wife divorced me, taking my baby son. She allowed neither me nor my mother to see him. When I was exonerated and transferred back to Shanghai, she asked to get remarried. I had forgiven her a long time before. She refused to let me see my son while we were negotiating our remarriage unless I agreed to all of her conditions, including forcing my parents to move from the room they had lived in for more than thirty years. Rooms, housing, I hate it! We got married because of a room, and we said good-bye over one.

The second reason your letter disturbed me was that I played such a stupid role in the independent-study plans you and your brother had, even though I did not realize it. I had forgotten whatever it was I said in the letter to Lao Mo, but I did remember your brother's letter with the quote from Galois, "Wherever there is sunshine, the violets blossom." You are too kind to save face for me, using Wu instead of Hu as my last name. I feel ashamed of myself.

Kang-li, Sun Tian, and Professor Shan are some of our country's outstanding intellectuals. I envy your knowing them. I was privileged to be so close to my mathematician friend, who was at least their level. Xiao Mo could well have attained such respect, but I? Of these Three Musketeers, one was beaten to death and one died of overwork, leaving only me, the weakest, most useless one. It is hard for me to believe in a generous, fair God.

When I described my picture of an ox, I only told you half. I am the ox, blocking the road for the young people who want to use it. This was the real reason I felt so depressed, but the recent ten days' hard work has proved that I still can do something useful.

I cannot waste your time and energies further. When my letter reaches you, it will be almost one month since you began sending me letters. You have won; my feelings are different now. Thank you, Xi-ou. Please tell me your opinion on naming my proof after your father, and please accept my very humble respects.

Sincerely yours,
Yong-hua Hu

Epilogue

Two months after I left China, Professor Lu died in the hospital. His wife and daughter wrote to me, saying that helping me get the chance to study in America made him more proud than anything else he had done in his later years. Professor Shan is still alive and well.

Kang-li died of a heart attack in the autumn of 1983. When the letter arrived at Princeton, it was already a cold, snowy winter. I wandered in the snowstorm for three hours, thinking of the first time we walked in the snow under her beautiful umbrella. She was my second mother, but I had been too shy to call her "Mother" while she was alive, and this disappointed her. In a condolence letter to her husband, I wrote, "I am sending this with daughterly love," without realizing it. I write to him three times a year, so I know that he and his three sons, now married, are all well.

It was said that Ah-liu lost control of the workshop soon after I left it. The young intellectuals who used to give her presents finally stood up to her. I even heard that one day when Ah-liu opened her lunchbox at noon, she found that someone had defecated in it.

Rei-qing still works as an interpreter at the steel factory, and Tao-ran is now a senior engineer. They are doing very well and have no political problems. In fact, the government has sent each of them abroad several times, including to the United States. Tao-ran visited me at Princeton, and Rei-qing and I spent a Christmas together in Los Angeles. You-pu is now the same age that I was when the Grand Cultural Revolution began. I write to him often, but I am not sure that he understands what we endured. He has everything we ever dreamed of having.

Jian-nan received a bachelor's degree in physics but was not interested in going to graduate school. He still works on his own theories in his spare time. He is married to a chemist, but they have no children yet.

Chi-kai came to the United States in 1985 and is nearly through with his Ph.D. in engineering. We see each other often. When he and I found Professor Hu's notebook at MIT, it had crossed my mind that it may have belonged to "Big Brother Wu," because I recognized on it the symbol of the two crossed swords. "Hu" and "Wu" are pronounced the same in the southern parts of China, including Shanghai.

When Professor Han had sent Father a card praising him for raising me, Father had said that it was society that had forced us children to respect ourselves and to work hard. He added that one becomes stronger through difficult circumstances, but too easy a life will kill one. From this I deduced that Father would not have accepted Professor Hu's generous offer, but I thanked him for it and suggested that he name his proof after his two lost Musketeers.

⚔⚔⚔ That autumn, I visited MIT and saw Professor Hu. We talked for hours while the leaves that had transformed the chill of oncoming winter into flaming brilliance floated down around us.